THE INVENTION OF SCOTLAND

THE INVENTION OF SCOTLAND

The Stuart myth and
the Scottish
identity,
1638 to the present

Murray G. H. Pittock

London and New York

First published in 1991
by Routledge
11 New Fetter Lane, London EC4P 4EE

Simultaneously published in the USA and Canada
by Routledge
a division of Routledge, Chapman and Hall Inc.
20 West 35th Street, New York, NY 10001

Typeset in Linotron Garamond by
Falcon Typographic Art Ltd, Edinburgh & London
Printed in Great Britain by
T. J. Press (Padstow) Ltd, Padstow, Cornwall

British Library Cataloguing in Publication Data
Pittock, Murray
The invention of Scotland: the Stuart myth and the
Scottish identity, 1638 to the present.
1. Scotland. Nationalism, history
I. Title
320.5409411

Library of Congress Cataloging in Publication Data
Pittock, Murray
The invention of Scotland: the Stuart myth and the
Scottish identity, 1638 to the present
by Murray G. H. Pittock.
p. cm.
Includes bibliographical references and index.
1. Stuart, House of. 2. Scotland – Historiography. 3. Scotland – Kings and
rulers. 4. Nationalism – Scotland – History.
5. National characteristics, Scottish. I. Title.
DA758.3.S8P58 1991
941.1–dc20 90-24511

ISBN 0-415-05586-5

To Ross

Contents

Acknowledgements   ix
Introduction   1

1   The divided myth and the drift to Union   7

2   Good corn upon the rigs? The underground world of
    Jacobite culture in eighteenth-century Scotland   41

3   The invention of Scotland   73

4   Reality and romance   99

5   A nation once again? Scotland since 1918   134

    Notes   166
    Select Bibliography   183
    Index   192

Hic jacet Arthurus, Rex quondam rexque futurus.

Surpassing the story even of Arthur and the Knights of the Round Table, because more near, more real and historical, the romance of Prince Charlie and the Highland chiefs has taken a lasting hold of the popular imagination.

Magnus Maclean, *The Literature of the Celts*

Acknowledgements

My thanks are due to many and to one. In particular, I owe thanks to Colin MacLaren for my free access to the MacBean Collection in Aberdeen University Library; to the staff of the National Library of Scotland, and to the British Academy whose research awards made research both possible and expeditious. My debts are due to the arguments of Frank McLynn, Paul Monod, and Willie Donaldson, who hitherto have made the closest approaches to the arguments enlarged upon here.

For permission to quote copyright material, I am indebted to Martin Brian & O'Keefe Ltd, the original publishers of the poems quoted from the *Completed Poems of Hugh MacDiarmid 1920-1976*, ed. Michael Grieve and W. R. Aitken (Penguin Books, 1978) and to Michael Grieve. Carcanet Press kindly gave permission to quote from Iain Crichton Smith's *The Exiles* (1984).

If these many made it possible to write the book, so did one, my wife Anne, who gave the time and peace to write it.

Introduction

Ancient traditions, when tested by the severe process of modern investigation, commonly enough fade away into mere dreams, but it is singular how often the dream turns out to have been a half-awake one, presaging reality.

T. H. Huxley

A people who lose their nationality create a legend to take its place.

Edwin Muir

Their lost realm has become our common heritage; and on the verge of despair we may find inspiration and comfort in the deep-seated conviction that sometime, somewhere, there will be a 'king over the water' to save the day if only we remain faithful to the noble dream of that lost dynasty which will live for ever in our hearts.

Pierre Joannon, writing in the *Royal Stuart Review*, 1988[1]

This is a book about the Stuart myth and its continuing power. It is not about tartan, whisky, or biscuit-tin depiction of the Stuarts, though these uses and abuses of the dynasty's image will be discussed. Rather it is about the unique fascination exerted by the Stuarts in their day and our own, and the contribution their propaganda, ideology, origin, and character has made to understanding the Scottish identity. Indeed, to enable that identity to understand itself the Stuart myth is one of the prime means of definition.

The British Isles are well-endowed with heroic legendary rulers, from Arthur to Cuchulainn to Fionn. It is said of many of these that they will return to lead their countries to victory at the time when they are most needed. Indeed, in the last hundred years, Irish nationalism has used such figures in support of its own claims. The statue of Cuchulainn in the GPO in Dublin bears witness to Patrick Pearse's supposed appeal to his spirit at the crisis of the 1916 Rising. Welsh nationalism makes use of the same kind of images, as the folk-song about Owain Glyndwr the Welsh hero makes clear:

> Owain is again ready for the day.
> From his hideout in Snowdonia

1

He will come with his faithful band
To lead us at dawn to a free Wales.

In similar vein, poems are found among young people in Wales voicing sentiments such as 'I believe with all my heart that Arthur is alive.' The legend of the returned Deliverer, Owain or Arthur, is traditionally strong in Wales.[2]

The argument of this book will be that the Stuarts long occupied a similar role in much of Scottish consciousness. In this they were unique among the legendary kings of the British Isles, for they were figures of documented and recent history. A dynasty of high ability and noted charm (as well as poor judgement), they seemed unworldly, even through the eyes of many of their contemporaries: mythic figures living in history. Those who came after them further mythologized them, as I shall demonstrate in the later chapters of this book. As time went on, a divided vision of them, always present, was confirmed and ratified. British history (partly because it was, as I shall argue, written by the victors of the 1688 Revolution) tended to disparage the Stuarts. On the other hand, their supporters (and those who had lost by the 1688 Revolution, where these were not the same) continued to eulogize them. It is remarkable that the response to historical figures should continue to be charged with such mythological or theological overtones. This is J. M. Charles-Roux, writing of Charles I (still an Anglican saint) in 1986:

> First, just like the Messiah who, from the beginning of his time on earth, as on several occasions He told His Disciples, knew that He would have to die the death of the Cross, so Charles I had a premonition of what his own end would be. . . . Indeed, for him, as in the case of the Redeemer, in his doom was his duty; since he was predestined to regenerate the faith in his realms and to manifest to his own people through his personal belief, example and sacrifice, the truth and value of Christian doctrines. . . . So like Christ sold to the Sanhedrin by one of His Disciples, was Charles sold to the Parliamentarians by the closest to him of his people, the Scots . . . the royal and anointed incarnation of Scotland, England and Ireland.[3]

It is hard to believe that such sentiments could be expressed about a king from any other historical British dynasty. Similarly, the kind of antipathy shown to the Stuarts by writers of opposing sympathies demonstrates that it is still difficult to evaluate them from a dispassionate viewpoint.[4]

The Stuarts themselves did much to bring this about. They were of the opinion that it was their manifest destiny to be kings of all Britain; and their ideology and propaganda after 1603 contained strong elements of mythic and sacred imagery intended to bolster both the claim to be all-British kings, and the idea that they were so by divine right, especially manifest in them. The images they adopted proved uniquely powerful and influential on posterity, as did the political analysis which went with them. Partly this was because the Stuart ideology was not decorative merely, to be abandoned in favour of *realpolitik* whenever that should prove necessary: it was an integral part of the dynasty's own faith in itself. For this reason, it had more impact on history than court ideologies usually do: the events of 1638 and 1688 can be directly linked to the ideals projected through Stuart politics.

The Tudors had previously adopted similar propaganda aims. Henry VII liked to stress his Welshness, and the manner in which he fulfilled Merlin's prophecy that a Welshman would wear the crown of England. Calling his eldest son Arthur was a sign of Tudor identification with Welsh mythology. Later, Elizabeth projected herself as the Virgin Queen of the English nation, a sign of the great destiny of Anglicanism: that church's own especial Virgin head. But Tudor symbolism, potent as it was, rarely expressed itself in political action or real belief: it was a facade, a celebration of the monarchy's aims and claims. There was no necessary correspondence with a real agenda. Henry may have been Arthur returned in an official capacity, but he and his successors were hard-headed politicians who appear to have used symbolism as a political tool, not as a means of self-expression.[5]

With the Stuarts, it was otherwise. They inherited some Tudor iconography, but from the beginning made more potent use of it:

Henry VII had declared that he was restoring the kingdom of Arthur, and the association was spontaneously made in James's favour: he was hailed in masques and pageants as the heir of Arthur or, as the climax to centuries of expectation, as Arthur's self returned.

From at least the beginning of the dynasty's reign in England, the Stuarts were strongly attracted to Messianic symbols of themselves at the Once and Future King, Arthur, or even Christ. Once they were exiled, their dispossession seemed a proof to some of heavenly support for this status:

By 1746 this vision . . . had matured into a mystical interpretation of the significance of the Jacobites . . . in terms of martyrdom and witness. The theological basis of this belief lay in Matthew v.10: 'Blessed are they which are persecuted for Righteousness sake: for theirs is the kingdom of heaven.'[6]

The idea of death and resurrection became linked to the idea of exile and return: Christ's Second Coming with Arthur's. The returning Stuart monarch would bring back true peace and a reign of perpetual righteousness over Great Britain, one country with two parliaments (England's and Scotland's).

The equation of British kingship with Arthurian status was made from the beginning by James VI and I:

> The fact that, from his accession, England, Scotland and Wales were thenceforward called Great Britain was another reason for hailing James as Arthur. In April 1603, the Venetian Ambassador wrote that the King's naming the kingdoms 'Britain' was like the decision of 'the famous and ancient King Arthur to embrace under one name the entire kingdom'.

Subsequently, it was to be 'those who supported the Divine Right of Kings' who 'upheld the historicity of Arthur'; whereas those who did not turned instead 'to the laws and customs of the Anglo-Saxons'.[7] Arthur remained a figure central to Stuart propaganda. Stuart iconography celebrated the habits and beliefs of the ancient Britons. In particular, the Royal Oak, still a central symbol of the dynasty, was closely related to ideas about Celtic fertility ritual, and the king's power as an agent of renewal: 'The oak, the largest and strongest tree in the North, was venerated by the Celts as a symbol of the supreme Power.' It was thus fitting that an oak should protect Charles II from the Cromwellian troops who wished to strip the sacred new Arthur of his status. The story confirmed the king's mystical authority, and also his close friendship with nature. Long after 1688, the Stuart dynasty was to be closely linked with images of fertility. In literature, Arthurian images of the Stuarts persisted into the nineteenth century.[8] This 'Welsh messiah, the warrior who will come to overthrow the Saxons and Normans', was an icon of the Stuarts' claim to be kings of all Britain, both 'Political Hero' and 'National Messiah' in Arthurian mould.[9]

Arthur's status as a legendary huntsman ('the figure of the Wild Huntsman is sometimes identified with Arthur') was also significant. The Stuarts made much of hunting: it helped to confirm their heroic status as stewards of nature and the land. In doing this, they identified themselves not only with Arthur but also with Fionn, the legendary Gaelic warlord who was in the eighteenth century to be the subject of James Macpherson's pro-Stuart Ossian poems. Fionn, legends of whom abound in Scotland, was also, like Arthur, scheduled to wake and deliver the nation when danger threatened. In identifying with both figures, the Stuarts were able to simultaneously present themselves as Gaelic and British monarchs.[10]

This symbolism was used with peculiar adroitness in Ireland, where the Stuarts were almost never identified with Arthur, but rather with Fionn and heroes from Fionn's own time. Charles Edward was compared to Fergus, Conall, Conroy, and Aongus Oge, while his grandfather became for some a symbol of Ireland itself, a Fenian hero in the making, a foreshadower of the sacrificial politics of such as Pearse: '*Righ Shemus*, King James, represented the faith of Erin, and so became her comrade in martyrdom.'[11] In famous eighteenth-century songs like 'The Blackbird', Ireland was presented as an abandoned woman, waiting for the return of her hero-king. The same symbolism was used in Scotland. 'The Gaelic messianic tradition' of Fionn suggested that the Stuart king would one day return to bring light and fecundity to the land. In the Highlands of Scotland, the events of Jacobitism themselves passed into folklore, like the older stories to which they were related.[12] More educated Jacobite sympathizers compared the Stuarts to the heroes of the Roman Republic, to Aeneas, or to the saints. But the view of them as sacred monarchs of folkloric tradition and power was one which endured among all ranks.

There is of necessity a gap here between history and the perceptions of the Stuarts which grew up, fostered by the dynasty's propaganda. But undeniably, the loss of the Stuart dynasty heralded a major constitutional change the effects of which are still with us. I will argue that the loss of Scottish independence was seen at the time as being closely bound up with the loss of the Stuarts, while in Ireland, songs about William, James, and 1689–90 are still common political currency. So the loss of the Stuarts was more than a dynastic upheaval: it was the occasion for lasting constitutional change, and the submergence or loss of national identities. Their loss was also accompanied by the sense, true or false, that an older, antiquarian, sacred, and mythic set of values had gone for ever. As Yeats was to put it: 'In 1690 the Battle of the Boyne . . . overwhelmed a civilisation full of religion and myth and brought in its place intelligible laws planned out upon a great blackboard.'[13] The Stuarts represented this lost heritage in political action. I will argue that in Scotland, if not in Ireland (where the case is more complex), their politicized mystique helped to preserve the identity of a nation struggling against considerable pressure to conform to the new British norms. Perhaps the legacy of the Stuart myth can also be seen in the mythopoeic faculty of the Scottish imagination, so often (for example, in the literature of the twentieth century) creating pasts to mourn the loss of. Noteworthy also is the Scottish concern with myth in anthropological study: 'The list of Scottish contributions to the rise of folklore, social anthropology, and sociology in the second half of the nineteenth century is formidable.' Perhaps even J. G. Frazer's dying king in *The Golden Bough* carries in him some echo of Stuart ideology and symbolism.[14]

The Stuart myth and the Scottish identity are closely linked through the loss of Scottish independence and its relationship to the loss of the Stuart dynasty. Mythology can be a kind of history favoured by the dispossessed; and it helps to read influence of the Stuart myth in such a light. Lack of independence goes along with a lack of independent means of securing one's own history. In such circumstances, in the eighteenth century and afterwards, the mythology and ideology of the Stuart cause became a kind of protest history, a self-expression of identity on behalf of those whose identity was under threat. In this underground history, many of the ideas still current today concerning Scotland's place in the Union came into being. Like Fionn and Arthur, the Stuart myth belongs in some respects to a glorious past. But like them also, its analyses did and do not fail to suggest that there might be some kind of reawakening, no longer of the Stuart kings, but of their mythical values, like Fionn's heritage to the Fenians:

> Gaelic popular tradition has it that they [the Fianna] are not dead, but sleeping under great green knolls somewhere in the Highlands, and that one day they will awake to restore the Gael to his ancient power, just as the Cymri look for the return of Arthur.

Just as, indeed, the British National Anthem betrays its origin as a Jacobite song in the phrase 'Send her/him victorious'.[15] Sent, that is, home from exile to victory.

1

The divided myth and the drift to Union

THE CLAIMS OF THE KING

Then from your fruitfull race shall flow
    Endless succession,
Scepters shall bud, and Laurels blow
    'Bout their Immortal Throne.

CHORUS

Propitious starres shall crowne each birth,
Whilst you rule them, and they the Earth.
                    Carew, *Coelum Britannicum* (1634)

The *Martyr's blood* was said of old to be
    The *seed* from whence the *Church* did grow.
The *Royal Blood* which dying *Charles* did sow
    Becomes no less the *seed* of *Royalty*.
                                    Abraham Cowley

We fought no crownes . . . we loved no new masters. Had our throne
been voyd, and our voyces sought for the filling of Fergus's chaire, we
would have died ere any other had sitten down on that fatall marble
bot Charles alone.
            Rev. Robert Baillie, speaking of the Covenanters[1]

As I suggested in the Introduction, the roots of the Stuart myth lie in the
history of the dynasty, not in the later accretions of sentiment. No British
royal family were praised as they were praised; none denigrated as they were
denigrated. Charles I was to his courtiers, poets, and apologists the ruler of
the stars, to be praised above them; to the regicides he was the Man of Blood,
chief of the Malignants, the unflattering term bestowed on all who actively
supported him.

He was not alone among his dynasty in being described in terms of
paradoxical extremes. James VI and I is famously known as 'the wisest
fool in Christendom'; Mary of Scots, Charles's grandmother, is judged
controversially by posterity as by her contemporaries: was she foolish

murderess or wronged beauty? It was seriously proposed that James II be canonized; yet to many of his subjects he was an arbitrary tyrant. Even Charles II, the least unpopular of his dynasty in England, was the Merry Monarch to some, and the 'mansworn tyrant' to others. The Earl of Rochester characterized his mercurial temperament in the famous lines:

> God bless our good and gracious King,
> Whose promise none relies on;
> Who never said a foolish thing,
> Nor ever did a wise one.[2]

In popular tradition, Charles II and James I are seen as the secular Stuarts, contradictory creatures of folly and wisdom. Charles I and James II are seen as the sacred Stuarts, contradictory creatures of sanctity and tyranny. One became one of the few distinctively Anglican saints; the other was proposed for canonization. On the other hand, both were unable to keep their thrones despite ruling one of the most socially and politically conservative countries in Europe: England.

Neither this chapter nor this book will deal with the Stuart myth in England, which, long neglected, is now a province to which other pens are heirs. However, it is important to realize that the cult of Bonnie Prince Charlie is not unique. The doom-laden prince aspiring to a glory nearly attained, but by fate placed beyond his reach, is not an image confined to the sentimentality of Scottish shortbread tins. It is something endemic in the reaction of both contemporaries and historians in Scotland, England, and elsewhere to the family of Stuart itself and its fatal attraction:

> Si quelque chose . . . justifie ceux qui croient à une fatalité à laquelle rien ne peut se soustraire, c'est cette suite continuelle de malheurs qui persécute la maison des Stuarts pendant plus de trois siècles.
>
> Voltaire[3]

Voltaire was an ardent supporter of, and propagandist for, the Stuarts. Charles Edward appears in *Candide* as an example of the most unfortunate of kings. Voltaire shared the fascination which many of those who fought or wrote for the Stuarts experienced: their charm and their misfortunes, their sacred convictions and earthly defeat, their willingness to put principle before pragmatism in their politics, marked them out as different. This mystique persists: historians of the present century have often been as pro- or anti-Stuart as those of the past.[4] Until we understand this, we cannot begin to understand the Stuart myth, nor the manner in which it competes with the myths of the Glorious Revolution, Imperial Britain, and Unionism which officially superseded it.

'Myth' is the appropriate term: none of the concepts mentioned above have settled interpretations. Our attitudes to them all fluctuate from generation to generation, and passionate convictions, scarcely rooted in historical fact, sway the minds of many on these issues.[5] The relevance to Irish politics (in symbolic rather than factual terms) of the years 1689–90 is only one example.

The Stuart myth is no accretion of sentimental Jacobitism: it was contemporaneous with Stuart rule, not merely nostalgic. The Stuarts were, from 1603 at least, clad in a mystique they did much to design. The facts of the Cavalier or Jacobite cause are ultimately incomprehensible without reference to the motivating ideology of sacred kingship, antique right, and manifest destiny which the Stuart kings developed. The images and beliefs they nourished are not, even now, without continuing power. In Scotland these still haunt the concept of national identity itself. That is a measure of their enduring effect, and the subject of this book.

History's temptation to design its conclusions through hindsight can tend to abandon any sense of contemporaneity with events in favour of an orderly reading of them. The orderly reading of the Stuarts which has been long available is that of the Lost Cause: the story of a dynasty doomed by incompetence and circumstances. Recent historians have challenged this argument from results in suggesting that, right into the eighteenth century, there was no *contemporary* sense that the Jacobite cause was fated to defeat.[6] While this view has proved a valuable corrective to the traditional one, it is nevertheless the case that the Stuart cause itself had a strong sense of history and hindsight. Some supporters of the Stuarts *did* dwell in the past long before their cause was lost, because the past was part of the validation both of the antiquity of their royal line and of the sacred and priest-like nature of their kingship, which in part derived from the ancient ideals of the Old Testament. Nostalgia characterizes lost causes: but in Stuart ideology it was an antecedent fact. The deplorable pictures of the Scottish royal line which hang in Holyrood, commissioned in 1684, are a display of this concern with sheer antiquity, paralleled in England by James and Charles's claims to descend from Trojan Brutus, and their resultant manifest destiny as kings of all Britain. They were indeed to be Arthur returned, the saviour-rulers brought by destiny.[7]

The masques performed at Charles I's court presented the monarchy as 'a compromise between the Neoplatonic extremes of Ideal Forms and the diminished reality of earthly appearances': a kind of *realpolitik* Platonism, with the Stuarts as philosopher-kings.[8] The visible beauty of the masques served as spiritual propaganda for a myth of an elevated, glittering, spiritually and intellectually aloof monarchy. Charles's interest in and commitment to iconic representations of himself in literature and painting had become an overt element in court propaganda by the late 1620s.[9] Not only was the monarch depicted as a Platonic hero, a philosopher and judge in his temporal body; his timeless body too, that of the king as symbol of God's power on earth, was held up for veneration by the ecclesiastical establishment. Archbishop Laud's enthusiasm for visible decoration in the Anglican church was summarized in his tribute to 'the beauty of holiness'. The phrase came from the Psalms, but Laud's 'understanding of it was informed by . . . Neoplatonic commonplaces'. Thus a complementary ideological vision of a supreme king representing supreme authority and beauty both in Church and State was worked out. Charles was constitutionally head of the Anglican church. Now he was symbolically head of it too: 'Laud's faith in the power of beauty was the religious analogue to Charles's reliance on icons as a means of governing.'[10]

King and Archbishop worked in tandem to provide an invulnerable image of the monarchy as 'God's ruling agent . . . bringing together heaven and earth'. The 'enraptured union' of State and Church was represented by the iconic images of Stuart majesty,[11] sometimes showing Charles seated upon a white horse, as is the Word of God, 'Faithful and True', in the Book of Revelation:

> I saw heaven standing open and there before me was a white horse, whose rider is called Faithful and True. With justice he judges and makes war. His eyes are like blazing fire, and on his head are many crowns. He has a name no-one but he himself knows. He is dressed in a robe dipped in blood, and his name is the Word of God. The armies of heaven were following him.
>
> Revelation 19: 11–14 (New International Version)

If this kind of symbolism was in Charles's mind, it can be said that his descendants did not abandon this self-image; and when Charles Edward rode into Carlisle to take possession of the city in 1745, he chose a white horse as his mount.[12] Charles I took pains to present himself as the 'white king': crowned in white he was later buried in a snowstorm, his robe too literally 'dipped in blood', that of his martyrdom.[13]

The Stuart family's power to fascinate was not born with Charles I, but his ultimate personal defeat tempts us to underestimate the enduring power of his propaganda, and the sway it obtained not only over his own, but future generations. 'Divine Right' was not a governmental formula: it was a sacred talisman. Moreover, it was one with actual transforming power:

> Our Charles, blessed alchemist! (though strange
> Believe it, future times!) did change
> The iron-age of old
> Into an age of gold!

Cowley's view of Charles as a 'blessed alchemist', who could transmute base metal into gold through holy power, is an example of the view of the Stuarts as fertility magicians; kings who could deliver countries from famine to prosperity, returners of a pastoral golden age.[14] This view became popular in eighteenth-century Scotland, when the Union was blamed for the economic state of the country.

There is no need to dismiss Cowley's praise as poetic flattery. It is too frequently paralleled elsewhere by less interested parties. Charles's enthusiasms for art and literature were like his enthusiasms for masques and Laudianism: an enthusiasm for the portrayal of his kingship, through the nearest things to the modern media available in the 1630s. This is not to say that Charles was calculating, and had no genuine feeling for what he professed. He reached back into antiquity to justify in the depictions he authorized the sacred and stable nature of his regime. The Anglican church was given a more catholic atmosphere in order to recall the orthodoxy of the past, and Charles's patronage of art and letters revived earlier royal practice reaching back to the age of Augustus. As king, Charles sought to show himself as the renewer of the life of the state; as head of the church, he displayed himself as a renewer of the life of the spirit. The power of beauty conveyed in the slogan 'the beauty of holiness' governed both: 'In the whole picture of the Cavalier world there is a grace in life and in death which must appeal to those who love beauty in the reality and the spirit.'[15] It was the power of beauty which the king's image emphasized in both sacred and secular propaganda.

Helped by a long period of peace, Charles's efforts in the direction of image-building were successful: 'O those were Golden dayes!' was not an infrequent reaction to the period of his rule. Once the Civil War had supervened, such reactions intensified, and the past 'acquired a magical beauty' in the eyes of Royalist sympathizers.[16]

The Civil War *did* supervene of course. In terms of the image of the Stuarts, one of the war's main legacies was to emphasize their role as guardians of a peaceful, fertile land, an 'ideal landscape . . . a state of Nature', which enshrined both the qualities of tradition and those of renewal to be found in the Caroline government's administration.[17] The 'incensed, stormie Age' rendered a cult of rural retreat both a symbolic statement and a political necessity for alarmed Royalists:

> Where shall I goe
> Or whither run
>   to shun
> This publique overthrow?

asked Robert Herrick.[18] The answer lay in rural retreat, and privacy relative to the urban uncertainty of Parliamentary London and Covenanting Edinburgh.

Divine right theory's implications for the positive values of the hierarchy to be found in Nature and rural society had appealed to pro-Stuart writers from Ben Jonson onwards, and gave rise both to the 'great house' and the topographical poem. Place and locale were important to Stuart concepts of identity: they were possessed of traditions (folktales for example), and remained unaltered through time despite the changes in the lives of those who lived in them. To the Stuarts, divine right had this kind of unchanging and natural authority. Their apologists associated the dynasty closely with metaphors of the enduring and renewing powers of Nature. The threat to traditional communities and landholdings voiced by more extreme elements in Cromwell's army underlined this connection. Perhaps as a result, 'the number and quality of retirement and garden poems' in the period 1640–60 show a marked pro-Royalist stance. In the central years of the period 'political disaster is commonly presented as a Fall, ruining the landscape as the first Fall was supposed to have done.' This theological interpretation of Stuart collapse was an evocation of precisely the ideology Charles had done so much to propagate. It was one shared by many writers, who projected 'a dream of undiminished squirearchy' and other strategies as an attempt to preserve human stewardship of the collapsing Eden of Britain. Herrick is one of the first to adopt the oak (an ancient pagan and Christian symbol) as a symbol for the Stuart king (thus associating him with longevity, stability, and natural force). John Denham's famous topographical poem 'Cooper's Hill' 'brings into focus the scattered . . . themes of earlier poetry – Jonson's moralized estates, Drayton's loose blend of regional history and geography, Waller's praise of royalist architecture.' In this context the liberty and fertility of the land plays a central role in defining the Stuart identity in terms of ancestral community (Jonson's 'estates', Drayton's 'regional history') and innovative renewal and preservation (Waller's 'praise of royalist architecture'). It is a 'myth of origin', but also one of continuity: 'the hyperbolic landscape . . . embodies the desire to invest the state with the qualities of nature, innocent, self-renewing and inviolable.'[19]

This rural ideology had its counterpart in Stuart political practice, which frequently sustained such images in action. One of the charges brought against Archbishop Laud before his execution in 1645 cited his opposition to enclosures, the early capitalist transformation of the use of land which was driving peasants out of their old communities. This opposition, although not consistently part of Stuart practice, was characteristic of the support their regime wished to be seen to offer to traditional habits and customs. This was, as we shall see, one of the prime causes of the enduring influence of the Stuart myth in Scotland: the importance of tradition, and the abstraction from it of positive values for the present. In Laud's case, his opposition to the enclosure movement has been taken as a judgement which can be extended to include opposition to the Highland Clearances. The Gaelic poet Sorley MacLean has recently made the analogy specific.[20]

The identification of the Stuarts with rural renewal or retreat is displayed with exquisite ambivalence by Andrew Marvell in his garden poems and in his Horatian Ode, a popular and predominantly Royalist poetic vehicle of the early 1650s. In addition, Abraham Cowley's *Davideis* (1656), later loved by Pope (himself a propagandist of rural retreat), was to provide a typology for Jacobite propaganda of exile from a land of milk and honey well into the following century. Both the image of the king as restorer of the land, and that of him as God's Anointed, were conjoined in the poetic, but also in the popular imagination. During the Interregnum, solitude and retreat begin to constitute major literary themes, with images of Charles I ' "in his solitude", implying an unjust separation from royal privilege and honour'.[21] The restoration of Charles II was celebrated as a restoration of Paradisiacal unity to the fallen land:

> Our land (like Eden) flourish'd in his time,
> Defended by an Angel's Sword,
> A terror 'twas to those abroad,
> But all was Paradise to those within.[22]

The iconography of praise is a continuous one; Charles II defends the earthly paradise his father's images were designed to evoke. Such imagery was to provide a continuum for Jacobite complaint after the Revolution of 1688–9: and the memory of a lost Eden, or a lost vision of Eden, haunts Jacobite thought thereafter.

THE SCOTTISH REACTION

I believe that there is a Church-militant . . . which like the Ark must lodge in its bowels all such as are to be saved from the flood of condemnation; but, to chalk out its bordering lines, is beyond the Geography of my Religion.

Sir George Mackenzie, Lord Advocate

Dissent, not satisfied with toleration, is not conscience but ambition.

Edmund Burke[23]

Scotland's National Covenant, and the rejection of the Prayer Book in 1638 and the years that followed, made possible the English Civil War. The Covenanters viewed 'the armies of heaven' (Revelation 19) as their own, not those of Charles. The king's attempt to extend his dual authority over secular and sacred issues into Scotland foundered on the differing inheritance of the Scottish Reformation, born as it was out of the failure rather than the success of royal authority in a previous generation. Charles's and Laud's search for spiritual authority was a development of the relationship between crown and church made possible by the policies and example of Henry VIII and Archbishop Cranmer. Within an English context, Charles's church policies could be made to appear consistent with previous practice, the validation of antiquity by which the Stuarts set such store. In Scotland, he was operating in violation of the lessons of history: the disasters of Charles's grandmother and great-grandmother (Mary of Scots and Mary of Guise), and the narrow successes of his father. Church government by bishops was not as unpopular as has been supposed, especially in the north. But what was unpopular was a church enforced in its practice to conform to the edicts of royal design; a reformed kirk bowed under the dictates of Erastianism, the state interest and control in despite of which the Scottish Reformation had been largely conducted. The authoritarianism of the Anglican state was the sticking point for the Scottish church, and the reasons for the ultimate fate of Episcopacy are to be found not in arguments over church government, but in the responsiveness of its bishops to an Anglocentric concept of control. When Presbyterians objected to Erastianism, they were not complaining of the church's subjection to the state in principle, but were opposing themselves to the Anglican power-structure, and the king, in so far as he was its head and representative. A Scottish polity where the teaching of the church was absorbed by a governing state would have been unobjectionable enough; but the nature of the Scottish kirk's development set it at odds with the authoritarian conjunction between prelate and monarch in the English state.

There was great social pressure to sign the Covenant. Charles's response was extreme: he considered the signatories as little short of treasonable in their designs. This has been thought an over-reaction. Yet it accurately diagnosed what the 'Covenanting dynamic' signified: a symbolic *and* concrete challenge to the Stuart image of authority, a rejection of the political and spiritual design Charles and Laud were interweaving in church and state.[24] The Scottish reaction was rooted in a popular history going back to the Reformation and perhaps beyond, to the thirteenth-century concept of the Community of the Realm of Scotland, and the limitations in the remit of the monarch's authority implicit there and in documents such as the Declaration of Arbroath (1320).[25] The Scottish nobility were often ready to take up factionalism in support of their right to participate in government, and the religious reasons for the Covenant should not blind us to the manner in which it reflected a long-standing tradition, alien to Stuart concepts of central authority. Scotland's response to Charles's policies in 1638–41 derived itself from notions of antiquity, both native and Jewish (the Covenant), and from resultant ideas about the rights of people against the monarch. Control of the presentation of religion through the media of decor and liturgy was the desire of the Stuart image-makers, and in Scotland they failed comprehensively. King Charles had relied on his traditional role as head of the Church of England, and had built on it too: but in Scotland such assumptions were inappropriate. He had used executive powers conferred on him by tradition to demarcate an extended field for the operation of sovereignty: in the country of his own birth, his images, icons, and arguments were rebuffed. In relying for support for his image-making on English and Continental traditions, Charles damaged what had seemed to many Scots in the early seventeenth century a proto-British identity.[26] He reminded Scotland that it was different, and awakened the Scottish subconscious: a deep-seated disorder as far as the creative acts of kingship were concerned. The Covenant was not a political or religious gesture alone: it was symbolic, psychological. No other explanation will do. The legacy of 1638 and the years that followed has left its mark on the consciousness of the British Isles to this day. In his assumptions and designs, Charles awakened a divided consciousness which until then had not known itself fully divided. He tried too hard to impose unity, and so emphasized disparateness. For fifty years Scotland was divided militarily; the political and psychological division lasted incomparably longer. There were those for King Covenant; those for a Covenanted King; and those who believed the King made the only legal covenants. The king and his icons faced the iconoclasts. 1638 was the crisis year for the Stuart myth and the Scottish identity.

Nevertheless, it is easy to be too decided in our judgements concerning the conflict between the king and the Covenanters. It has, in its turn, been mythologized, though that mythology has now only a local and limited role in comparison with the many domains and disciplines in which the Stuart myth itself has developed an influence. The Jacobite risings ensured that the story of the Covenanters would be overshadowed by the greater story of their adversaries. The strong opposition of 1638 had in any case divided by the 1640s, as the Reformation tradition on which it drew became a premise for fanatically innovative action. The desertion of Montrose to the Royalist cause so early in the Civil War period was significant in undermining the ideal of a unified Scottish response. His series of smashing victories, fought largely with Highland soldiers, won their own mystique, and he subsequently entered Stuart hagiographies. From almost the beginning, the symbolic political acts of 1638–41 were destabilized in their role as metaphors for a nationalist resistance to Stuart tyranny. After Cromwell's victories confirmed the ascendancy of a schismatic (to the Presbyterians) and triumphalist English army, the wheel had turned almost full circle, and Stuart rule was clearly the patriotic option.

But 1638 still gave rise to a sequence of events which confirmed the presence in Scotland of a religiously authoritarian culture, distrustful of the kind of marriage of secular and sacred values Charles had sought. Both the union of church and state and the propaganda means by which it was to be achieved were distrusted by the Presbyterians. Artists and writers, largely supportive of the Stuart regime, were only one of the objects of attack. Culture and beauty were after all the values of patronage, not only corrupted by Erastian politics, but also tainted with the values of the Greek and Roman worlds. To the champions of intellectual and artistic culture, Presbyterian domination was a philistine threat; and the inheritors of such culture have often continued to see it in the same light, as will be discussed in Chapter 5: 'with the revolution of 1638, Scotland plunged into an era of *Unkultur* from which it did not recover before the defeat of the last Jacobite rising.'[27]

Certainly the Covenant had a profound and rapid cultural impact. Earlier generations of religious reformers had been markedly pro-English; this was no longer possible given Charles's approach to church government. Instead the Covenanters sought internal uniformity to deal with the external threat. Zealous attempts to impose this sense of unity in all Scots awakened, in their turn, hostile responses from hitherto constitutionally quiescent groups. One of these was the Gaeltacht, where at least a third of the population of Scotland lived. A rapid rise in 'Scottish Gaelic vernacular poetry' appears to have occurred as a means of orchestrating a Royalist response to the 'Covenanting dynamic', one reinforced by the bloodthirsty triumphalism of some of the Gaelic poems which greeted Montrose's victories. The Covenanters demanded assimilation of the rural hinterland and the Gaeltacht in their drive for victory against the king:

> For over thirteen years . . . until the battle of Worcester on 3 September 1651, the Covenanting Movement exerted unprecedented pressures on the Scottish localities in an effort to establish and maintain constitutional checks on an absentee monarchy.[28]

In response to this, 'folksongs in Scottish Gaelic' begin to 'accord greater priority to political propaganda and social comment than to artistic standards'. This is also apparently true of the song culture in Lowland Scots. The literary organs of Stuart propaganda without royal encouragement spontaneously found their role as voices in opposition to the social didacticism of the Covenanters. 'Poetry and songs were . . . transmitted outwith the townships and the territories of their kindred' in an effort to oppose the political ascendancy of the Covenanting forces within Scotland.[29] Moreover, elements in these forces undermined their own authority by pushing the case for resistance to the king too far. The Solemn League and Covenant (1643), which attempted to commit England to Presbyterianism, was a mirror-image of Charles's own policy of the 1630s. It rather alienated than rallied many of the forces in Scottish society on which the Covenanters needed to depend. By 1647–8, 'Scotland was a country divided as it had hardly been since Pinkie, a hundred years before.'[30] In England, Laud's execution (or martyrdom) in 1645 was followed by that of Charles in 1649. His son, Charles II, was crowned in Scotland on condition he accepted the Covenant; but after his defeat at Worcester in 1651, Cromwell became master of Scotland. He reduced it, as he did all Britain, to a state of military government and control. Charles fled abroad, and only on his return in 1660 was the Scottish parliament restored, and after it Episcopacy.

Charles II did not rule Scotland untroubled, but Episcopacy survived. The Covenanters had lost much of their support furth of their heartlands, and despite Drumclog and Bothwell Brig (1679), remained more of an irritant than a major political threat. The toleration of loyal Presbyterianism (1667) eased matters significantly for many; otherwise, the government might have been wiser to ignore than repress. The previous ascendancy of the Covenanters had, however, guaranteed at least one thing: the commitment of the clans to Scottish politics, made in reaction to Covenanting pressure. This was to be one of the most important military facts in Stuart politics for the next hundred years.

Charles II was, perhaps through circumstance, a more self-consciously intelligent man than many of his family. He did not have his father's capacity for self-valorization; or he did not consider it safe to display it. James, his brother, always differed, and was inclined to think that their father had given in too much, rather than too little, to the demands of his opponents. The myth of the martyr–monarch, the artistic and sensitive hero-king, had survived and outgrown the various attacks on it from Scottish and English quarters in the previous thirty years. But it was already itself a nostalgic story. The 'golden dayes' of Charles I had gone for ever. Charles II did not choose to extend or resuscitate the mystique his martyr father had conceptualized and delineated, except in selected and unobtrusive areas (his large-scale use of the Royal Touch for sacred healing, for example). James had grander plans.

He was sent to Scotland late in 1679 to keep him out of the way during the Exclusion crisis in England, when many wanted James kept from the throne because of his Catholicism. In Scotland, he had a freer hand, and he made use of it to rebuild and extend the Stuart mystique in the very country which had proved so antipathetic to its claims forty years before.

James was in Scotland for three years. He determined to make Edinburgh an intellectual centre of Stuart Royalism. Indeed it can be argued that the roots of that apparently mysterious growth, the Scottish Enlightenment, which 'sprung up ... by a sort of enchantment, soon after the rebellion of 1745', were planted by James's patronage of the arts and professions.[31] The Duke of York (as he then was) laid a typically Stuart stress on the antiquity of kingship and its resultant patriarchal rights. This ideology was reflected and developed by the Lord Advocate, Sir George Mackenzie, in his *Ius Regium*. As a benevolent patriarch, the father of his people, James was partly or wholly responsible for the institution of the Advocates' Library and the Royal College of Physicians, as well as the Order of the Thistle (1687). He was attempting to reinforce Scotland's cultural heritage, at the same time altering it subtly by clothing it in institutions and forms which stressed the pro-Stuart values of order, inheritance, and establishment. He was seeking to provide Edinburgh with an ideology of learned elitism far from the democratic Scripturalism of the Covenanting divines. In doing so, he emphasized ancient and by implication pre-Reformation traditions: the Order of the Thistle is a good example, with its overtones of aristocratic patriotism, so well exploited by Sir Walter Scott in his novel *Redgauntlet*. The cult of the virtuoso, 'the Royalist intellectual model', was encouraged. The powers and reputation of the University (first called so at this time) were extended, despite its doubtful sympathies in regard to the royal duke. James did not meddle with its curriculum, unlike the Presbyterian regime in the 1690s.

By his attention to the arts and professions, and in reinforcing the claim of the Stuarts to rightful authority by virtue of ancient lineage and traditional sympathies, James attempted to win back an intellectual and symbolic high ground which Charles II had cautiously abandoned. His actions in the Scottish capital between 1679 and 1688 were 'intended to make Edinburgh a fitting capital for the Royalist aristocracy', but were also intended to rehabilitate the heroic image of his dynasty as great patrons and benefactors, deriving authority from the teaching and example of the past on which they built.[32]

James's accession in 1685 was popular on both sides of the Border. Unfortunately, he misconstrued the underlying sentiment as a licence to assert his powers. It would be rash to venture here on a full assessment of his controversial rule; but his support for religious toleration, whether fundamental or contrived, was an attitude centuries ahead of that of his subjects in both England and Scotland. He was far from merciless against Covenanters who were not caught in arms against the government, expressing the opinion that they 'deserved a Bedlam rather than a gallows'.[33] With respect to English Nonconformity, his mass release of Quakers from prison in 1686–7 earned him credit in their ranks.

Yet history has long recorded James a tyrant, and his religious toleration plays no small part in this assessment. The Declarations of Indulgence in 1687–8 violated the very link they were meant to preserve: that between sacred and secular authority. Like his father, James was concerned to present himself as sovereign in matters both sacred and secular, and to regain the ideal of the myth of sacred kingship his father had subscribed to. As a Roman Catholic, he could not seek that sovereignty through the Anglican church. Charles I had sought a mystic headship of that church: but James was not even a member of it. Instead, he sought the mystic overlordship of his subjects through the medium of toleration: he was wise enough to realize that the imposition of Roman Catholicism was, even had he wished it, an impossibility, though there were fashionable conversions at Court. Instead, the king would stand for toleration between faiths, showing both his sovereign mercy and his sovereign authority towards and over all his subjects.

In Scotland, he had constructed and encouraged patterns of antiquity and tradition in the development of intellectual and other institutions designed to reinforce his family's claim to hereditary authority and role as guardian of the nation's material and spiritual well-being. By concentrating in this on developments more in consonance with the pre-Reformation past, he combated more recent changes in Scottish culture in a manner designed to support an Episcopalian intellectual elite of classicists, lawyers, theologians, and senior professionals. These sought for precedent and prerogative for Stuart rule and Scottish independence over the next sixty years, in the process erecting a series of complex cultural typologies which were antipathetic to the more radical aims of Presbyterians and Unionists.

This policy had considerable success in Scotland. On both sides of the Border, toleration was a different matter, since it struck at the spiritual authority of the Anglican church, and the king's part in that authority. James had supported toleration for almost twenty years; as soon as he attempted to introduce it, his constitutional position as head of the Anglican church was fatally compromised. Despite his hostility to Louis XIV's maltreatment of Protestants, James convinced few that he was acting as a patriot king should in undermining the central role of the Church of England. His even-handedness contributed nothing to his hoped-for status as sacred father of his people, at that time better based on clerical imperialism than toleration. Relief for the Huguenots was forgotten in the reaction to events such as the public reception of the Papal Nuncio in 1687. The Three Questions, which attempted to elicit whether those in public authority supported James's religious policies, received a mixed reception. In the English counties 26 per cent consented to the repeal of anti-Catholic legislation; in Wales 22 per cent. Many responded ambiguously or did not reply. James went ahead, and 'by August 1688 toleration was . . . established, in a fuller form than at any time in the next 150 years'.[34]

Meanwhile James reinforced the Stuart image of the sacred king by popular encounters as well as through structural reforms. Touching for the King's Evil was an important element in the outward manifestation of Stuart spiritual power (it is significant that this practice stopped altogether after the Stuarts, for it belonged to their ideology of kingship). James was as enthusiastic for it as his brother Charles (who touched 100,000) had been: he spent more on it than he did on promoting his own religion.[35] At Oxford in September 1687, James touched 700–800 people in two days, and there were other like occasions. This was effective spiritual propaganda for thousands; those who were touched, families, spectators, and those to whom the story was passed on.[36] When today a political candidate's personal visit to a few hundred homes can win an election in a constituency with tens of thousands of voters, how much more effective was the public act of the Touch conferred on thousands then? It was not the ordinary people who threw James from his throne.

Toleration in Scotland was not open to the remaining Covenanters, who themselves would hardly have offered it had they been in a position of authority. But James's support was declining in Scotland in any case, and the Estates in Edinburgh rejected toleration by a large majority. Concern was growing that it was a cloak for a Roman Catholic spiritual coup, and this fear was focused on the presence of Catholics in James's standing army. There were widely believed to be many of these; but this was in fact untrue, save in Ireland, where so many of the population were Catholic in any case. The commanders of the Scottish forces were all Protestants, and it was well said of the army in Scotland that 'the hundredth man . . . is not a Catholic, and we have scarce any officers of that persuasion'.[37]

But the truth of such matters did not overly concern those who were suspicious of the *innovatory* (and the word is worth stressing) nature of James's government. The weakness of toleration was that it undermined tradition, not reinforced it, as Charles's sacred Anglican cult had tried to do. The Stuart king in this generation was not calling on the practice of ages to 'Vindicate his . . . Right',[38] but was bent rather on altering the established precedent of the Constitution by undermining Protestant Episcopacy. In so far as there was a traditional dimension to this kind of political action it was (as in the image-building in Scotland from 1679 to 1688) concerned with a tradition which was the *status quo ante*: Roman Catholicism. John Dryden, the poet laureate and James's propagandist in religious matters, put it thus:

> What weight of antient witness can prevail
> If private reason hold the publick scale?

The 'antient witness' Dryden speaks of in his poem 'The Hind and the Panther' is a concept which, we have seen, is a fundamental part of Stuart claims to authority: the precedents and statements of antiquity and tradition. But in Dryden's poem it is indicative of spiritual authority also; and that authority belongs to the Roman Catholic church. Many of James's contemporaries less sympathetic than Dryden detected a traditional return to that 'antient witness' under the guise of the innovatory policies of toleration. Certainly the Stuarts' sympathy towards Catholic practice (Anglican or Roman) was the natural concomitant of the force of their reverence for traditional methods and sources of authority, and a significant element in their image of themselves as sacred monarchs. Dryden wrote thus of the king who was 'God's Image, God's Anointed':

> Let his Baptismal Drops for us attone;
> Lustrations for offences not his own.[39]

The sacred act of baptism was itself a sign of the power of the Stuart monarchy, the 'just and legal Succession of the sacred Line', 'unalterable by any human Jurisdiction', as the Scots Estates expressed it.[40] Senior heir of the houses of Tudor and Plantagenet as well as of Wessex and Stuart, James VII and II was a living embodiment of the 'Sacred Authority and Power' vested in all English kings since the Saxon royal line (via Queen Margaret, wife of Malcolm III Canmore) and all Scottish kings since the Bruce. In England, the Stuarts were the first dynasty since the Conquest to be free of competing claims to the throne. James was the rightful inheritor of every royal line with a claim: there was none other by virtue of hereditary right. Small wonder that the Stuarts saw themselves as the destined kings of a united Britain, a dynasty who were the consummation of all the royal houses who had gone before. To overthrow them would be an especial blasphemy.[41]

This was to be accomplished in 1688, when William of Orange landed in the west country and marched on London. He received substantial support from the powers that be for his opposition to James. But he and his supporters showed the depth of their awareness of the strength of the Stuart claim to the throne through their propaganda. The 'warming-pan story', which suggested that James's son, born in June 1688, was illegitimate, was an attempt to undermine the overwhelming legitimacy of the Stuart claim to the throne by a crude smear which it is clear William himself did not believe.[42] His behaviour was 'incredible': 'James can hardly be blamed for finding it difficult to believe that his kingdom would be invaded by his son-in-law, with his daughter's approval.'[43] William's declaration acknowledged the Stuart image of kingship ironically in the very crudity of its accusations, speaking as it did of James's 'worst betrayal of his sacred crown by putting forward a base-born heir'.[44]

James's own behaviour verged on mental collapse. Like Lear, he was deserted by his daughters, and his new-born son was sneered at by them and his son-in-law. He could not bring himself to make a coherent attempt to defend his kingdoms and fled. What a contemporary historian calls 'the symbolic date' of 1688 had ended the tenure of the dynasty which above all others had paid attention to its own symbols and the creation of its own myth.[45] The Scottish Estates' proud boast of tradition and allegiance, made in 1685, states that 'This nation hath continued now upwards of two thousand years in the unaltered form of our monarchical government.'[46] Four years later this boast was virtually abandoned, and a train of events set off which would lead to the end of Scotland's independence. From now on, our concern will be entirely with what happened north of the Border. 'Our holy king' had fled.[47]

THE DRIFT TO UNION

Halloo! the Hunt's begun
Like Father, like Son!

So the Whigs sang during the early 1680s.[48] The song proved prophetic. Although the attempt made in England at that time to exclude James from the throne had resulted in a strong loyalist backlash, his flight in 1688 wrongfooted his supporters by leaving them without a figure to rally round. The runaway ruler was a less credible icon than the martyr–monarch. In England, there was virtually no armed resistance, and it is from this fact that the term 'Glorious (i.e. bloodless) Revolution' is derived.[49] In Scotland, anti-Catholic riots in the capital served to underline the Estates' decision of spring 1689 to recognize William as king in Scotland. The extent to which

Williamite support was bound up with pressure for a restored Presbyterian ascendancy was underlined when the Scots parliament abolished Episcopal church government on 5 June that year. Henceforward the Episcopal church, which William himself had been initially willing to recognize in the interests of continuity and order, was disestablished and its ministers dispossessed. It had remained loyal to James, and so the new king abandoned it. For the next century, it, and not the Roman Catholic church, was to serve as the theological and political focal-point for Jacobite ideology north of the Border.[50]

Even while its fate hung in the balance, jubilant Covenanters were harrying Episcopal ministers out of their charges in the south west of Scotland, where there was little sympathy with the bishops. In the areas where native as opposed to imposed Episcopacy was stronger, such as the north east, ministers were sometimes not dispossessed for many years, particularly if the local laird lent armed men for the preservation of their charge. In co-operation with such Jacobite defiance, an Episcopal ideology was developed based on Stuart ideas of tradition and sacred kingship, which challenged the right of the Presbyterian establishment (and, after 1707, the British Parliament) to rule over Scotland.

During 1689, however, the church and its leaders were paralysed: 'the Kirk invisible', one of James's chief supporters called them.[51] They could not halt the political events of that year, which began with William's letter to the Estates in March 1689 recommending Union between Scotland and England. There was renewed interest in the topic, to judge by contemporary pamphlets, interest which was directed against the restoration of Stuart rule:

> for if the *King* [James] return wee . . . Cut of all Hopes of an Union with that *Nation* [England], and thereby Deprive our selves of an unspeakable Advantage, which would redound to all sorts of People, and would be the only means to support an Impoverish'd and sinking Nation.

This 'letter' was sent 'By a Lover of His Religion and Country'.[52] The two had gone together in Scotland in the most peculiar and unsatisfactory respects during the seventeenth century. It was not untrue that by 1689 Scotland was 'Impoverish'd and sinking' compared with England, a situation which was to intensify during the famine years of the 1690s and through the financial misery of the Darien venture. Such a situation had developed naturally enough out of the extended period of civil war and religious uncertainty which had begun half a century before. The original Covenanters of 1638 had rejected the aspiration of the Stuart kings to incorporate Scottish religion into the pattern of Anglican authority. In so doing, they led both nation and religion into a state of civil war. Just as Charles had chosen to ignore part of the traditional inheritance of the Scottish Reformation in his insistence on his sacred authority, so the Covenanters, in his reign and during the reigns of his sons, chose to ignore the nature of royal authority in the interests of religious resistance. They complained of Erastianism; but in a sense they were by nature Erastians, mixing questions of church and state with an ease which allowed them to be regarded as rebels with so much reason that further repression was inevitable. Out of that further repression yet further resistance was born. In 1689, Scotland had been suffering from this vicious circle of events for far too long. Religious and secular politics, never distinctly separate at this period in any case, had been so ruthlessly conflated by both sides that parts of Scotland seemed in perpetual rebellion against the king (God's Anointed) on behalf of God. Others, on behalf of God and the same king, saw these rebellions as the political acts in reality which they were only metaphorically to those who prioritized the God of the Covenant, a God of Israel's chosen status and armed resistance. Many Covenanters saw secular acts as religious; and their opponents took an opposite view. Between such positions there could be no compromise, and Scotland lay exhausted in the effort to find one.

The political problems were real enough. In his letter to the Estates, William displayed more skill than was to be found in the rival letter which purported to be from James, but was probably written by one of his more gung-ho advisers.[53] William was conciliatory, and his recommendation of Union may have seemed an opportunity for Scotland to divest itself of internal conflict through turning its attention to a wider horizon. That this horizon would be even more restrictive of Scotland's political rights than Charles's sacred union had been of her religious ones is certain; but it was a plausible line to pursue in the willing ear of the parliament of an exhausted nation.

The Bishop of Edinburgh (as he then still officially was) 'prayed God to have Compassion on King *James*, and to restore him', but such an event became less likely when the rival letter was produced. Though fair in tone, it contained too many threats of justice hereafter to be thought diplomatic. These threats were also too reminiscent of the period of conflict Scotland had just passed through. The letter may not have been James's own; but it made no matter: William carried the day.[54] The Duke of Gordon was still holding the Castle for James, but he, like many others, seemed to have little stomach for a fight. Outside the parliament in Edinburgh, the propaganda pamphlets against the late regime beat their insistent drum: '*Popery* and *Slavery*', '*Popery* and *Tyranny*', forcing home the message that James was an arbitrary tyrant, and that the Stuart reliance on tradition concealed a sympathy for pre-Reformation religion and primitive and arbitrary habits of governmental decision-making.

James was also associated with opposition to any proposed Union. In 1689, that might have been a black mark: it was not to be so in the years to come. During the 1690s William was not notably enthusiastic either, and left the Scottish noble factions to govern their country in much the same way as their predecessors had done.[55] Before the end of his reign in 1702 he became interested in Union again; for left to themselves, the Estates became gradually alienated from the English polity. Their eventual unwillingness to guarantee the Hanoverian succession may be seen as evidence of the growing unease with which the constitutional consequences of the 1689 settlement were regarded. On a broader front, England sought to stifle Scottish colonial and mercantile expansion, and to reverse the Stuart policy of 'keeping out of Europe's power-struggles'.[56] The fierce opposition to France implicit in the terms of the Glorious Revolution, though politically almost inevitable, was bad for Scotland's trade and traditional contacts on the Continent. Moreover, although Presbyterianism was popular in the central belt, it was less so elsewhere in Scotland (and this at a time when the majority of Scotland's population lived north of the Tay): 'The Nobles and Gentry are generally Episcopal, and so the People especially Northward', wrote a pamphleteer in 1690. The religious divide still gaped beneath the shaky brig of the 1689 settlement. Scottish pamphleteers compared the sufferings of Episcopacy to those of the Christians under Nero (as in 'A narrative of the late treatment of the Episcopal ministers'). The view from the south, that 'the *Revolution* is the great aera of English liberty', was not one shared by all, especially not after the Union.[57]

The process of alienation was, however, gradual. In 1689, only Viscount Dundee's army of 2,500 fought for King James in Scotland, winning at Killiecrankie, and losing at Dunkeld to one of the most extreme Covenanting forces of all, the Cameronians. Dundee was hated by them, and his predominantly clan-based army attracted comparatively little support. James gave him little help: he had his hands full in Ireland fighting the battles and sieges which would perpetuate the Stuart myth of Irish patriotism as far as the reaches of contemporary politics. The defeat of the Jacobites (as they were now called) in Ireland came in 1691 at Aughrim; in Scotland in 1690 at Cromdale. W. B. Yeats wrote that the defeat of the Jacobites in Ireland spelled the end for Irish Celtic civilization;[58] in Scotland, the myth of the Stuarts became bound up with the idea of a *restored* Celtic civilization. As Scotland drifted into England's orbit, there was an attempt (which continued long after the Union) to reach back into the past in order to invent a community-based organic society, free of conflicts, which was represented in the persons of the Stuart kings and the status of an independent Scotland.[59] This vision of a true, ideal Scotland persisted in many forms, as we shall see in the chapters to come. The society the Stuarts had sought to create by their appeals to tradition, their heroic iconographies, and their presentation of themselves as sacred patriarchs, became the image accepted by hindsight, as if they had succeeded in engendering it. The Stuart image became a dominant Scottish memory. As resentment grew against Scotland's marginalization in terms of predominantly English mercantile and strategic interests, so did the view of Scotland as the inheritor of a unified past, and 'Scots of every kind

. . . began to consider themselves as part of an essentially Celtic nation',[60] a nation unified by a long history of resistance to England. This change was slow in coming, and never incorporated groups such as the more committed Presbyterians, nor was it held by all with equal intensity. But during the eighteenth century it was to begin to change the way Scots regarded their own national culture and its apparently divided expressions. At first it was a view of Scotland popular only among Jacobites, but the measures leading to Union widened its appeal, and it continues to exist both in the sentimental cult of tartanry and in a more elusive, but positive, search for political and cultural identity.[61]

'King William's lean years', which began with the harvest of 1696, were seven bad years of famine for Scotland. They intensified the economic crisis in the country. Some blamed them on God's displeasure concerning the overthrow of the Stuarts; but in practical terms, they destabilized even further the prosperity of the Scottish polity.[62]

As well as economic, there were also constitutional developments which warned of coming economic crisis. The Act of Settlement of 1701, narrowly passed by the English Parliament, guaranteed the succession of the House of Hanover. The Act excluded the Stuarts for ever if they remained Catholic, and by excluding Catholics from the throne, prevented not only James's son James VIII from succeeding, but also fifty-six members of European royal families closer in blood than George. The Act represented in practice a volte-face from William's offer of the late 1690s to bring up the young James in England. By so doing, he recognized the legitimacy of the Prince of Wales, a decade after he and his supporters had so cruelly and publicly doubted it. But their religion was always the price the Stuarts were not prepared to pay: their sacred kingship could brook no compromise with earthly realities.[63]

Although the governing classes of Scotland, now officially a Presbyterian country, might have been expected to abhor the restoration of the Stuarts even more markedly, there was strong feeling against the Act of Settlement. It seemed as if England high-handedly expected Scotland to follow suit, and accept the Act. It did not. In 1703, the Act of Security was passed, and this, in conjunction with the Act anent Peace and War, represented a twofold challenge to the power of the English Parliament. The Scottish Estates reserved the right for Scotland to keep a separate foreign policy and adopt a different monarch.

The Act anent Peace and War was intended to distance Scotland from England's growing imperial strategic interests, by underlining Scotland's right to pursue a distinct path in the political conflicts of Europe. Combined with trading and colonial adventures abroad, it underlined growing reservations concerning the necessary convergence of Scotland's and England's political futures. If it was an Act which reserved a sovereign right to Scotland, the Act for the Security of the Kingdom claimed the choice of the sovereign himself. The Act of Security was a challenge to the constitutional privileges the English Parliament was demanding by virtue of the Act of Settlement. It effectively stood in opposition to the Settlement's encroachment on Scottish political jurisdiction in the same way that the National Covenant had barred the way to Anglican constitutional supremacy a lifetime before. Once again, an English government was attempting to extend its own constitutional resolutions to Scotland: not openly or aggressively, as Charles had done, but surreptitiously. The Act's supporters seem to have tacitly assumed that the Scottish Estates would follow the English lead, as they had done in 1689.

Rather, the Act of Security claimed Scotland's right to choose its own monarch, 'being always of the Royal LINE of *Scotland*', and a Protestant. Despite this latter provision, it was believed in Scotland that the measure effectively favoured the Stuarts. Certainly, the country was distancing itself from the English constitutional revolution of 1688–1701. The provision for a successor of 'the Royal LINE of *Scotland*' was in any case threatening to Hanover, since if it did not point to the Stuarts, it could be applied close to home in the person of the Duke of Hamilton. The Hamiltons had been close to the throne before, through their descent from a daughter of James II of Scots. Now the Estates passed legislation which opened the door to one of their number. But Hamilton was distrusted. He wheeled and dealed but did not know when to strike, and sat on the fence too long, through the Union of 1707 and the Jacobite Rising of 1708, both crucial times for Scotland. His lethargy did him no good, and compromised the Stuart cause, which was the only one with a real hope of success. Despite the alarm bells it rang in England, the Act of Security did not go far enough to secure the Stuart succession it was seen to imply; and the claim of Hamilton hung like chains on attempts to defeat the looming Union by Jacobite means.[64]

The Act of Security nevertheless challenged the English government. They responded by renewing the pressure for Union from 1705 onwards. For some time previously, however, there had been a propaganda war concerning the respective constitutional positions of England and Scotland, with English pamphleteers claiming long-standing feudal suzerainty over Scotland. Edgar, the Saxon king supposedly rowed down the Dee by eight subject kings, was one example used; Henry II's and Edward I's partial control over Scotland were others. It was as if the ideological ground for Union was being prepared long before the political necessity for it actually arrived.[65] Perhaps the propaganda of the pamphlets and books was an attempt to consolidate the apparently joint settlement of 1689. The Estates had agreed to most of the outcomes of the Glorious Revolution, but they had not initiated them, and the difference was profound. Scotland was following England: the opposite of its actions in the age of the Covenant. In the Covenanting era, Scotland had initiated significant political action, both in support of and in opposition to the Stuarts and their rule. Now the inheritors of the Royalists were the Jacobites, who of necessity opposed the English government; the inheritors of the Covenanters were also dissatisfied with the moderate but obtrusive

Erastian and Anglican priorities of the London administration. The Estates themselves were tagging along at the heel of English constitutional reform (at least until 1702), which thus had the capacity to alienate both the Stuart/authoritarian and Covenanting/radical wings of Scottish opinion, because it was an alien process conceived and executed furth of Scotland in the interests of certain groups in English society. The class base of pro-Revolution opinion in England served to stoke popular Jacobitism in the English provinces;[66] in Scotland it presumed an authority which, at first welcomed in the establishment of Presbyterianism, had after fifteen years lost its glamour. The house guest of the 1689 Settlement had decided to take over its host's living room, and settle the Elector of Hanover at the head of the table. If this was not enough, the propaganda of the English and pro-English pamphleteers increasingly suggested that Scottish co-operation was only the legitimate development of Scottish subjection. Famine, and the collapse of colonial experiments such as Darien, underlined a divergence in the prosperity of the two countries which appeared a metaphor for that subjection. Scotland was poor, and Scotland was inferior.

Scottish writers responded to these suggestions vigorously. Sir Thomas Craig's *Scotland's Soveraignty Asserted*, largely written almost a century before, was published in 1695 as a rebuttal to claims of long-standing Scottish feudal subjection. Craig points out that homage in Saxon times was technically impossible due to a lack of feudal machinery, and parallels Scottish homage for Cumberland and Westmorland to Denmark's acknowledgement of the Holy Roman Emperor as lord over the *Distmarsh*.

Craig's work predictably mentions William Wallace, though in a position subordinate to the esteem in which he is now generally held. Although Wallace is like 'the Antient Hero's', when his part in the Battle of Falkirk (1297) is mentioned, he appears only as the last of three commanders, '*John Cummin . . . John Steward* and *William Wallace*.'[67] Wallace receives limited attention compared to that he was accorded in the Middle Ages, and was to inherit in the eighteenth century, when Jacobite interpretations of Bruce and Wallace underlined their positions as national heroes anew. The view of loyal Bruce and Wallace inherited by the Victorian age was conditioned by their incorporation in the Stuart myth of the national identity engendered in the popular literature of the eighteenth century. Wallace became a designer-hero appealing to the radical, while Bruce appealed to the royalist in Jacobite image-projection. Their struggles for independence were adopted as one of the central chapters in a story of Scotland based on struggle, and their achievements and aims were aligned with those of the Stuarts. As I shall argue, since only the Jacobites had a developed ideology of response to Scotland's loss of political power, their projection of Scotland's historical struggle with England is the one we inherit. Their talent for promoting iconographies of tradition provided a heroic history for a country shorn of its present identity in the years following 1707.

27

Whereas Craig's views were a century old, Scotland's constitutional counter-propaganda claimed the service of many living writers. James Anderson, whose *Scotland Independent* appeared in 1705, a significant year for the constitutional debate, 'received the public acknowledgement and thanks of the Scottish Parliament' for his book. Written in response to a work by a Mr Atwood which argued the case for English constitutional supremacy, it engages with his claims in polemical style, dismissing especially the old canard about Edgar: 'the vain whim of *Edgars* being row'd over *Dee* ... devised by the Monks'.[68] Historical examples like this one, and the Scottish counter-arguments against them, crop up again and again in the propaganda battles of the period. It is quite clear from the discussion that two conflicting ideas of British history are embattled. After 1707, as might have been expected, the English interpretation gained the upper hand. Well into the twentieth century, histories of Britain made great play of the constitutional significance of episodes like the one quoted above. This book only deals with the Stuart myth and the Scottish identity: but in passing it should be noted that a competing British imperial myth of manifest destiny and British unity was created by historians out of the slim evidence of the pro-English writers in the short-lived pamphlet wars which led up to the Union. The winning side of the political controversy contributed substantially to British history and to the idea of Saxon supremacy.[69]

While they raged, the pamphlet wars provided plenty of evidence for historical interpretation. History, tradition, and the lessons of antiquity were indeed uppermost in the arguments of the Scottish writers. Thus Scotland's identity was projected in the same manner as the Stuart identity had been: through the medium of past practice. James Dalrymple's tract, *Collections Concerning the Scottish History*, also written against Atwood, was published in 1705. William Nicolson, a pro-English writer, who had attempted to impugn the legitimacy of the Scottish royal line in a book of 1702, was answered by Robert Sibbald's *Liberty and Independency of the Kingdom and Church of Scotland*, which was directed in succeeding editions against the arguments of both Nicolson and Atwood. James Drake's *Historia Anglo-Scotica* went so far as to entirely fake a chronicle history of Anglo-Scottish relations in order to argue for English supremacy. On the other hand, books such as George Ridpath's *An Historical Account of the Antient Rights and Power of the Parliament of Scotland* were encouraging the Estates to act more independently.[70] The debate took a concrete and contemporary shape as the prospect of Union loomed, and the years after 1701 witnessed extended conflict between Scottish and English political interests disguised in the language and issues of the past. The battle of the books raged as tension between the two countries mounted. The winner would be able, literally, to make history.

Significantly, the interest in defining the status of Scotland in the present in terms of what was or was not the fact in the past, involved arguments relevant to both church and state. This is not surprising in the light of the Scottish conflation of church and state in the definitions of identity of the seventeenth century. Wars had been fought over the subordination of the former to the latter. The independency of the Scottish church and the Scottish state were seen by many of the tracts as different ends of the same axis. The Covenanters had defended Scotland's right to exist as the intimate relation of the Scottish church's special status. This had effectively led to the exaltation of the rights of the church above those of the commands of the state. Church and State were conflated, but in the interests of the former: that was the lesson of the Covenants of 1638 and 1643.

The failure to define the difference between ecclesiastical and political questions cost Scotland dear in the seventeenth century. It was a response to Charles I's attempt to do the same thing; but as head of the Anglican church, he had had more constitutional grounds for his religious actions. In any case, the Stuarts had now gone; but the same failure of differentiation continued in Scotland, and contributed signally to the Union. By its guarantee of the continued status of an independent and Presbyterian Scottish church, the Union preserved itself against the overwhelming opposition it would otherwise have faced. The promise of independence in the church was enough to prevent the Presbyterians rallying to the defence of the state, despite the fact that the axis of Scotland's religious and political identity now ran loosely behind the driving wheels of English constitutional ascendancy. The Scottish church preserved its identity, as did established interests in the Scottish state, but the driving force of government was gone.

This settlement did not please all the Presbyterian party; but it was acceptable to many. Naturally, Episcopalians saw things differently. They too had accepted the interdependence of church and state, but on more equal terms, and governed through the person of the sacred king. For them, the Union confirmed their dispossession, and underlined their desertion by Anglican England. At the Revolution, six hundred Episcopal ministers had refused to swear allegiance to William; and in England, a similar number of Anglican priests did the same. Naturally these, the Nonjurors, represented a far smaller proportion of the whole. Most of those in Anglican orders were keener to keep their livings than their principles. The stance of a whole generation of Anglican clerics is described in the popular song, 'The Vicar of Bray':

> And whatsoever king may reign
> Still I'll be Vicar of Bray, Sir.[71]

Anglican doctrines of loyalty to the Stuarts were exposed as flags of intellectual convenience, as churchmen voted with their feet for ecclesiastical advancement.

Scottish Episcopalians remained loyal to the Stuarts in overwhelming numbers. The years after 1689 showed that the Revolution's heirs regarded the preservation of the Anglican polity (a major premise for the Revolution itself) as a partial exercise. The price of Scottish co-operation was by and large the abandonment of Scottish Episcopacy. The Revolution may have killed the Catholic hind, but it scotched the Episcopal panther. A large proportion of Scottish society was religiously and politically dispossessed. Such suffering further underlined the economic misery of Scotland which was diagnosed by writers like Nathaniel Johnston as a punishment for abandoning the Stuarts: 'a long Train of War, Famine, Want, Blood and Confusion, entailed upon us and our Posterity . . . as God's punishment for the sin of rebellion'.[72] Many Episcopalians shared this point of view.

The fact that Johnston's and similar prophecies were borne out in Scotland's situation was a destabilizing factor. Poor and under pressure, Scotland's statehood by 1703 was so compromised as to draw Episcopalian and Presbyterian interpretations of events closer for the first time. The former saw the state of affairs in their country as a punishment for transgressions; the latter saw it as a decline in part engineered by English interests, particularly after Darien. Both had reservations over England's role in Scotland's affairs, and for a while after 1700, hostility towards England was greater than it had been at any time since the Middle Ages. England's only long-term answer to the growing reservations over its influence was Union. The Presbyterians were incorporated in this end through preservation of their privileges, which predictably overrode for them the Erastian risks of London government. The Episcopalians got nothing save a few religious concessions from High Church Tories in the south.

Long before this point, however, their interpretation of political events had effectively barred the Episcopalians from any non-Stuart settlement. They clung to the traditions of an independent Scottish polity as depicted by the Stuarts, who had done so much to forward the interests of their church. The concept of divine right and 'the King's two bodies', sacred and secular, earthly ruler and holy hero, became metaphors for two Scotlands, a heavenly and an earthly one.[73]

The heavenly aim of the Episcopalians was to preserve the image of sacred kingship and the idea of the Stuarts as saviour-kings for a distressed and suffering nation. In order to do this they perpetuated and developed Stuart iconography and traditional typologies which supported the ideals of sacred kingship. Their earthly aim was to restore James VIII to his three kingdoms. This twofold aim of Jacobitism, both idealistic and pragmatic, was 'the mysticism that lies at the heart of Jacobite political culture'. It was an ideology of ideality, where the ideal and the real merged in aspiration towards eternal goals which could nevertheless be temporally expressed.[74] Lord Pitsligo, General of Horse in the 1745 Rising, gave as his reason for following the Prince the words 'This is the heir. Let us kill him', part of Jesus's parable about His rejection by men.[75] It was part of Episcopal practice to conflate the suffering God and the suffering king in this way.

After all, the idea of the king's two bodies derived in the first place from 'the two-fold nature of Christ'.[76]

The idea of the state which Episcopal ideology expressed was exemplified in hierarchy, loyalty, and an iconography of tradition: all the values on which the Stuarts had relied. It was shattered after 1689, and fragmented by the Act of Union, which destroyed even the idea of a Scottish state on which such ideological premises could be based. Henceforward, the Episcopalian idea of the king's two bodies was propounded in a hieratic form through sacred Jacobite poetry, with its confidence in God's inner purposes, and in an emotive form through erotic Jacobite poetry, where the land is the abandoned lover, calling after her fertile and far-off king. In these songs, the king is presented through a range of images from Christ-figure to simple lover – who might have come from any Scottish folk song.[77] I will return to the ideological importance of Jacobite poetry later, when I come to discuss how this literature maintained a vision of the Scottish polity which was enabling in allowing the Scottish identity to survive: 'Jacobite verse, designed not so much to argue as to seduce, unashamedly bares the King's two bodies in all their glory and absurdity.' Already in the 1690s, such poetry was sending out a decisive message. 'Jacobite verse . . . made every attempt to associate the Revolution with the Civil War', and William was portrayed as the anti-hero of Jacobite satire, a Prince of Darkness, inverting all order: 'William has turned things into their opposites; in his Orwellian kingdom, meaning is undermined, war becomes peace, and love is hate.'[78] Such interpretations foreshadow those of Pope's *Dunciad*, where '*Dunce* the Second reigns like *Dunce* the First' – a polity where the betrayal of constitutional integrity has led to irreversible moral decline in the state:

> Thy hand, Great Anarch! lets the curtain fall,
> And Universal *Darkness* buries all.[79]

Jacobite/Episcopalian propaganda linked 'a healthy constitution with a mystical and hereditary kingship'. Queen Mary, William's consort, was herself 'anathematized as "The Female Parricide", a "monster" unique in history except for the Roman Tullia and King Lear's daughter Goneril'.[80] Her betrayal of her father was a betrayal of the state.

Whether it was the deposition of James VII and II or the approach of the Act of Union which set the seal on the betrayal of the state, concern in both Episcopalian and Presbyterian camps in Scotland reached a pitch in the early years of the eighteenth century. 'That most obnoxious of measures', as P.H. Scott later called the Union, approached by stealth. In 1705, few thought it could be passed. By 1707, it had been.[81] It is no part of the task of this book to enter into the whys and wherefores of the passage of the Act. Others have done this in more detail in greater space than can be afforded here. It is enough to say that the 'fight against the Union' was 'in the cultural sense' a 'struggle [which] truly enlarged Scotland's intellectual horizons'.[82]

31

To many it now began to appear that the battle between differing interpretations of Scotland's identity, religious and otherwise, was a waste of time if Scotland no longer existed. *The Smoaking Flax Unquenchable* (1706) is an example of a Presbyterian tract which 'compares the lesser evil of being ruled by a Stewart king with the greater evil of being suppressed by an English-Hanoverian dynasty and parliament':

> For this nation is so foolishly gadding about to change their way some for the Union, some for the pretended Prince of Wales [James VIII and III]. Now these are but Egypt and Assyria, which is hard to know which of them we shall have most cause to be ashamed of. For it is hard to know wether [sic] the 5 or 600 Brambles England (to ring over us) shall be the worst, or the one Bramble in France.[83]

To the radical Presbyterian, the Anglican English Parliament could be a more potent threat than the Catholic Stuart king. Such views were expressed widely, and in 1708 some of the old Covenanting areas were ready to rise for James VIII.[84]

Most Scots had at least reservations over the Union. An influential body of opinion, spearheaded by Fletcher of Saltoun, called for a federal union, which would at least preserve elements of Scotland's constitutional identity. The complete failure of this argument to succeed against the representations of interested parties shows how much the Union was the fat end of the constitutional wedge of domination being pushed home at last by a triumphant English and pro-English lobby. The process had begun in 1689 when the Estates agreed to the settlement of the crown on William and Mary. The Act anent Peace and War and the Act of Security had threatened the development of that process in the wake of the Act of Settlement. They were the last constitutional threats to English domination of the British Isles, and the Union was the means to end their challenge.

The propaganda war fought for and against Union grew more specific as the time approached. *Villpone* (1707), after claiming that the Union desired under William had a greater respect for the Constitution than the present one, argues for:

> an Union like that of Marriage, not only honourable in its self, but where the Individuality of the Persons is preserv'd, and the great ends of Society taken Care of; not like the monstrous Union of an Hermaphrodite, where both Sexes are confounded, which is the Reproach and not the Advantage of humane nature.

The author's arguments are largely constitutional. He suggests that the 1689 Claim of Right promises a Scots parliament under the terms of the Queen's coronation oath. In putting forward the case for a federal union, he prophesies that any guarantee of independence for the Kirk offered in an incorporating one may in the end prove illusory:

> It's true indeed they have taken some care to swear succeeding Princes to preserve the Government of their Kirk, but I find nothing of any Obligation demanded for what they have reserv'd as to their Civil Constitution.

In other words, the Covenanter's nightmare may come true, and the Scottish Kirk be swallowed up in an Anglican-dominated British state.

The arguments of *Villpone* are found in many tracts written at this time. However, *Villpone* itself is more than ordinarily interesting as an example of its kind. Two aspects of its critique foreshadow the nature of the interpretation which was in later years to colour nationalist views of the Union: the treachery of the Scots Parliament, bought and sold for English gold', and the degenerate/doomed nature of the Scots nation.

Villpone argues that the conduct of the 'Treacherous and Mean' Scots Parliament should be compared unfavourably with the proceedings of their 'Ancestors', and accuses the current administration of being 'Men [who] degrade their own Country'. This interpretation of events was to prove attractive to future generations, with the dominant popular account of the Union (an account containing a great deal of truth) being that which envisions it as the action of a corrupt clique of self-seeking noblemen, their pockets lined with English bribes. The positive, British-oriented account of the Union, on the other hand, portrays it as the act of far-seeing statesmen aware of the necessity of history, which was all the time bringing both nations closer together. But the anti-Union account, as evidenced in the pages of *Villpone* and other tracts, survived. The idea of the Union as a corrupt and morally bankrupt Act was to endure.

So also was the other idea put forward in *Villpone*, that there was 'some great fatality on that Nation' of Scotland, which was dooming it to vote for its own extinction.[85] Both suggestions, that of a faithless parliament and that of a fated nation, took root in the Scottish consciousness at about this time. The former compared the present Estates unfavourably with the heroic deeds of their ancestors: in doing so, it lent itself to pro-Stuart (that is, pro-ancestor and pro-traditional) propaganda. The idea of the past as a better guide to action than the present was deep-rooted in Jacobite political culture. The Union was a betrayal of all the past, in the sense that it betrayed Scotland's very identity: it was thus foregrounded along with the deposition of the Stuarts in the Jacobite world-picture. If the Estates had betrayed tradition enough to depose a king of their own race, was it so surprising that they had betrayed their nation also? 1689 and 1707 could, on this view, be aligned as joint betrayals, despite the fact that the Estates had passed many measures in the interim calculated to defend Scotland's interests. So the vision of the Union as corrupt political degeneracy, common to anti-Union writers of both Jacobite and non-Jacobite inclinations, lent itself more readily to the ideology of the latter.

The second suggestion that surfaced at this time was that Scotland was fated and had no future. This was not only a gloomy prognostication; it seemed borne out by the incredible bad luck of the Jacobite risings which were to come. It was to prove perhaps even more influential than the idea of the Union as a sellout: for it was to feed both nationalist and Unionist interpretations in the years to come. For the former, it might be a conviction held by many Scots but of no objective validity, a mental block which had to be overcome (or a religious block where predestinarian Calvinism was held to blame for this sense of doom). For the Unionist, dedicated or reluctant, it was a conviction that Scotland's historical fate was submergence in the British state. Scott held this view. The characters in Scott's novels who represent the values of a positively Scottish identity, Jacobites and nationalists, are all figures from a bygone age, isolated anachronisms abandoned on the shores of progress by the receding saltires of history's tides. In a version of the myth of the fated nation, Scott outlines a future where for Scotland to retain its identity at all, it must do it on a local and not a national level.[86]

Both these suggestions shared a common premise: the superiority of the past over the present, ancient over modern Scotland. These grounds of argument suited the purposes of the Stuart apologists. It was the Stuarts who represented the past and its values; it was the Stuarts who had not betrayed their ancestors but had suffered for their principles. It was the Stuarts who opposed the Union. Unfortunately, it was also the Stuarts who seemed strangely fated to be unsuccessful in the pursuit of their political ends. Their association was not only with the state, but with the fate of their country; for they also seemed fated, although perhaps not as early as 1707.

One of the results of the association between the Stuart cause and the state of Scotland was that the propaganda war against the Union contained a strong literary and antiquarian contribution. A move was initiated towards 'a regional vernacular poetry in a spirit of sociological condescension, patriotic feeling, or antiquarian revival' – 'the development of Jacobite sentiment into Scottish national feeling was a direct consequence of the debate about the Union.'[87] Indeed, the interpretations of Scotland's position and the position of the Stuarts were so cognate as naturally to gel, and to gel moreover in exactly the kind of antiquarianism and rage for the past which the growing nationalist identity espoused. 'Scottish nationalism in the eighteenth century inevitably became associated with antiquarianism', and this antiquarian tradition belonged almost overwhelmingly to pro-Stuart nationalists.[88] It was not, however, to be a litany of loss but a major element in attempts to subvert the ideology of the early British state. This was recognized by the authorities. Jacobite literature, such as song books, was a dangerous thing to have in one's possession; that is one of the reasons why relatively little survives in its original form. What seemed simply to be works of antiquarian interest were viewed by government as subversive – for example, in 1752, Alexander MacDonald's *Revival of the Old Scottish Tongue* was 'burned by the common hangman in Edinburgh'. Whether in 'popular song' or 'heroic legendary history', the praise of Scotland past was a dangerous thing in the eighteenth century.[89] It only became acceptable in the nineteenth after the direct political threat of Jacobitism was no more. In the eighteenth century nationalists praised the past; in the nineteenth, Unionists. Perhaps this shift explains some of the present-day nationalist neglect of cultural issues, tainted as they are with over a century of Tory sentimentalism. I shall be returning to this topic in Chapter 4.

For eighteenth-century Scots like Pitcairne, Watson, Ruddiman, and Ramsay, the past was a more serious business. They sought to portray the Revolution and Union as having 'brought about the decay of learning and civilised accomplishments'. In response they purveyed 'literary patriotism',[90] an early version of which is found in this poem of Archibald Pitcairne's on the death of Viscount Dundee, written in Latin and translated by John Dryden:

> Oh last and best of Scots, who didst maintain
> Thy country's freedom from a foreign reign,
> New people fill the land now thou art gone,
> New Gods the temples, and new Kings the throne.
> Scotland and thou didst each in other live,
> Nor wouldst thou her nor could she thee survive.
> Farewell, who dying didst support the state,
> And could not fall but with thy Country's fate.[91]

The ideas displayed here of the supremacy of the past over the present are typical. Dundee is the 'last and best of Scots' (an epithet itself taken from Tacitus, the Roman historian). Things have changed since his death. 'New people fill the land', who are not Scots (at least in their patriotic spirit, or the lack of it); and the fate of Scotland and of Dundee (as a representative of the Jacobite cause) are linked in the last two lines. The heroism of the past he represented is now lost, and this has helped to seal 'thy Country's fate'.

Pitcairne wrote in Latin; he intended not to be obscurantist, but to emphasize the long Scottish classical tradition. Jacobite writers used the Latin language, and compared Scotland with Rome, in order to emphasize that Scotland's fate was similar to that of the Roman Republic, overthrown through its weakness and division and the abandonment of its traditional ideals. In this reading, Dundee could be last of the Scots, as Brutus had been 'ultima Romanorum', last of the Romans, last of the patriots. On the other hand, the typology could be reversed, with Scotland portrayed as the betrayed Caesar (slain by Brutus), as it was in Lord Belhaven's famous speech against Union:

THE INVENTION OF SCOTLAND

Lord Belhaven's speech to the Parliament of 1706, which sought to shame the Scottish sense of nationhood, through a series of elaborate Roman parallels [included] . . . the famous vision of 'our Ancient Mother Caledonia, like Caesar sitting in the midst of our Senate . . . breathing out her last with a *Et tu quoque, mi fili*'.

Belhaven's speech was widely versified by Jacobite pamphleteers, and popularly broadcast in poetic form.[92]

The adoption of Roman models was strongly bound up with images of retreat from the corrupt cities to the fertile countryside, such as had prevailed in England during the Civil War period. The famous Jacobite Thomas Ruddiman's belief that 'luxury and vanity' had replaced 'primitivism and simplicity' was a touchstone of this tradition; the view it represented was that Scotland's agricultural purity had been corrupted by the imperial consumption of a greater Britain.[93] This was a potent metaphor: before the Union Scotland had relied on exchanging basic produce and raw materials for sophisticated goods abroad.[94] Ruddiman's argument belonged to the bribe-based school of interpretation of the Union, holding that Scotland had deserted such pre-Union integrity for the sake of a share in the luxuries of imperialist Britain. Both Ruddiman and the poet Allan Ramsay glorified the simple peasantry and the ancient rural life of Scotland. This view of a lost community of heroism and purity was to prove enduring. No less a figure than Charles Edward Stuart was in later years to make use of the idea of a vanished rural and Roman-style pastoral purity in his portrayal of himself as a restorer of lost Republican ideals to French thinkers and Scottish nationalists alike. Strange though it may seem that a claimant to the throne should appear to favour Republicanism, such images, drawn from classical sources, were part of the iconography through which Jacobite propagandists portrayed the fitness of the Stuarts for power.[95]

At the time of the Union, Scottish foundation myths and the traditional and long-standing nature of Scottish kingship were emphasized in a way they had not been since the Wars of Independence.[96] 'Loyal Bruce and Wallace' were invoked on numerous occasions, and their achievements and heroic destinies compared with those of the 'Royal STUARTS'. A 'golden age of political independence, social autonomy, and pure uncomplicated heroism' was recalled and invented in the years around the Union.[97] Belhaven's speech against the Union was only one among many declarations in the argument that the Scottish polity was about to abandon the values of its history:

> Oh fy for *Bruce* and *Wallace* now
> For *Randolph*, *Montrose*, *Airly*,
> This wicked *Generation's* curst
> And hes done nothing fairly.

Once again we notice the curse motif. This falling away from heroism and patriotism seems so marked it might also seem to be fated. The contemporary suggestion, even when not fatalistic, returned again and again to the accusation of political jobbery, as in 'A Song on the Treaty of Union – 16th April 1706':

> Fy let us all to the treaty
>   For ther will be wonders there
> Scotland's to be a bryd,
>   And married be the Earle of Stair.

Stair was one of the prime movers in the pro-Union negotiations.[98]

'The New Dame of Honour' was among the majority of songs which adopted a yet more direct attack on the 'Promiscuous union', involving both the ideas of betrayed tradition and sexual corruption:

> Since now our Nation's bought and sold,
> And Scotland has no name;
> Since honour's cast in a new mold,
> And chastity's a staine . . .
> How men and women did behave
> I'll tell you, Sir, the manner,
> When Wallace and the Bruce did live,
> When I was a Dame of Honour.

The past is 'bought and sold', and the world of 'Wallace and the Bruce' disappeared for ever. The manner of the buying and selling is depicted in greater detail in poems such as 'Verses on the Scotch peers' (1706):

> They sold the church, they sold the state and natione,
> They sold their honour, name and reputatione,
> They sold their birthright, peerages and places

In another poem, William III was attacked posthumously as the 'most cruel foe/O! Starved in Caledon, and martyred in Glenco', references to the famines of the 1690s and the 1692 massacre. It is interesting to note that the writer of these verses is prepared to call the MacDonalds of Glencoe, proverbially one of the most lawless of all the clans, 'martyrs'. This underlines the way in which Jacobite nationalism was painting a picture of Scotland which glossed over the divisions of recent history in favour of a unified picture of a martyred and oppressed nation. There was to be only one version of the past: that of a noble, loyal, liberty-loving people sold into bondage. Scotland was Israel to England's Egypt.[99]

At the time of the Union, it was the Scots who were not Presbyterian who predictably reacted most angrily to the incorporation of a Presbyterian establishment in the Union settlement as a clerical carrot to balance the constitutional stick:

From a Laodicean's hodge-podge reformation,
Who banish'd dear prelacy out of the nation,
Then left our church sitting without a foundation,
                              Libera nos Domine.

Supporters of 'dear prelacy' could only hope that 'if there's truth in heaven, as sure there must, / God will support the race of James the Just'.[100]

If the attacks made in popular songs and scurrilous poems on the Presbyterian party were bad, those in prose could be even more vindictive:

> Take five pints of the bitterest Envy with three pounds of hypocrisie and as much pride as you please and take three pounds twelve ounces of Uncharitableness with two pounds of Rebellion and a good handful of truckling abjuration beat all in a Mortar of Violence and boil them for three hours upon a fire of Vain Glory with a quantity of Animosity in a kettle full of all Sorts of Wickedness and give the patient a Doas of it every hour of the Day for the space of a Week and that will make as true a Whigg as ever beheaded a king murdered a bishop or abjured a Lawful Prince &c.[101]

The vicious nature of propaganda like this was a sign that its authors were on the losing side. After the Union was passed, more and more of the plaints against it formulated by the opposing Episcopalian/Jacobite/nationalist party were carried on in private, written explicitly in commonplace books, and publicly expressed, if at all, only through the codes of classical history or Scottish antiquarianism.[102]

The exception to this trend towards codes and secrecy was the popular song, which prevailed especially in areas dominated by Episcopal lairds. Local fiddlers played Jacobite airs, and the local populace sang various sets of words to them. Songs new and old were put up in inns or distributed by hand in small print runs totalling up to five hundred copies, as well as being transmitted orally. Where it was unsafe to sing them, the tunes could be played or whistled. Since these tunes were often held in common with non-political songs (the words only differing), Jacobites had a means of public communication even where they could not make their sympathies explicit. This song culture was to prove a powerful and popular propaganda weapon in eighteenth-century Scotland, as we shall see. In the post-Union period, when so much of the opposition went underground, it maintained and developed the ideologies and images of Jacobite political culture. The popularity of the contemporary Jacobite song to this day is a tribute to its influence and power.[103] Jacobites are reputed to have said to Queen Anne, 'Suffer us to make the songs of our country, and do you make its laws'.[104] It was a fitting comment.

The Unionists of course had their own propaganda, in songs and elsewhere. It is not intended to deal with this in detail here: its legacy has, in subtly altered form, penetrated the popular history books which portray Scotland's history as one of perpetual disunity and violence.[105] In such readings, the conflicts of the seventeenth century are seen as endemic in Scottish society. Paradoxically, pro-Union historians sometimes find heroes among that group of Scots who did most in the seventeenth century to promote division and disunity – the Covenanters. No less a historian than J. A. Froude claims great things for the influence of 'radical presbyterianism':

> The covenanters fought the fight and won the victory; and then, not till then, came the David Humes, with their essays on miracles, and the Adam Smiths, with their political economies, and steam engines, and railroads, and political institutions, and all the unblessed fruits of liberty.[106]

Such 'liberty' as is described here is never Scotland's political liberty; it is merely a gift of Scotland's to the world. This view subsumes Scotland under a British idea of liberty, where those who rebel on Scotland's behalf as did the Jacobites are stigmatized as 'barbarians', or viewed as noble but misguided at best. Indeed, 'little-Englandism . . . has long treated "English history" as a virtual synonym for the history of four nations – England, Wales, Ireland, Scotland'. In this picture, the idea of a post-Revolution growth of British liberty (to which Scotland, as part of Britain, contributed) flourishes by ignoring the imperialist nature of British practice in Scotland and Ireland. Such views of 'British history' find 'the dismissal of Jacobitism . . . of peculiar polemical importance'.[107] This is for the simple reason that Jacobitism represented, as Irish nationalism was later to do, a profound ideological challenge to the foundation myth of the modern British state, which relied (and to some extent relies) heavily on a positive reading of the Revolution and the Union. In 1707 and the years that followed, many Scots felt they had lost liberty, not gained it. Jacobitism was now the hope that focused national aspiration on the Stuart claimant. Although James VIII and III was claimant to the thrones of England and Ireland as well, there was little doubt among many Scots that Scotland offered the best opportunity of a restoration. As Simon Fraser, later Lord Lovat, put it:

> Tho I be no prophet I dare boldly affirm that Christ Jesus will come in the clouds before an Inglish people or party call home the King; and it is as clear as the sun to any that knowes the countrey that Scotland is the only kingdom willing and capable to restore him, and establish his Majestie sure and absolut in spite of Ingland.[108]

'Scotland is the only kingdom'. This was to be a focal concept expressed in the images of Jacobite ideology in the years after 1707, when the Stuarts became increasingly associated with an iconography of Scottish patriotism. This will be discussed in Chapter 2.

In this chapter I have tried to outline the main themes of the history of the 1638–1707 period in Scotland and elsewhere, and to show how the ideological pretensions of the dynasty which raised such opposition in power grew in appeal after 1688. In Scotland, the constitutional pressure exerted by post-Revolution England lent enchantment for many to the distant view of Stuart rule; and the disestablishment of the Episcopal Church converted its already pro-Stuart membership into the eighteenth-century spiritual shocktroops of the Jacobite cause. Above all, impending Union forced Scots to come to terms with what they were losing – in particular, the long history of a struggle for liberty in which Scotland's kings had played no little part. Jacobites compared Bruce and Wallace to the exiled Stuarts. As the Union cast the reasons for that struggle into oblivion, an appeal was made against the betrayal of the past on behalf of the past. Tradition became, as the Stuarts had tried to make it, a primary vehicle for identity; and the tradition that served as that vehicle was not the complex one of Scotland's internal divisions and cultural clashes (though that was exploited by the opposition), but the simple model of Scotland v. England. Scottish history was thus the history of the fight for liberty; and the Stuarts' long-standing ideological association with the past and its values fitted easily into this nationalist viewpoint. The paramountcy of the past was the measure against which the Union was judged and found wanting by those who put Scotland's existence as a nation ahead of any contemporary political or economic problems. First among these were the supporters of the Stuarts.

2

Good corn upon the rigs?
The underground world
of Jacobite culture
in eighteenth-century Scotland

FERTILITY IMAGERY AND POLITICAL REALITY

> But to wanton me, but to wanton me,
> D'ye ken the thing that wad wanton me?
> To see gude corn upon the rigs,
> And banishment to a' the Whigs.[1]
>
> 'To daunton me'

Perhaps a hundred thousand Scots had died in the years of famine which ended William's reign. Such suffering certainly lent material force to the symbolic politics in which the Jacobite analysis of post-Revolution and post-Union society was couched. Famine seemed a sign of retribution: 'The old historians always observe that God blesses the reign of good princes by a succession of peaceful and abundant seasons.'[2] This traditional view was still strong in Scotland, and its expression animated Jacobite propaganda for more than fifty years. As it became less and less acceptable to voice opposition to the Union publicly, there was increasing resort to the symbolic association of Scotland's economic poverty with the state of its political repression. By 1745, anti-Union arguments which remained in print were nearly all from a strongly Presbyterian viewpoint. Jacobite argument, more of a threat, and thus unsafe to print, had taken refuge in allegory.[3]

The Jacobite interpretation was thus thrust underground. But like buried seed, it sprouted. Appropriately enough, one of the main forms it assumed was that of a fertility myth, which associated the Stuarts with a golden age of plenty. The suggestion was that the restoration of the sacred monarchy was a precondition for the resumption of normal relations between God and His disloyal people Israel/Scotland. The Stuarts, who had in any case always tended to glorify their own image in the interests of projecting a hagiographical view of monarchy, supported this mystic interpretation through their own actions. In exile they retained the use of the Touch and the iconography of sacred kingship. Both were used as propaganda vehicles; the one through pictures and medals, the other through personal anecdotes which came from the stream of people going abroad to receive the ancient cure for the King's Evil.[4]

41

Other images associated with the Stuarts by their supporters already carried a powerful message of fertility and strength, such as the oak, both a Christian and pagan symbol – 'the smiling king in the flowering tree was the reverse of the suffering king on the barren crucifix'. Charles II's escape after Worcester, traditionally accomplished by hiding in an oak near Boscobel, could be iconographically contrasted with Charles I's martyrdom. The old king dies; and the new king is reborn. The symbolism was that of the crucified and resurrected Christ on a Christian level, and of the dying and reborn year on a pagan one. This interpretation was reinforced through the days the Stuart calendar celebrated. Charles I was executed on 30 January, in midwinter. Even his coffin was covered by a snowfall, suggesting both purity and the coldness of death. Charles II, on the other hand, was restored on 29 May, in the middle of spring. Thus his restoration was both a fact and a sign appropriate to the returning season. Moreover, the Stuarts were sympathetic to traditional spring festivals, and May Day and the maypole were associated with the pro-rural aspects of their governmental image. They were 'tied . . . to May-day, a natural liaison considering their primary feast fell in the same month, and to the return of the vegetation god (Pan)'.[5]

Thus not only did tradition associate good kings with fertility and renewal, but the Jacobites were able to nurture this tradition as peculiarly relevant to the Stuarts. Their existing association with spring and renewal had seemed almost providentially intensified when James, Prince of Wales, was born on 10 June 1688. The 10th of June, White Rose Day as it became, fell almost exactly between Restoration Day and the summer solstice. It was 'depicted as a feast of returning nature, a celebration of "Flora"' by Jacobite ideologues:

> But there's a bud in fair Scotland,
>   A bud weel kend in glamourye;
> And in that bud there is a bloom,
>   That yet shall flower o'er kingdoms three;
> And in that bloom there is a brier,
>   Shall pierce the heart of tyrannye,
> Or there is neither faith, nor truth,
>   Nor honour left in our countrye.

The image of the bud and briar was the twofold image of the Stuarts, an icon of the king's two bodies, timeless and temporal. The bud was the talisman of sacred or legendary ('glamourye') renewal, just like the oak, with its overtones of spring and sacrifice. The briar was the sign of the secular arm of Stuart power – the earthly arms which would restore the sacred monarch to his throne. The Jacobite rose was not 'sine spina', without a thorn; it was not entirely metaphysical. Rather it had its active, violent side:

Let our brave loyal clans, then,
　　Their ancient Stuart race
Restore with sword in hand, then,
　　And all their foes displace.
All unions we'll o'erturn boys,
Which caus'd our nation mourn, boys,
Like Bruce at Bannockburn, boys,
　　The English home we'll chase.[6]

This song, 'Come let us drink a Health, Boys', is a song of 1714, the year before the first major rising. It belongs to the practical side, as 'But there's a bud in fair Scotland' belongs to the mystical side of Jacobite song culture. Invoking all the talismans of nascent Scottish nationalism, the 'ancient Stuarts', the Union, Bruce/Wallace, and 'The English', it uses another image which was eventually to be more potent than any of these, not just in Scottish society, but in Britain as a whole. The 'brave loyal clans' were a major innovation of pro-Jacobite literature and propaganda. The legend that only Highlanders supported the Jacobites is still a prevalent one, and historians are not altogether to blame. The Jacobites themselves broadcast their movement in such a way as to suggest that the Highlander was the type of the true patriot. Wild and free, he was the kind of hero all Scots used to be (so the story went), before the sapping betrayal of the Union. For the Jacobites and those who inherited or borrowed their analysis, the Highlander as patriot became a type of an older, nobler Scot, disassociated from the betrayal of nationhood it was felt that 1707 represented. The Noble Savage, in the more refined form of the Noble Hero, existed as a propaganda concept long before Ossian. The 'brave loyal clans' were the heroes of many songs, from 'The Clans are Coming' to 'The Highland Laddie' cycle, which viewed the Highlander as not only a patriot, but the fecund renewer of a barren land also: a green man from a green glen. In this guise of fertility motif, the Highland hero was conflated with the Stuart hero to present a picture of Charles Edward as the archetypal 'Highland Laddie'. Charles himself did much to foster his representation by this image. The defeat of the Union was seen as possible primarily through the restoration of a predominantly Celtic Scottish state, its fertility restored by a sacred chief, Charles, who was also its earthly lover:

I crossed *Forth*, I crossed *Tay*;
　I left *Dundee*, and *Edinborrow*,
I saw nothing there worth my stay,
　And so I bad them all Good-morrow.

O my bonny, bonny Highland Laddie,
　O my bonny, bonny Highland Laddie,

> When I am sick and like to dye,
>   Thou'lt row me in thy Highland Pladie . . .
>
> Princely is my lover's weed,
> Bonny laddie, Highland laddie,
> Fu' his veins o' princely blude,
> My bonnie laddie, Highland laddie.[7]

'Dye' is a metaphor for the sexual act which renews the spirits of the 'Lawland lass', who is the speaker in this poem. She leaves the Lowlands because she feels them sterile and stultified, and journeys to the Highlands to experience fertility and excitement. This comes courtesy of the Highlandman who is in his turn a metaphor for the fecund Highland Prince Charles, just as the 'lass' is a metaphor for a Scotland suffering erotic loss through the absence of the renewing power of nationhood. This metaphor is replicated throughout the corpus of Jacobite song:

> 'Oh hey! oh hey!' sang the bonny lass,
>   'Oh hey! and wae is me!
> There's siccan sorrow in Scotland
>   As een did never see.
> Oh hey! Oh hey! for my father auld!
>   Oh hey! for my mither dear!
> And my heart will burst for the bonny lad
>   Wha left me lanesome here.'

The 'sorrow in Scotland' is that of the lass who is left 'lanesome'. In songs such as this, personal affection for the king over the water is blended skilfully with public need. The country itself is in love with him, and so, individually, are its people, as in 'Charlie is my Darling' or 'Great James, come kiss me now':

> Great James, come kiss me now, now,
>   Great James, come kiss me now:
> Too long I've undone myself these years bygone
>   By basely forsaking you.

In this song the loved nation, as well as longing, is penitent for the past injustices committed against her faithful lover, the king. Should the sacred lover whose return is implored take back his bride, Scotland, the land will be startlingly renewed:

> Come, all brave *Scotsmen*, and rejoice
>   With a loud Acclamation;
> Since Charles is come over the Main
>   Into our Scottish Nation.

> Let Hills, and Dales, and Mountains great,
>   And every Wood and Spring,
> Extend your Voices to the Clouds
>   For Joy of Stewart our King.
>
> Ye Nightingales and Lav'rocks too,
>   And every Bird that sing,
> Make haste and leave your doleful Notes,
>   And Royal Stewart sing.
>
> All Beasts that go upon all Four,
>   Go leap and dance around;
> Because that the curst Union's broke,
>   And fallen to the Ground.[8]

The image of the sacred king's restorative power was rarely put more touchingly.

But it was not only Charles and James who were celebrated as the renewing lovers of the land. Other Cavalier or Jacobite heroes were occasionally shown fulfilling the same role. For example, in 'The Haughs of Cromdale', where Montrose's victory at Auldearn in 1645 is conflated with the Jacobite defeat at Cromdale in 1690, the Marquis appears as a returning hero-figure, avenging the latter defeat by having his victory transposed into the future:

> Thus the great Montrose did say,
> I say, direct the nearest way,
> For I will o'er the hills this day,
>   And see the haughs of Cromdale.
>
> They were at dinner, every man,
> When great Montrose upon them came;
> A second battle then began,
>   Upon the haughs of Cromdale . . .
>
> The loyal Stewarts, with Montrose,
> So boldly set upon their foes,
> And brought them down with Highland blows,
>   Upon the haughs of Cromdale.

The disastrous defeat of Cromdale is exorcized by its repetition in tandem with the talismanic name of the Great Marquis, who crosses the hills with a large clan army to destroy the forces who have dared to defeat the Jacobites forty years after his death. 'The Haughs of Cromdale' is a song where Montrose is a figure like Finn, a hero who sleeps to wake, an ever-present figure among the mountains which his victories have made his own.[9]

Up to this point I have outlined the basic themes of love and loss, death and renewal, war and liberation, which are expressed through the popular Jacobite literature of eighteenth-century Scotland. Before I go on to discuss the ideological development of these themes, I shall suggest a basic method of categorizing the songs themselves, the better to understand the thrust of their arguments.

One of the features which shows Jacobite song as ideological rather than occasional, and thus an element in a political argument, is the patterning present in its analyses. There are three major types of Jacobite song: the aggressive, the erotic, and the sacred.

The first type merits least discussion on an ideological level. It usually deals with a call to arms, or with a description of a battle. 'Hey, Johnnie Cope' is one of the prime contemporary examples. Because it is a type of song with such direct aims it normally includes little in the way of imagery or conceptualization. Normally it tells the tale, and its variations are of tone rather than metaphor:

> The Chevalier being void of Fear,
> Did march up *Birsle* Brae Man,
> And through *Tranent* e're he did stent,
> As fast as he could gae Man,
> While General *Cope* did Taunt and Mock,
> Wi' mony a loud Huzza Man;
> But e'er next Morn proclaim'd the Cock,
> We heard another Craw Man.

Such songs have often remained popular, as they convey the story of the cause to future generations in a direct manner.[10]

The sacred and erotic categories of song are closely related, and both can be traced from the Revolution, if not from the Civil War period. The sacred song tends to adopt Christian typology (the absent lord, the deprived king, the prophet without honour in his own country), and the erotic song puts these or similar types in the role of lover. In the former, Scotland was the forsaken Israel, in the latter, the abandoned lassie. The concepts were not distant from one another. The Jacobite song only followed in a long tradition of the use of erotic metaphors for sacred relationships, dating back to the Bible itself.

Nevertheless, the two types of song, though related, were distinct. The erotic tradition was freely adopted by sentimentalists, and post-eighteenth-century composers of Jacobite lyrics. This was perhaps because it was the more neutral of the two kinds of song. It had always existed by kidnapping traditional airs and words to express political sentiments. It could thus, however flimsily, disguise its subject as a conventional love song. This option was not open to the aggressive, descriptive tradition (though by setting songs such as 'The Braes o' Killiecrankie' and those on Sheriffmuir in terms of a dialogue between a moderate Whig and a

Jacobite, they occasionally attempted neutrality). The sacred song did not conceal its intentions either, being written, as it generally was, from a strongly Episcopalian standpoint.

In the process of adapting existing airs, the erotic song decisively changed some non-Jacobite love lyrics into Jacobite ones. Among the most famous of these is 'Loch Lomond': the lover who once appeared 'in the gloaming' becomes instead the Stuart soldier, bound on 'the low road' of death for king and country. He looks back to a lesser erotic cause (his sweetheart), as he perishes for a greater (his king). Other famous songs in the erotic tradition, which indubitably became and remains the most popular form of lyric Jacobite expression, include 'The Blackbird', 'The Highlander's Farewell', 'Jamie Come Home', 'Will Ye No Come Back Again?', 'The Moorhen', and, of course, the 'Highland Laddie' cycle. Some, such as the 'Broom of Cowden Knowes', the Jacobite version of which was traditionally written by Lord Duffus in 1716, became popular in both Whig and Jacobite forms, as part of a propaganda of vilification and mockery against those who had failed one side or the other during the Fifteen.[11]

The sacred lyric could not easily be adopted, and was less often mocked, by the opposition. It was too uncompromising and specific. There are obvious and explicit attacks on the London Whig regime, which draw repeated attention to its hypocrisy and greed, and accuse it of enshrining that arbitrariness it had supposedly created a Revolution to prevent. The sacred Jacobite lyric had no doubts that the Revolution had brought little liberty: only the language of freedom with the practice of oppression. This the songs saw as a Pharisaic and corrupt rhetoric, cloaking an oppressed Scotland in the praise of a 'free' Britain. The sacred lyric thus notably prefigures recent developments in historical scholarship which play down the positive aspects of the Revolution.

The songs in this tradition establish a picture of heroic and Christian fortitude struggling against a mercantilist society sold out to foreign interests and mercenary values, greedy yet wasteful, engaged in endless European wars. Against this, noblesse, honour, and the values of traditional and ideal heroic culture are expressed and exalted. The image of a self-sacrificing timocracy becomes the expression of the Episcopal church in internal exile, a dynamic projection of the Jacobite ethic:

> Long have we groaned under the yoke
> Dear Sovereign now relieve us
> From Tyrants that oppress our Lands
> And Horned Beasts that grieve us.
>
> Come over James come over
> Brave Royal James come over
> And take possession of thy throne
> Usurped by Hannover.

The product of our Country's tax'd
   With grievous impositions
And Strangers Lord it over us
   With rigid Dispositions.

Chorus

Our Liberty & Trade is gone
Our Gold all carried over
To forreign Lands now to maintain
The Beggars of Hannover.

Chorus

Thou Father of Our Country art
Thou will do thine endeavour
Our freedom now depends on thee
O Heavens conduct thee over.
           – 'General Cope's Defeat at Gladsmuire'

This impassioned plea in a song of the 1740s (to the tune of 'Away with Prince Hannover') shows the depth of feeling which motivated sacred Jacobitism. The 'Horned Beast' is a reference to Daniel 7, where it is an apocalyptic symbol of approaching tyranny. The promise is, however, that 'the saints of the Most High shall receive the kingly power and shall retain it for ever' (Daniel 7: 18), so the song hopes that the victory of the Hanoverian Beast will only be temporary. The view of the Hanoverians as satanic is not untypical, and the belief that the Jacobite king, 'Father of our Country', would rid Scotland/Israel of their bondage was widespread. The Stuart monarch is called on to return or restore to health a violated natural order.[12] Sometimes he is portrayed as a Christ-figure, sometimes more daringly as a figure who shares the characteristics of both Christ and Pan:

   ... his Friends hold him in scorn,
They give him Honey mixt with Gall,
They turn'd him out in Grief and Thrall,
Although they do my Love disown,
I'll drink his Health in the Month of June.

The Christian sacrifice is associated with the coming pagan festivities of spring. The unity of these elements allowed the love expressed for the sacred king to be sacred and profane simultaneously. Thus there is a contiguity between the sacred and erotic in the Jacobite song.[13]

   This combination of various religious symbols of renewal was potently allied with the idealized rural landscapes inherited from a previous generation of pro-Stuart writers. Sacred Jacobite songs adopted images of rural renewal because this allowed them direct reference to contemporary political issues (famine, the malt tax, the replacement of a domestic by an imperial economy, and latterly, exile and the Clearances). Such images also conferred a thematically rich vision of a lost paradise of landed nationhood. Moreover, their use aided the songs in that it made them more communicable to English Jacobites, who spoke the same symbolic language.

For English Jacobites, an urban-based Whig revolution was undermining inherited values, values based on the traditional practices and loyalties of a landed society.[14] Poems such as Pope's *Windsor Forest* expressed the values of a landscape politicized in the Stuart cause, the idea of the British nation as 'a federation of rural communities'. Such writing was characteristic of the pro-rural anti-urban analysis made by Jacobite writers in England. In Scotland, the enormous shift in the post-Revolution political world which the Union represented rendered similar arguments more dynamic and less nostalgic. The relationship between mythology and ideology is more tense and less playful or self-reflexively ironic than in English Jacobite writing. Dryden celebrated James II's love of hunting and rural pursuits; Pope denigrated the post-Revolution financial world and praised retreat while being a public figure and playing the stockmarket. Both were principally elegiac in their opposition to the post-Revolution world. Neither could be called an active Jacobite.[15]

Those who wrote in the same vein in Scotland often implemented their principles. In the work of poets such as Alexander Robertson of Struan (Colonel in the Atholl Brigade, 1745), rural retreat is not a symbolic gesture but a political necessity. In 'Struan's Farewell to the Hermitage' (Struan models his poems self-consciously on Herrick and the Cavaliers), the pastoral retreat collapses into an anti-world like that of Pope's Dulness, but under the attack of Hanoverian soldiers rather than Hanoverian scribblers. Such poems foreshadow the Clearances:

> A barb'rous unrelenting Throng,
>   Cuts down your Bow'rs with every Tree,
> Ravaging your melodious Song,
>   Meerly because you sung for me . . .
>
> Thy cooling Rills, thy murmuring Noise,
> Where often, with a Health to JAMES,
>   Thou could'st revive our scanty Joys,
> Be muddy still, if any Wretch begin
> A Health to Tyrants, or Success to sin.

Such verse is far more explicit than that Pope could have afforded, or wished, to write.

In his 'Advice to a Painter', Struan makes this rural violation a metaphor for a national one, as he reviews Scotland's fate in terms reminiscent of those the prophets use to describe suffering Israel in the Bible:

Limner, would you expose ALBANIA's Fate,
Draw then a Palace in a ruin'd State,
Nettles and Briers instead of fragrant Flow'rs,
Sleet, Hail and Snow instead of gentle Show'rs,
Instead of Plenty all Things meagre look,
And into Swords turn Plough-Iron, Scythe and Hook.

The word-picture of desolation seems a lament, but it suddenly reverses itself to take on the form of a call to arms in the last line. The prophecy of Isaiah, that swords will be turned into ploughshares, is reversed to illustrate Jacobite militancy. The land is barren, and the instruments of harvest are useless; before the land can be fecund again, blood must be shed: the blood of the tyrant and the 'strangers' who support him. 'Would that kind Pow'r . . . send us Home the man we love' (the messianic figure of Charles Edward), then no longer would the people of the land Struan celebrates be oppressed:

Lo! while the furious Horsemen prance,
    Poor Peasants gasp beneath their Feet;
Yet cruelty sits smiling on their Cheeks,
To hear the Orphan's cries and Widow's shrieks.

Instead, 'Show'rs of Rain' should 'exalt' the streams of Scotland, Oxford (a noted Jacobite centre), and London.[16]

Although it is the absence of the Stuart family from the land which has led to Scotland's violation and oppression, Struan is careful not to blame them for their absence from the scene. Rather he suggests that they withdrew into exile as sacred figures must in a profane world, though their exile itself is to be regretted:

When honest PAN withdrew from factious State
(Curs'd was the Hour, and fatal was the Date)
When virtuous SYRINX, vilest rage to shun,
Fled to preserve herself and infant Son,
Then our unguarded Flocks became the Prey
Of rav'nous Wolves, and men more Wolves than they . . .

This is sacred Jacobite poetry. The identification of James with Pan and Mary of Modena with Syrinx is suggestive of the fruitfulness of the king's sacred presence, and his concern with the well-being of nature. In Christian as opposed to Hellenic typology, the flight of the royal family echoes the flight of the Holy Family from Herod's Massacre of the Innocents. The reference to the sheepfold, from the Gospel of St John, casts a sidelong glance at Whig commercialism as manifested in the figure of the hireling shepherd, who leaves the flocks unguarded. The critique of the Whig society as one imposing commercial values on traditional lifestyles was common to Jacobites in England and Scotland. Only in Scotland, however, was this

50

critique bound up with the inescapable political fact of the Union and 'the treacherous . . . ENGLISH Gold' which had then secured the Scots Estates to act against the desires of their countrymen and the examples of their ancestors.[17]

Struan is one of the only poets writing sacred Jacobite poetry in English or Scots whom we can name. Most of the songs and poems are anonymous, by accident or design. Their interpretation of events gave rise to a rich imagery of suffering, struggle, and renewal, which formed the premise for a positive nationalist ideology. The sacred Jacobite song and poem are contemporary, immediate, direct. They have no need to take refuge in the oblique antiquarian nationalism of Ramsay, or the embedded codes of Pope and Swift. Their poetry is an underground history which appears to have spread farther by word of mouth and manuscript than it ever did in printed collections. Hogg's *Jacobite Relics* itself covers the sacred lyric sparsely: perhaps because of its overwhelmingly Episcopalian nature, for Hogg himself was a sympathizer with the Covenanters. Because the sacred lyric was not tied to specific exploits and campaigns, and lacked the delicate but diluting ambivalence of the erotic tradition, the analysis it provided survived the occasions of its production and remained a symbolically potent force in Scottish patriotism long after the Jacobite cause was politically dead.[18]

The sacred lyric contained, as I have argued, both Christian and pagan themes of resurrection and renewal. Often these are conjoined. Where they are separated, the Christian themes tended to occupy the higher registers of Jacobite discourse, appearing in commonplace books rather than being transmitted orally or via the broadsheet, as were the fertility songs:

> It's Geordie he came up to the town,
> Wi' a bunch o' turnips on his crown.

In this famous song, 'The Sow's Tail to Geordie', traditional Scottish plants and vegetables (such as kail and thistles) have been replaced by the foreign and low-class turnips of Hanover, which have undermined the agricultural traditions of the land. 'Geordie', clumsy, cuckolded, foreign and rude in every sense, is the Lord of Misrule, the (hopefully temporary) representative of evil and disorder in the polity, as Cromwell once had been:

> Where Oliver and Willie Buck
> Sit o'er the lugs in smeeky muck,
> Wi' hips sae het, and beins sae bare,
> They'll e'en be blythe when Geordie's there.

Enormous numbers of this particular poem, 'Geordie Whelps' Testament', were circulated throughout Scotland.[19] The Christian lyric, if full enough of hellfire, could be popular. 'Geordie' is the king who exchanges 'saut' for 'kail', creating a Satanic barrenness through excise taxes and perceived (if not actual) discrimination against Scottish produce. In retaliation, the land itself, unnaturally abused, is seen as joining the risings against his rule. Scotland's

> ... ancient thistle wags her pow,
> And proudly waves o'er dale and knowe,
> To hear the oath and sacred vow,
>   'We'll live or die wi' Charlie!'

Charles himself was aware of this theme in the analyses of his supporters, and he cultivated it by both singing and encouraging the performance of such songs, as well as by presenting himself in the light of their symbolism. Reputedly, his favourite was 'This is no my ain House', a poem which indicates the pressure the Scottish identity is under:

> O this is no my ain house, I ken by the biggin o't;
> For bow-kail thrave at my door-cheek,
> And thristles on the riggin' o't.[20]

Once again the implication is that the native vegetation has disappeared along with the native political identity. The return of the Stuart 'vegetation god' was required to allow them to flourish once again, and cast out the turnip, a 'symbol of George's mediocrity ... a perfect metaphor for the supposed vulgarity and silliness of the Electorate'. By contrast, James and Charles not only encouraged their portrayal as native and renewing heroes by the 'itinerant "singing men"' who performed Jacobite verse 'in taverns and alehouses', but developed, as Charles I had done, a personal iconography which strengthened and preserved the association of the Stuarts with both sacred and secular authority.[21] James 'III' was portrayed as Hercules on the medals 'minted at his birth in 1688'; subsequently, he was presented as a dual 'Phoebus-Apollo' and 'Christ figure'. His sympathy with the feminine was emphasized; indeed, Jacobitism in many ways set out to attract women to its cause: 'the Pretender was represented as a handsome knight or shepherd, and his restoration was connected with images of feminine fertility. By contrast, the Revolution was depicted as an act of rape.' The Stuart King was a good shepherd in other contexts also. High Church paintings show a close association with Jacobitism in this period, and 'the influence of mediaeval church images' was powerful, not only in the portrayal of Charles I as 'the man of sorrows', but also through the association of Charles II with the oak-tree painting tradition. The oak icon was revived by Charles Edward; James 'III' was portrayed with a sun shining behind him, a promise of renewal – and this in a journal as popular in England as *Mist's*, which had a circulation of up to 10,000 copies. Charles Edward developed more complex images of resurrection and renewal:

> By the early 1750s, Charles Edward had established a unique icono-
> graphic place for himself. His images were more human, more active

and less authoritarian than those of his father. They mingled Republican classicism with tinges of romanticism to create the concept of a bold and virtuous 'patriot' Prince.[22]

This partial shift from sacred monarch to the combined image of sacred monarch and patriot hero was one calculated to appeal to the intelligentsia and to seize the intellectual high ground. Connected with the belief of the Scottish Latinists, discussed in the next section, that Scotland had declined from classical purity, such images were by this stage adopted more in order to lead English than follow Scottish opinion. England was Charles's primary ideological target after 1746.[23]

The association of the Stuarts with spring and renewal was one which was popularly understood. Jacobite activity frequently accompanied 'seasonal change'. Jacobite associations with groups like the Freemasons and the Templars were reflected in symbolism such as 'The cycle of death and rebirth, of revolution and restoration, [which] was represented in "Scottish Rite" masonry by the self-consuming snake, as it was in the [Jacobite] Cycle Club of 1770, whose origins may have been Masonic.'[24] Both in private and in public, such symbolism constituted a settled code of Stuart political and ideological claims.

The Stuarts were fortunate in being able to ally their iconographic, sacred, and traditional presentation to a list of real political grievances. These were especially strong in Scotland after 1707, and Ireland after 1689, but were also present throughout Britain. Too many accounts of the Glorious Revolution omit the dispossessed in their excitement over Parliamentary sovereignty. There is another side to the question, a side the culture of Jacobite letters addressed:

> The Toleration Act of 1689, compared to James II's Edict of Toleration, looks like a step backwards for freedom of religion. . . . The post-Revolutionary judiciary appears to have been as pliable as ever. *Habeas Corpus* was suspended so often under William III that it seemed to be in almost constant abeyance. Freedom of the press meant as little to the executed William Anderton in 1694 as it did to Whig pamphleteers in the 1680s. . . . The 'despotism' of James II appears amateurish beside . . . the Riot Act, the Registration Act, the Constructive Recusancy Act, the Septennial Act, the Smuggling Act, the Peerage Bill, the 1722 levy on Nonjurors and Catholics, and the Black Act.[25]

Small wonder the Stuart claimants remained a viable option, and that their overt supporters longed for a renewal of their authority:

> The lads took heart, and dressed themselves
>   In rural garments gay,
> And round about, like fairy elves,
>   They danced the live-long day,

Around, around an oaken tree
They danced with joy, and so do we.[26]

This was the image of the innocent land, a folkloric Eden.

ALLAN RAMSAY AND HIS CONTEMPORARIES

I'll prove the Moral is prodigious strong:
I hate to trifle, Men should act like Men,
And for their Country only draw their Sword and Pen.

Ramsay[27]

In the years after 1707, the defence of Scottish culture and the Scottish language were in themselves nationalist acts. The revival of antiquarianism at this time was overwhelmingly political.[28] Nevertheless, where it was a public revival, it was constrained in its patriotism through the need to compromise with the new political world of the British state. As a result, its analysis of Scotland's situation was blunt and sanitized in comparison with that made available through the underground culture of Jacobitism. The only way in which a continuing consciousness of Scottish history could be made acceptable to the London government and its Scottish allies lay in a policy of distance lending enchantment to the view. Many of the antiquarians, even those such as Ramsay, who was clearly a Jacobite, consigned the lessons of history to history, and largely forbore from publishing contemporary political lessons from their renditions of the past. Instead, 'Scottish national feeling' became 'elegiac and literary'. In this case, the pen proved to be not a superior ally of the sword, but a poor one. Allan Ramsay, who had visited Charles Edward in the safe haven of Rome in 1736, was nowhere to be found when the Prince entered Edinburgh in 1745.[29]

The literary culture of printed books nurtured the view of Scotland as fated, which dated from the debates surrounding the Union, while the fugitive broadsheets tended to deny it.[30] The idea that Scottish history was over, and that the only suitable manner of recollecting it was elegiacally, was a strong influence on the work of generations of Scots writers to come, finding its fullest expression in Scott. The apparently strange dual loyalty it created, to Scotland's past and Britain's present (Bruce and Wallace on the one hand, England and Empire on the other), was one that endures to this day. It was ratified not only by the antiquarianism of the eighteenth century, but also by the jingoistic commitments of the nineteenth. On the one hand, Brigadoons, on the other Brigadiers: Scots supported both Kailyard and King, with Scotland representative of childhood and Britain of adulthood in the loyalties they learnt to proclaim. It was only in the twentieth century, with the decline of Empire, that Scots at large no longer rejoiced in the title of Englishmen. The view of history they inherited was one where Scotland became automatically obsolescent after 1707.

It was this ambivalent attitude to the relevance of Scotland's history among Ramsay and his contemporaries which led to his position as 'a champion of Scottish folk-song and a wrecker of scores of such songs'. On the one hand he preserved, and even innovated, by rewriting old songs or writing new ones; on the other, he overlaid an inappropriately urbane tone on some of the songs he rewrote, thus rendering them inoffensive in the new, British, context. Moreover, his service to the Scottish vernacular was handicapped by his determination to civilize it and render it more comprehensible in the emerging Anglophone environment.[31] Both these decisions can readily be associated with Ramsay's desire to conform to the expectations of a society which now revolved round London – a society where Scots were outsiders freshly admitted, and those who spoke their own tongue were accused of bad English. The eighteenth century saw the publication of a stream of Scottish songs, old and new, but there was an accompanying trepidation in their presentation, a side-long glance at the new standards the metropolitan colossus of London had imposed on post-Union Scotland. Book-length publication was liable to the jurisdiction of a centralizing cultural agenda. Only the radical propaganda of Jacobites and Presbyterians (and most markedly the former) succeeded in fully disengaging the expression of Scottish culture from the grasp of British priorities. Although some elements of the Jacobite song were later to join the 'torrent of tartanry' which was the sentimentalized culmination of the elegiac approach to Scotland's history and identity, other elements developed strongly enough in the eighteenth century to leave a different, unofficial, ideology behind them. Such development was especially strong in Episcopalian households where 'the older traditions of music and poetry were more likely to be preserved, especially in the north east'.[32]

One of the products of the north-east's milieu, Thomas Ruddiman, printed the poems of Allan Ramsay, which first began to appear in the 1720s. Ramsay himself, born in 1684, had been in his youth a member of 'the Easy Club of young nationalists', which disbanded in 1715.[33] A staunch defender (under the conditions above stipulated) of the Scottish vernacular, Ramsay exploited post-Union resentment in his poetry. Although his claims for Scots are cautious, they are definite.[34] Moreover, Jacobite themes, only lightly camouflaged, are found throughout his extant work. For example, his espousal of the Highland plaid as one of the main symbols of Scotland and Scottishness directly connects to the Jacobite analysis of the Highlander as patriot which enabled the pro-Stuart faction to identify Scotland as a predominantly Celtic nation. Since the Highlanders had little or no part in the Union, they could be shown as the pure and uncorrupted patriots of old, rather than the bribe-taking betrayers and weaklings of the present generation. Ramsay is alert to these nuances:

> The Plaid's Antiquity comes first in View,
> Precedence to Antiquity is due

The Jacobites, of course, often made great play of the ancientness of the Stuart dynasty, with the resulting 'Precedence' it had. Ramsay declares the plaid 'O first of Garbs! . . . So long employ'd of such an antique Date', and recollects that it was part of the dress of that ancient Scotland which has passed away for ever:

> We'll find our Godlike Fathers nobly scorn'd
> To be with any other Dress adorn'd;
> Before base foreign Fashions interwove

The mention of 'foreign Fashions' is an obvious allusion to the Union, while the phrase 'Godlike Fathers' reminds us of the contemporary Jacobite propaganda which sought to argue that Scotland was a nation in decline from the great standards of its past (until it should restore the Stuarts).[35]

But although this poem may appear Jacobite, we should note that it is written in 'correct' English, which may partly neutralize its implicit aggression. Ramsay further distances himself from the Jacobite implications of the poem by suggesting that the hardy heroes of Scotland would make excellent soldiers in the British government's war against France (Scotland's traditional ally):

> With such brave Troops one might o'er *Europe* run,
> Make out what *Richlieu* fram'd, and Lewis had begun.

'Tartana, or the Plaid' is a poem careful to celebrate antiquity while neutralizing the implications such celebration might have for national-ist/Jacobite feeling. Rather there is a comforting congratulatory tone which does not rock the political boat. Even the association of the Stuarts with fertility and renewal is rendered in a fashion too homely to warrant suspicions of rebellion:

> If lin'd with Green *Stuarta's* Plaid we view,
> Or thine *Ramseia* edg'd around with Blue;
> One shews the Spring when Nature is most kind

Far from the renewing imagery of overt Jacobite patriotism, Ramsay's 'Nature' is a tame creature. She withdraws from the symbolic language of national revival; serving instead as a comforting adjunct to a local Scottish pride, set snugly within a British consciousness.[36] Ramsay portrays Nature in contemporary English terms, terms which emphasize how well she has been tamed, not how wild and free she is. The overt Jacobite analysis of Nature as a potent and autonomous force personified in her spring season by the sacred and victorious Stuart king has far more in common with Ossian and the Romantics than it does with the kinds of discourse available to the

Scottish writer of the early eighteenth century with a British market for his work.

It would be wrong to castigate Ramsay because he was forced to compromise. Moreover, the nature of that compromise was not uniform. His Scottish songs, as opposed to his other poems, were privileged in that they were descended from native traditions less open to the pressure to conform to English models. It is claimed that Ramsay wrote many of the songs which appeared in *The Tea-Table Miscellany* (1726), and subsequent collections.[37] If this is the case, it allowed him to maintain and extend a tradition which lay outside the forms demanded by English cultural norms (this despite the fact that Ramsay did in part anglicize the songs). Whether these songs were only altered by Ramsay or were originally written by him, their impact was considerable. Songs such as 'The Highland Laddie', 'The Bony Scot', and 'Lochaber no more', a song of exile, were speedily adopted by the Jacobites after their publication in 1726. Ramsay almost certainly intended some of these songs to be read as encoded Jacobite statements, but it is hard to be sure when he is doing this, and when, on the other hand, he is merely publishing a song the air of which has been already usurped by Jacobite propaganda.[38] Despite these uncertainties, Ramsay's uncollected and manuscript poems show that he remained strongly pro-Stuart in his sympathies, as evinced in 'A Marching Song' and 'Ye Gods who Justice Love':

> Ye gods who Justice Love look down
> and as you promised heretofore
> would you all Scotland's wishes crown
> James with his Golden Reign restore

But this is Ramsay in his closet. Only in a few songs does the antiquarianism made available for public consumption become revolutionary rather than nostalgic. Otherwise, Jacobite statements are hidden in code, as in poems like 'The Vision', with its critique of the Hanoverian state presented in the guise of a commentary set in the time of the Wars of Independence. Appropriately, the poem is a dream vision, itself a nostalgic form.[39]

As well as the vernacular and traditional antiquarianism of Ramsay, classical typologies maintained a strong presence among Scots with reservations concerning the Union. Figures like Ruddiman, Freebairn, and Watson not only supported the idea of 'the Scots language as a means of asserting Scotland's identity', but attempted to regenerate and preserve the 'Scoto-Latin culture' of the Renaissance.[40] This was, of course, a culture with which the Stuarts had strong ties: James I, James IV, V, VI, and VII, and Charles I were all among its exemplars. The identification of Charles I with the murdered Caesar dated back to 1650, and the Horatian Ode, a predominantly Royalist genre, reflected such typology, later confirmed by the popularity of Horace among eighteenth-century pro-Jacobite writers, including Ramsay.[41]

Classical parallels were also drawn with other writers and figures. King

James could be any heroic Roman, such as Cato – a guise in which he frequently appeared, despite Joseph Addison's attempt to seize Cato for the Whigs in his 1713 play. Virgil's *Aeneid*, arguably the greatest poem of political exile, became virtually a Jacobite document from the time of Dryden onwards. The exile of Aeneas, faithful to God and duty, was a frontline Jacobite image, appearing in works such as *Aeneas and His Two Sons* and *Ascanius, or the Young Adventurer* (1746). Charles Edward himself tried his hand at writing in this vein; and Aeneas' Jacobite role was only enhanced by the fact that the names of Trojan heroes were traditional among the Jacobite clans (Hector MacLean, Aeneas MacDonald).[42]

Thomas Ruddiman, brought up in 'the North-East's traditional cult of Latin', was one of the chief of the post-Union Scoto-Latinists. Ruddiman's circle believed that the Revolution and Union had 'brought about the decay of learning and civilised accomplishments'. In response to this, they purveyed 'literary patriotism' dominated by 'the Scoto-Roman ethos'. The glorification of an ancient Scotland of 'primitiveness and simplicity' was set against the corrupt, duplicitous world of post-Union politics. Those who subscribed to this analysis were subsequently able to adopt figures such as Wallace as representatives of the stern purity of the past, a parallel with legendary Romans such as Scaevola and Horatius.[43] Wallace's victory at Stirling Bridge with an army composed of the 'poor commons of Scotland' (rather than the corrupt and treacherous Anglo-Norman noblemen) thus partook of Roman Republican overtones in the Jacobite analysis of the past, overtones Charles Edward was later to draw on.[44] Wallace symbolized popular resistance to imperial power.

Despite its origins in the elite intellectual world fostered by the Stuart kings to the time of James VII, the Scoto-Latinist ideology contained the potential for radical leanings through the Republican nature of some of its interpretations of Scottish heroism. The nostalgia was for the simple life of peasants and heroes, for a Scotland uncorrupt and free from imperial responsibilities.

The earlier generation of these writers were sometimes active Jacobites, often due to their links with the north-east, Episcopalianism, or both; though this tended not to be the case as time went on (figures like Lord Pitsligo, Scott's Baron Bradwardine, excepted). In 1715–16, 'Ruddiman's own regent [at King's College, Aberdeen] . . . went with a deputation of professors to greet James Stuart at Fetteresso'. Archibald Pitcairne, Ruddiman's older contemporary, lamented the loss of Scotland's 'aristocratic culture', symbolized by figures such as Claverhouse, George Lockhart of Carnwath, and George Mackenzie, all defenders of the Stuart cause. Both Pitcairne and Lockhart, whom he admired, displayed their opposition to Union through classical codes, and Lockhart through political action also.[45] The use of such codes to defend Scotland's glorious past against the demands of a British future, was developed by Ruddiman during his time as 'Keeper of the Advocates'

Library' (where he preceded Hume). Ruddiman 'inspired a movement of Scottish patriotic publishing which at one time looked as though it would represent a major reaction to the Union'.

Although this partial renaissance in Scottish culture may have had some influence on the poetry of Fergusson and 'the vernacular classical architecture of some Edinburgh building in the 1760s', in the long term it was doomed to failure. Its role was always in the celebration of the culture of the past with little thought of the politics of the future. Its support of 'primitiveness and simplicity' was an inadequate bulwark against the restlessly complex demands of British culture. Such Jacobite or nationalist message as it possessed was diluted as the century progressed. Those who reached adulthood much after 1715 did not act out the political implications of these cultural arguments.[46]

Yet unlike the 'genteel versification, done by the book' of some of the writers of the Ramsay school, the ideas of the classical antiquarians were reflected by official Stuart propaganda. James 'III''s 'CUIUS EST' medals drew on the divine iconographies of the Roman emperors in portraying the king's physical self on one side of the medal, and his nation, the spiritual self, on the other.[47] James indeed wanted to see himself as father of the fatherland.

Later, Jacobite allusions to Roman examples centred on the idea of a vicious and degenerate nation, which required the restorative genius of a young Charles Edward. Charles's portrayal in Republican guise, mentioned above, was one of the chief features of this propaganda campaign. As the genius of the kingdom, he represented himself as encapsulating both Republican and royalist sentiment. By this time, however, such arguments were directed more towards French *philosophes* and English sympathizers than towards the fading ideological charms of the Scoto-Latinists. On the opening of the Radcliffe Library in Oxford, Dr William King commented 'Redeat Ille Magnus Genius Britanniae' ('Give back that great genius of Britain'), a characterization of Charles Edward which showed how effective his classical propaganda had become by the middle of the eighteenth century. Charles has consistently been underestimated as an architect of his own propaganda. The idea of a patriot king blended with Roman Republican virtues such as patriotism, steadiness, and learning was one carefully cultivated.[48]

The Royal Stuarts were thus not only compared with Scottish heroes such as Bruce and Wallace (respectively the aristocratic and radical aspects of their image), but also with the exemplary figures of classical culture. To these accessible reference points were superadded the majestic typologies of Christian and pagan gospel and legend. The more remote the Stuart claimant grew from contemporary politics, the more encompassing became his claim to represent the true (ancient) spirit of the Scottish nation. The strength of hard-line Presbyterian opposition to the Union had been diluted by the Erastian compromise which the Church of Scotland accepted in order to partake of the advantages brought to it by Union. The Stuart king, who promised deliverance from English bondage, freedom and leadership in religious matters, protection for traditional ways of life, and the preservation of a distinctively Scottish learned culture, came for many to represent the most immediate manifestation of national consciousness available. He was David; his psalms were the songs of the Jacobite broadsheets and local composers. He was Cato; aloof, unselfish, uncorrupt, and patriotic. He was Caesar, murdered by his own political dependants (the Scottish Estates). He was Aeneas, doomed to exile, yet beloved of the gods. He was Bruce, the patriot king and lover of Scottish liberty; and Wallace, the radical with the interests of the common people at heart. He was Augustus, the bringer of light to the land celebrated by Horace and Virgil. He was the genius of that land, its fecund identity. And the Stuart king was the king of sorrows, the sufferer for his people Israel/Scotland.

The regenerated king was the regenerated nation. The range of his surrogate identities was a measure of his range of appeal: to the historical, the classical, the folkloric, and the theological in Scottish culture. The erotic Jacobite lyric, by its 'wholesale pillage' of the 'central canon of Scottish love song', subliminally suggested that the cycles of common life themselves, loves, hopes, and hungers, were devoted to the sexual politics of a renewing restoration.[49] The sacred lyric, although it also spoke of renewal, was often sustained as an interpretation by the 'martyrdom and witness' of those who died for the Cause on the scaffold. Indeed, the theatrical and propagandist use of public executions made by Jacobite victims foreshadows the publicity machine of the IRA in our own day. On most occasions, Jacobites were executed confessing no treason and asserting their own righteousness. Their last words, particularly if they were famous Jacobites like Townley or Balmerino, were printed, and treasured by fellow adherents. As the martyrdom of Charles I gave an example to some, so that of Montrose inspired others. Even when exile or death threatened the sustaining ideology of the Jacobite lyric, a positive reading of renewal was usually available to compete with defeatism.[50]

The classical and historical perspectives showed implicitly marked defeatist (or realist) tendencies from an early date. Traditionalist antiquarians, forced to compromise with the Union, or at best writing in the codes of patriotic and classical typology, made less and less headway against the British priorities they opposed as the century advanced. After 1715, few who belonged to the patriotic/classical group remained active Jacobites. Naturally, their analysis, despite sharing some features with that taken up by the Stuarts in their own propaganda, began to seem increasingly forlorn in political terms. Only in the relatively more underground world of the Jacobite song did a lively invention persist, and it was there that the ideologies and typologies of the Stuart cause best flourished. The Jacobite song, as I shall argue, went on to be a major force in the positive, hopeful reading of the Scottish identity. On the other hand, the antiquarian wing tended to take on more and more the shape of Tory sentimentality as the years progressed. In doing so, it was to partly adapt and rewrite the Jacobite lyric to suit its own purposes. But in its contemporary manifestation, that lyric, along with other kinds of popular propaganda, formed the basis for a more regenerative view of Scotland's potential, through keeping alive anti-Union politics long after the antiquarians had diluted them in favour of a cultural argument which their absence vitiated. Cultural images of renewal inevitably carried political implications if they were to be used effectively. As Lord Pitsligo, the Prince's General of Horse, wrote in 1745:

> When I heard of the Prince's landing in the Highlands, I found an inclination to give him what small assistance was in my power. . . . These words, 'this is the heir, let us kill him' are often applied, I only repeat them.[51]

For Pitsligo, the cultural symbol of the Stuart kings as the rejected Christ was powerful enough to encourage him to take up arms, even though nearly 70 years old. Such was the gulf between the polite antiquarians and real Jacobite culture by 1745.

THE AGE OF CULLODEN

Sin' Charlie he is landed,
  We ha'e nae mair to fear;
Sin' Charlie he is come, kimmer,
  We'll hae a jub'lee year.
                  'What's A' The Steer, Kimmer?'

Oh! here no Sabbath-bell
  Awakes the Sabbath-morn,
Nor song o' reapers heard,
  Among the yellow corn:
For the tyrants voice is here,
  And the wail o' slaverie;
But the sun o' freedom shines
  In my ain countrie.
                  'Oh! Why I Left my Hame'[52]

Culloden and the period thereafter was the end of an era, though this was not fully realized at the time. The profound savagery of the government troops fulfilled the worst predictions Jacobite propaganda had made of Hanoverian oppression. London's reaction made compromises between cultural nationalism and the demands of a British identity harder to sustain. The ferocity of the British state turned even politically moderate writers such as Smollett against the actions of a government hitherto increasingly regarded as legitimate.

Jacobite reaction was at first predictably savage, and then gradually became sentimentalized, even perhaps in the Gaeltacht.[53] By 1760, it seemed that the Cause was lost; by 1780, this was unquestionably the case. But the Jacobite song, despite being rewritten and redrafted by sentimental Jacobites, maintained a continuous critique of Scotland's place in the British state throughout the period, which is otherwise for so many associated with the Enlightenment and the intellectual success of a Scottish culture which acquiesced in British cultural norms. For the Scots killed or transported in the aftermath of the Rising, such norms would be unavailable. Jacobites who went into exile and later returned often treated the society they returned to with a degree of cynicism or rebelliousness. Allan MacLean, who fought at Culloden and was subsequently a colonel in the British Army, used to lead his men into action in Canada in the 1770s wearing a white cockade, to the disgust of his superiors.[54]

Those who remained in the desecrated or despoiled parts of Scotland also often had little alternative but to join the British Army. It was one of the few acts which could clear them of the suspicion of treason: indeed, many Jacobites captured during the Forty-Five were pardoned on enlistment. Those who continued to protest in terms of a pro-Stuart analysis of Scotland's plight (and some did) produced a more plaintive articulation of their grievances than their predecessors had done. In part this was due to their own defeat; in part to the increasing role exile had to play among the communities who had supported the Jacobite cause. When the Clearances came, and it was not till the end of the century, they supported this doleful interpretation. Like Culloden, they were seen as a fulfilment of the gloomy prophecies of Jacobite propaganda. In popular tradition and popular history alike, the Clearances are still frequently assumed to have succeeded Culloden almost immediately in time. This is not the case, but the enduring popularity of such conflations of events is a tribute to the transforming analysis of Jacobite propaganda, and its effect on the understanding Scots have of their own history. It argued that both the Clearances and Culloden shared the common denominator of anti-Scottish oppression, as did many other events:

> On Darien think, on dowie Glencoe,
> On Murray, traitor! coward!
> On Cumberland's blood-blushing hands,
> And think on Charlie Stuart.[55]

Jacobite songwriters frequently brought together events such as Darien and the Forty-Five, which had only the most tangential relation to each other, as elements in the litany of protest against oppression.[56]

The Jacobite analysis of events did not die out after Culloden. Rather the events of the Year of the Prince reinforced that analysis. The lack of practical interest which the English Jacobites had shown in the Rising underlined the nationalist ideological element of Scottish Jacobitism: the idea of the pro-Stuart faction as a smallish but pure band of martyrs and heroes, fighting for Scotland's freedom. The English propaganda image of the Highlander as child-eating savage and lawless bandit was turned on its head by the Jacobite vision of the Highlander as patriot, who alone clung to the heroic standards of the Scotland of Bruce and Wallace.[57] This Jacobite propaganda image blossomed spectacularly among the camouflaged Jacobitism of Macpherson's Ossian poems, helped by the military reputation 'reclaimed' Jacobites were earning for themselves in the British Army. The degree to which the Jacobite idea of the Highlander as patriot survived and influenced the writers, politicians, and historians of subsequent generations was profound, and it will be a subject of the next chapter. It was Jacobite ideology alone which maintained a coherent framework in which to define the identity of Scotland and the Scots in an era of national and cultural flux.

This uncertain flux was accentuated by the events of 1745–6. For the first time since the Union, Scottish and Stuart arms seemed poised on the brink of success; and yet suffered their most catastrophic failure. The popularity of Charles Edward, and the survival of his charisma to this day, are largely due to the epiphanic potency of his campaign, which galvanized sympathizers and opponents alike. After it, nothing was the same.

It has often been argued that Charles stood no real chance of success had he marched on from Derby. Both historical and military experts continue to differ in significant numbers from this pessimistic analysis. Charles had an immense propaganda advantage; he was throwing London's financial system into turmoil; he had speed, surprise, and a record of success. Few had joined his army in England; but then few had joined Charles II on the way to Worcester in 1651, and that betokened no great love of Cromwell. Possibly more significant is the fact that few opposed him. Only the militia at Finchley, whose low morale has been immortalized in a painting by Hogarth, stood in the way of the Jacobite army. As George V put it in conversation to the Duke of Atholl: 'Your ancestor was wrong. . . . Had Charles Edward gone on from Derby I should not have been King of England to-day.'[58] Whatever the myths and the might-have-beens, part of the enduring attraction of the Forty-Five is that it contained the chance of victory as well as the reality of defeat.

When Charles entered Carlisle on a white horse, he imitated the iconic symbolism practised by his great-grandfather, Charles I. Throughout the first half of the campaign, he acted as a fulfilment of the propaganda dreams of his supporters, through his dress, pageantry, concern for tradition, and opposition to the Union. This was, whether he believed in it or not, a well-calculated course of action: for he had supporters from all over Scotland, who would respond to such symbolic sensitivity over presentation. Many of the contemporary songs bear witness to their appreciation. Indeed, poets such as Alexander Robertson and John Roy Stewart served in Charles's army; and the poets of the Gaeltacht, in particular, welcomed him in terms more extravagant than any that had been used since the days of Montrose.[59]

From the beginning of the post-Culloden period, the Year of the Prince wore a romantic aura. Years of propaganda based on images of noble patriots, sacred kings, forsaken nations, and betrayed churches were conflated with the undeniably charismatic reality of Charles's campaign. The idolization of the Highlander as liberator and patriot continued to develop. Charles's army had been a mixture of Highland and Lowland, English, French, and Irish in its composition: but this was forgotten in the emergent story of its having been a Highland army alone, a last heroic attempt by an antique culture to throw off its new masters. The army, at its maximum strength, had had 5,710 men in predominantly Highland, and 4,220 men in predominantly Lowland regiments, besides 1,200 English, French, and Irish. It had secured the support of Lowland noblemen such as Perth, Atholl, Strathallan, Pitsligo, Viscount Dundee, Kilmarnock, Balmerino, Elcho, Nairne, and Lord George Murray. But the Highlander had become the Jacobite icon of patriotism; and a Highland battle Culloden became. It remains so in the popular imagination to this day.[60]

The Highland icon was, in the aftermath of 1745, taken up in many quarters. Tory gentlemen in England, who had done little to assist the Rising, wore tartan waistcoats in the House of Commons, and tartan became a fashionable statement of opposition to the government. James Boswell, Samuel Johnson's biographer, helped to sentimentalize the noble and patriotic Highlander for a public for whom the Jacobite threat had receded. In Pasquale Paoli, the Corsican freedom-fighter, Boswell found a figure who reconciled 'Roman' and 'barbarian' (i.e. Highlander) images of Charles Edward: Paoli was noble like the Romans, and savage like the Gaels. This kind of identification of Jacobites and freedom-fighters later extended itself, for some Jacobites, into support for the American Revolution. Later, Byron's noble savages are attempts to portray the Highland icon in a European Romantic mould.[61]

Radical Jacobite activity was not dead, however, despite the use of Jacobite patriotic images in increasingly depoliticized contexts. The Jacobite lyric continued to imply rebelliousness as well as nostalgia, and the printing of Jacobite songs remained a dangerous activity, as some elements in government remained jittery about a possible pro-Stuart rising or invasion for many years after 1745–6 (the last Jacobite arrest was in fact made in 1817).[62] Many of the songs were thus collected in manuscript, and only a few such as *Loyal Songs* (1750) saw print. This continued fear on the part of government meant, however, that the Jacobite lyric was one of the last elements of Jacobite propaganda thinking to be subjected to the reactionary nostalgia into which the Cause was to be converted for the amusement of a public out of danger of a Stuart restoration. The song continued to develop, providing a radical critique later partly codified by Burns and Hogg. But Jacobite song was not entirely respectable until the Victorian period.[63]

The age of Culloden, during which the image of the Highlander/patriot underwent a savage challenge which was later to be subtly converted into a wide but uncommitted popularity, also witnessed the tail-end of non-Jacobite anti-Union radicalism. Works like *Scotland's Glory and Her Shame* (1745, 1786) are examples of late Presbyterian feeling against the Union. *Scotland's Glory* shares Jacobite assumptions concerning the motives behind the Union:

> Our leading men got money then
> to carry on this action;
> Thus for red gold was Scotland sold
> to sin and sad defection.

This has led to Scotland being 'an inslaved nation'. But the author denigrates subsequent Jacobite attempts to right this state of affairs. His only answers to Scotland's problems are theological ones; and the involved inwardness of his concepts in this area must seem inadequate to confront the real political problems arising from Scotland's loss of statehood. Increasingly voices like his, Presbyterians who had compromised neither with Jacobite nationalism nor with the Union, were becoming isolated. The writer sees 1638 and 1707 as turning points in the history of Scotland: but although he provides a similar analysis of Scotland's plight to that on offer from the Jacobites, he is unable to participate in their patriotic reading of Scotland's antiquity and traditions. The idea that Scotland is deteriorating because contemporaries are more corrupt and able to be bribed than were the heroes of old is one the author cannot agree with for a specific reason: these patriots were often Catholics. Writing of medieval Scotland, the time of Bruce and Wallace, this 'Well-wisher to the Good Old Cause' can only call it an age when 'dismal darkness did remain/and overspread the nation'; the 'darkness' of 'Palladins from Rome' and their 'prelatick scorpions'. The author's view of the history of an independent Scotland is coloured by his theology, and consequently biased towards the post-Reformation period, a period which was hardly the most successful in Scotland's history.[64] The signal role that the Roman Catholic church played in liberating Scotland during the Wars of Independence is a fact that the Jacobite analysis could accept, and that a Presbyterian argument like this one is forced to ignore.[65] Loyal Bruce and Wallace, the patriotic icons of Jacobite song and other propaganda, were potential embarrassments to such extreme Presbyterian writers. A Scottish patriotism which did not begin to take effect until the 1560s was bound to be less persuasive than one which unreservedly glorified the antiquity and tradition of Scottish kingship and culture. *Scotland's Glory and Her Shame* is an example of how the Presbyterian left of post-Union nationalism lacked arguments which were other than theologically convincing.

It was the Jacobite story of a lost history and discarded tradition which had proved more attractive. It is significant that the 'Well-wisher' who wrote the above book claimed he was provoked into doing so by hearing the Jacobite song, 'Whurry Whigs awa' man', on Halkerton Muir in 1745.[66] The Jacobites had already won the publicity battle, though they were to lose the war. Their myth that '. . . hardy loyal *Highlanders* alone/Restor'd the STEWARTS, and set them on the Throne!' was adopted as an image of the success of the Highlanders as noble fighting men in the British Army after 1746:

> O'er the bleak Mountains see the SONS OF FAME
> Fearless advance, and catch the glorious Flame

This 'Illustrious, but forgotten Race;/A Race that added to the *Brucian* Fame,/And rises now with no less loyal Flame' was identified with the patriotic spirit of Scotland and Britain alike. The battles the Jacobites had fought to deliver their country were translated to a sentimentally local patriotism, a need to be subsumed under the interests of imperial Britain. After the defeat of Charles, 'latest Son of Fame, Son of the BRUCE's Line', the idea of an independent Scottish polity was by many consigned to history.[67] The cultural nationalists and antiquarians became the inheritors of a hobby, not a movement. Although Jacobite writing and thinking continued among a minority through lyrical means and in oppressed Episcopal worship, the public voice of Scottish culture became more and more comfortably assumed into that of England. Attacks on the vernacular (for language guarantees identity) were strong; and Beattie's *Scotticisms* (1770) was a typical product of its day. The future lay in Britain; and the adopted icons of Jacobite heroism were frequently used only to denote a journey from active into sentimental patriotism.

There were exceptions to this trend, and the Gaeltacht (which had a third of Scotland's people) provided one of the major ones. The literary response of Highland Jacobite writers remained strident, in contradistinction to the sentimental approaches to Gaelic patriotism gaining ground elsewhere. Gaelic poetry shares many features in common with Jacobite propaganda being written elsewhere in Scots or English. It is noteworthy that it gives no indication of any distinction in the priorities of Highland and Lowland Jacobites: any Highland/Lowland divide is not evident in these lyrics. Rather their writers use images and appeals to tradition markedly similar to those made by pro-Stuart nationalist writers in other parts of the country. The fertility/infertility, light/darkness, purity/corruption, sacred/devilish, and retreat themes of the popular song and poem are echoed by many of the Gaelic and Irish lyrics. Gaelic poetry in particular is frequently marked by great bitterness as well as lively imagery such as Alexander MacDonald's description of George as 'a flatulent badger'.

Poets such as Col. John Roy Stewart, who wrote both in Gaelic and

English, sit astride both traditions. John Roy wrote sacred Episcopalian poetry in English and carried the same analysis through into his Gaelic verse in images of violation and lost fertility. In his Gaelic poem, 'Culloden Day', the state of Scotland is represented as '. . . foul weeds of charlock/Overcoming the wheat of the land'. The poet puts 'the curse of the fig tree' on the unholy oppressors who have created this situation.

Apart from the themes of overthrown fertility and the natural order, shared by many Gaelic poets, attention is paid to Whig commercialism and its threat to the cultural values of a society which sees itself in traditionalist terms. The writers of these poems share not only a substantial common ground with Lowland song writers, but also with English or Anglo-Irish critics of financial change and Whig hegemony, such as Pope and Swift. The presence of common imagery in Jacobite critiques from the West Highlands and London alike is remarkably suggestive of the presence of a fundamental Jacobite ideology which could be voiced by apparently culturally disparate groups.[68]

This manifests itself in a number of ways. The Whig state is seen as a 'greedy Egypt' holding Israel/Scotland in bondage. In the poetry of Alasdair MacMhaighstir Alasdair, Whigs are Judases, and Cumberland is the persecuting Nero of the Episcopalian kirk. Queen Anne is the 'borrowed sow', stealing in to her brother's kingdom. In 'Na Casagan Dubha' ('The Black Cassock'), the poet Rob Donn makes clear his interpretation of Scotland's plight:

> The Government read
> greed in those who had turned to them
> and gave avarice bait
> till you tore at each other.

This kind of view is consonant with the general Jacobite understanding of the Union as an act of avaricious fraud and corruption, which showed a falling away from ancestral standards, of which the patriotic Highlander was the symbol. Gaelic poets do not seem to have demurred significantly from this view. Alasdair MacMhaighstir Alasdair sees the Campbells as an exception to the traditional values of the clans (he would, as a MacDonald, of course). He believes that they have betrayed the clan system by yielding to the financial allures and opportunities offered by the British government. Like his Lowland counterparts, MacMhaighstir uses sacred metaphors:

> till a camel goes through
> the eye of a needle,
> no joy will ensue
> from treachery so vile

'What shall it profit a man, if he gain the whole world, but lose his own soul?' As a result of their action, the Campbells have joined the Whig underworld, and dwell in the darkness of the grave even before they are dead, taking their '. . . charters/to your beds that are narrow,/your wills all in order,/and your carcase for beetles . . .'. Their material gain is spiritual death. In contrast, Charles, 'Topmost grain of all kings', is the epitome of light, like the sun itself:

> Last night I saw in a vision
> Red Charles coming over ocean . . .
>
> As I woke in the morning early,
> Great was my joy and gladness
> To hear of the prince's coming
> To the land of Clanranald.

The Prince comes to destroy the dwellers in darkness, who 'faint and sad at sun-rise' as they face the reborn Jacobites, warriors of the light, will become prey for the ravens, kites, and vultures. Then they will return to their darkness, but now it will be the darkness of the grave, with Hell to follow:

> On Doomsday resurrection
> When George's folk, a-shake with fear
> Scream from their graves for mercy[69]

The subject-matter of much of the contemporary Gaelic poetry shares the sacred imperative of a Stuart restoration as the key to restoring Scotland's state and fortunes. Devotion to the person of the sacred king as a metaphor for renewed fertility is especially evident in poetry like that of Iain MacLachlainn:

> A change will come o'er barren lands,
>   No thorn on the ground but will fade,
> Every hill will be laid in smooth rigs,
>   And wheat will grow on the hillsides . . .
>
> Another tale that I'll not hide,
>   The woods will put leaves o'er our heads,
> The earth will yield crops without stint,
>   The sea's fruit will fill every net;
> Herds will give milk everywhere,
>   And honey on straw-tops be found,
> Without want, unstinted, fore'er,
>   Without storms, but every wind warm.[70]

Verse of this kind makes us understand how powerful both to Gael and Gall was the idea that 'the reign of a good king was distinguished by agricultural prosperity', the old theme on which such hopes drew. Tradition, as ever, was the talisman and guarantor of the Stuart claim to be both Scottish patriots and rightful kings, and it appealed to Highlander and Lowlander alike through fertility myths and the icon of the reborn spring king:

> Cold and wet each day,
> Each night is dark and stormy;
> Sad and dull each day,
> Close, misty, scarce a ray . . .
>
> With the King will come bright days,
> Frost and snow shall flee from us,
> Tempestuous skies he'll banish,
> With joy our pain shall vanish

('Oran Mu Bhliadhna Thearlaich': 'A Song about the Year of Charles')[71]

In bringing back the brightness of the land, Charles acted during 1745–6 as the legitimate descendant of an ancient traditional line: the 'Dear visage most royal, /From Banquo's proud lineage' as MacMhaighstir Alasdair puts it. As the spirit of returning spring, this anciently derived yet youthful prince acts 'Like the storms of March' in clearing away the wintry opposition of the Whigs:

> 'Dog-tooth' through the beating rain;
> Sharp blade in his hand for slaughter,
> Corpses hewn like autumn grain.
> In that day the man is fated,
> Who an ugly red-coat wears

The Stuart prince is an apocalyptic force, irresistible as the weather when he climbs to the zenith of his valour. He is both returning spring and the grim reaper. MacMhaighstir Alasdair's view of Charles as an elemental force is complemented in his poetry by the view of James as a gentler sacred king who can reassume his title when his son restores it, as he has restored spring to Scotland:

> Make haste, thou gentle James,
> Thou art our King and earthly sire,
> Under the holy heavenly One
> Thy pity we desire

The sacred monarch will forgive his erring people, a policy actually carried out by Charles, whose notable clemency on campaign was perhaps in part due to an identification of himself with the merciful and providential aspects of the sacred monarch:

> The health of King James Stewart,
> Full gladly pass it round:

But if within you fault is hidden
Soil not the holy cup.

The image is of the Eucharist: the conflation of Jacobite and Christian images could go no farther.[72]

In poems written substantially later than the battle of Culloden, strong nationalist sentiments survive ('Like lions rampant we shall rise'), along with both sacred and erotic attachments to the exiled Jacobite leader:

O come, beloved, lest we faint,
Before our courage sinks through fear;
As long as hearts are in our breasts
We're thine beloved, far and near.[73]

No one who reads such lyrics in Scots, English, or Gaelic can retain the view that Jacobite sympathies were predominantly cynical or sentimental. Nevertheless a strong nostalgic note soon crept in, as it became increasingly clear that 'June, the month of gold' (i.e. James VIII, who was born on 10 June) would not return to rule his people. William Ross's poem 'An Suithneas ban' ('The White Cockade'), an elegy for Charles Edward, displays a valedictory quality which even the most ideologically committed Jacobites could see was approaching more and more closely to what was true in reality. In the poem, Charles himself is characterized as 'the white cockade': the implication is that with him dies not only the symbol of the Stuart cause, but any real chance of a Stuart restoration:

Farewell to the White Cockade
Till Doomsday he in death is laid,
The grave has ta'en the White Cockade,
The cold tombstone is now his shade.

By using 'the white cockade' as a synonym for Charles Edward, Ross conveys a more general and complete elegiac note than could be sounded if the prince were named in person. Moreover, his elegiac note is also applied to the concept of exile, an ugly reality for many Jacobites besides the prince: something they had in common with their leader. The loss of the prince is a loss to the land, whose true character is now in exile from itself:

Each hill-slope and mountainside
On which we ever saw thee move,
Now has lost its form and hue
Since thou ne'er shalt come again.[74]

This Scotland is the 'poor land that is lost now'.[75] The Jacobites are in exile or dead, like their prince. The potential for renewal has been abandoned.

Such poems as 'The White Cockade' are relatively uncommon in Gaelic poetry, but the lament for exile and the loss of nationhood is found in much

Lowland Jacobite verse in the period after 1745, despite the survival of a more positive response, which continues to praise 'WALLACE' and 'great ROBERT' against the 'haughty' king of England, remembering the patriot Scots who fought:

> Whilst yet their country had a name,
> The foremost in the books of Fame,
> Unsacrific'd to gold.[76]

Increasingly, however, loss and exile become more potent themes. It is hard to date these songs and poems precisely, except where we can trace original manuscripts or broadsheets. But the trend is clear. One of the songs which exemplifies it is 'Jessie's Dream'. In it, an exiled woman dreams of a lost Scotland, and of a delivery from her present condition, which is effected by Highland patriot-figures. The poem opens with Jessie dreaming that 'awa' to bonnie Scotland has my spirit ta'en its flight, /An' I saw my mother spinnin' in our Highland home at night'. Though this is a Lowland song, its recollections are of a 'Highland home' – so pervading a symbol of traditional and patriotic Scottish behaviour had the Highlander become under the influence of Jacobite propaganda. Suddenly, Jessie hears a sound:

> I heard the tune the pipers play'd, I kenn'd its rise and fa',
> 'Twas the wild Macgregors slogan 'Tis the grandest o' them a'

Then she realizes that the sound she hears is a real one, and that the slogan of Clan Gregor is not just a lost dream from a (defeated) Jacobite childhood, but intrusive fact:

> Hark! surely I'm no wildly dreamin' for I hear it plainly now,
> Ye cannot, ye never heard it on the far-off mountain's brow;
> For in your southern childhood, ye were nourish'd soft and warm,
> Nor watch'd upon the cauld hillside the risin' o' the storm

She sees the Highlanders appear:

> An' nearer still, an' nearer still, an' now again 'tis
> 'Auld Lang Syne' . . .
> They're comin' now to dee wi' us, or save us at the last.

That this host of deliverance turns out to be reinforcements for the embattled British Army does not alter the fundamental tone of the poem, with its appeal to 'Auld Lang Syne' and the Highlanders as they used to be in Jessie's childhood: a Jacobite force, not come to save her in far-off Canada, but to deliver her nation of Scotland.[77]

This tone is one repeated in other late eighteenth- and early nineteenth-century songs such as 'Hame, Hame, Hame', and 'Oh! Why I left my Hame', one of the songs which heads this section. One of the most famous is the late song 'I Will Go':

> I will go, I will go,
> Now the fighting is over,
> To the land of Macleod,
> That I left to be a soldier;
> I will go, I will go.

Here the Jacobite clansman, recruited into the British Army, returns to find 'Our goods lay in the snow/And our houses were burning'. His family are victims of the Clearances; his return is an understated ironic reverse of the deliverance of 'Jessie's Dream'.[78]

The identification of the experience of exile from Scotland with that of the Jacobite experience was a powerful one. Nevertheless, the exilic experience did not voice a consistent political critique because it was often conflated with the actions of Scots exiled only temporarily and voluntarily in order to pursue imperialist aims rather than to fly a hostile British state. There are two kinds of exile: that of losers, and that of winners. That in songs such as 'Jessie's Dream' the two could make common cause (British soldiers come to rescue exiled Jessie) was due to the adoption of the Jacobite image of the Highlander as patriot by both parties. In the eyes of one group, he was still the archetypal Jacobite hero-figure; to the other, he was a new kind of *British* patriot – an image of political reconciliation manifested in the conduct of Highland regiments during the Seven Years' War. Confusion, deliberate and accidental, between the two kinds of political statement at stake in these uses grew as time went on. The Jacobite reading of the Scottish experiences was retained, but it was increasingly subsumed under a British context. During the 1760s and 1770s, the Jacobite note of loss became institutionalized by the imperial note of gain, which adapted some of its stronger images in the quest for an imperial identity into which Scotland would fit. This change in the understanding of the nature of the symbols of Jacobite loyalty was accompanied by a romanticization of its loss, found most notably in Macpherson. A succeeding generation was able to find room for both among the patriotic myths of imperial Britain: and such Jacobitism, castrated by sentiment, became politically mute and socially fashionable. Defeat at Culloden had removed the possibility of Scotland once again becoming a *Reichstaat*; the imperial myth was to seek to prevent her remaining a *Kulturstaat*. Her political identity lost, her cultural identity began to be absorbed.[79]

3

The invention of Scotland

MACPHERSON

By the third quarter of the century, Jacobite and anti-Jacobite sentiment
tended to become subordinate to a new loyalty to Scotland conceived
as part of the super-nation, Great Britain.

Tom Crawford[1]

Such, Fingal! were thy words; but thy words I hear no more. Sightless
I sit by thy tomb. I hear the wind in the wood; but no more I hear
my friends. The cry of the hunter is over. The voice of war is ceased.

Macpherson[2]

For a long time, James Macpherson has largely been written off as a fake
and a forger; but today it is increasingly recognized that his attempt to
create a Gaelic epic was one which drew heavily on existing poetic
traditions, of which he made a genuine if idiosyncratic use. His Gaelic
contacts certainly included Jacobite poets; and in the epic he chose to
create he adopts the post-1745 Jacobite tone of loss as a metaphor for the
whole Gaelic experience. While his subject matter might alert his Scottish
readers to Jacobite codes, his tone could comfort the English reader with
the thought that picturesque as the Scottish heroic age undoubtedly was,
it was now over and no threat. Macpherson's image of ancient Scotland
was related to that of the antiquarians: but it was a pleasingly remote
image, unlikely to stir any patriotic spirit to action. By packaging Scotland's nationhood in a safely fictive form, Macpherson's Ossian took the
world by storm. At the height of the Scottish Enlightenment, Scotland
was presented as an anti-Enlightenment culture, to the delight of all
Europe.

Macpherson himself was a member of a Jacobite clan, brought up in a
Jacobite area, Badenoch. His clan were unavoidably absent on Culloden
day, an absence reputed disastrous not only because of the resulting lack
of manpower, but also because it was reputed that the Macphersons could
not be defeated in battle while carrying their talismans, the Green Banner
and the Black Chanter.[3] Macpherson must have known of this story. The

Macphersons remained undefeated, and their chief, Cluny, was never captured, remaining loyal to the Stuarts.[4]

The Jacobite influences of Macpherson's childhood were Highland; those of his adolescence, Lowland. Through these dual experiences, he was uniquely situated among contemporary writers in his ability to straddle both cultures and to realize the similarity of the pro-Stuart political analysis available in both. As a child during the Forty-Five, he had witnessed two of the events of the Rising at his home in Ruthven: the advance of Cope in 1745, and Glenbucket's attack on Ruthven barracks in 1746. As a student at King's College, Aberdeen from 1752, he was able to experience the last flickerings of the north-east's distinctive political interest in Scoto-Latin culture, an interest nearly always accompanied by Jacobite sympathies. Here he absorbed the 'discipline of the classical scholarship of the Episcopal North-East', retaining also 'his interests in that civilization [of the Highlands], in the legends and the traditions of his own people, the farmers and cottars, the herdsmen and the hunters he had known from boyhood'. These interests grew into the raw material for his epic, an epic of the raw and uncorrupt Caledonians, pure in their native vigour, unseduced by rationalism and commerce. In recreating this distant society, he sought to give it contemporary significance:

> He wrote of ancient tragedies: 'A tale of the times of old!'; but the spirit which throbs through these lays is the dirge for the ancient civilization which in his own day and in his own strath he saw dominated and depressed by the coarse, dull emissaries of the raw materialistic civilization of the South.[5]

The language of Ossian and ancient Celtic mythology was to be a coded nationalist language for Macpherson, as it was for W. B. Yeats in Ireland 150 years later (Yeats in fact borrowed the refrain 'A terrible beauty is born' from Macpherson).[6] But for the Scottish writer, the nationalist note was to be elegiac, and set the seal on an image of a doomed and fated Scotland, present in Jacobite analyses since before the Union, and after the suppression of the last Rising, even more pronounced.

It was not only Macpherson who adopted this approach, as I have already argued. Besides the change of tone evident in the Jacobite song, works like John Home's *Douglas*, first produced at Edinburgh in 1756, show the stirrings of the valedictory school of patriotism, later so profoundly developed by Scott. Macpherson's poems were toweringly successful compared with other early efforts in this vein. He defined its possibilities. Henceforth, Scotland and romance were linked through the age of Scott and beyond:

> enthusiastic readers . . . responded to the vision of a strange, remote, exotic ancient world, peopled by grandly heroic characters who move with a kind of stately dignity across wild and barren landscapes of mountains, crags, rivers, seas, clouds, and mists.[7]

This was a lost world of superseded heroism with which the late eighteenth-century reader could sympathize, and over which he could grieve with the self-conscious 'sentiments of regret and melancholy' appropriate to his own cultural milieu. But in reading Macpherson, we must remain conscious that the pervading melancholia of the poems is not merely a marketing technique, but is also 'the spirit of the Scottish Highlands in the generation that followed Culloden'.[8] As a poet, Macpherson has been accused of misrepresenting Gaelic poetry; this is true, but fails to take cognizance of the special and distressing disadvantages under which Highland society was now labouring. Ossian was a reply to political repression, an 'assertion by the ancient civilisation of the North of the triumph of mind and spirit' over the seedy world of Hanoverian commerce and imperialism. Jacobitism was, even before Macpherson, a romantic political movement; it was alienated, revolutionary, nationalist, and daring and dangerous on a personal level. In drawing many of its strands together, Ossian symbolized 'the spiritual strength of the old Celtic civilisation of the Highlands of Scotland reinforced by the old scholarly civilisation of the Episcopal North-East'.[9]

There is no space here to discuss the texts of *Fingal* or *Temora* (1763) in detail. Instead I shall be examining the peculiarly appropriate areas of their subject matter, and how the career of their author reflected his political interest in the more sensitive areas of his epic.

Ossian, the Gaelic hero who survives the fall of the Fianna (Irish national-ists were proud to call themselves Fenians), was an emotive character on whom to centre these poems. Himself reputedly the last vestige of a lost culture, Ossian's lays told of the heroic culture of Fionn and the Fianna – this is the subject of *Fingal*. Macpherson's choice of subject matter becomes still more relevant when it is realized that right into the present century, Scottish Gaelic heroic ballads portray Fionn as a hero-king who in the hour of need will come to save his people:

> People . . . believed equally strongly [with the Scriptures] in the Gaelic Messianic tradition that puts Fionn, lying in Tom na h-Iubhraich, near Inverness, in the role of Sleeping Warrior who will one day reappear to restore the Gaels of Scotland to their former greatness.[10]

The analogy between Fionn and the Stuarts is clear from this tradition. Macpherson's 'research mission' in the Highlands in 1760–1 serves to emphasize the close sympathy he undoubtedly possessed with the traditions in which he grew up. They were elements in a consciousness which often made such analogies explicit. There is a legend of a man who intruded on the sleeping Fianna by accident during their wait under the soil. He was greeted by the 'awful imprecation' – 'You have left us worse than you found us.' Significantly, this phrase was and is also used about the Year of the Prince. It is headlined in the National Trust for Scotland display at Culloden. The Forty-Five was an inadequate return of the Fianna, a failed deliverance. This kind of thinking is evident in the Gaelic literary renaissance of the eighteenth century, as it is in the work of Macpherson himself:

> Surpassing the story even of Arthur and the Knights of the Round Table, because more near, more real and historical, the romance of Prince Charlie and the Highland chiefs has taken a lasting hold of the popular imagination.[11]

The central role of Jacobitism in eighteenth-century Gaelic poetry laid the foundation for Macpherson's mythic constructs. Poets like MacMhaighstir Alasdair 'found a way to fuse together ... [a] vision of the Stewarts, of Gaeldom, and of an ideal Scotland'. This was made easier by the 'Messianic nature of the Prince's appeal': 'the Prince will be crowned in triumph/in the White House where the heroes dwell' as a waulking-song from Barra puts it.[12] The quality of heroic description which implicitly or explicitly aligns Charles with the deeds of more ancient warriors reaches heights of clear personal dedication and great sweetness in some of these poems:

> 'Watchman, what do you see?'
> 'I see An Udairn and Rubha Huinis,
> Caolas Ronaidh with mist obscuring it.'
> 'Do you see the galley beside the Dun,
> flying the white banner of Charles Stewart?
> Mary Mother, may grace be doubled for him,
> a price on his head and the enemy hounding him;
> may the French host come over and help him!'[13]

Macpherson's references are far less specific than are those of the poems on which he drew; but he nevertheless provided a mythic framework in which such perceptions could continue to flourish. More importantly for a wider audience, he provided the pleasures of vicarious Jacobitism shorn of its dangerous politics:

> We sat. We feasted. We sang. The soul of Cuthullin rose. The strength of his arm returned. Gladness brightened along his face. Ullin gave the song; Carril raised the voice. I joined the bards, and sung of battles .... Battles! where I often fought. Now I fight no more! The fame of my former deeds is ceased. I sit forlorn at the tomb of my friends!

This passage can be seen as containing a passive rendition of the Jacobite spirit: its glory, its celebration, its failure, its suppression, and its lament. Elsewhere, Macpherson describes these lost battles. Here is a description of something which sounds very like a Highland charge:

> Ryno went on like a pillar of fire. Dark is the brow of Gaul. Fergus rushed forward with feet of wind. Fillan, like the mist of the hill. Ossian, like a rock, came down. I exulted in the strength of the king.

Many were the deaths of my arms! dismal the gleam of my sword! My locks were then not so grey; nor trembled my hands with age. My eyes were not closed in darkness; my feet failed not in the race!

The great days are remembered, but they are gone. 'The Highlands will rise no more' is the implicit refrain of this and many other passages. 'The cry of the hunter is over. The voice of war is ceased.'

The strong association of the Stuart cause with fertility is played on by Macpherson in the way he identifies (as other Jacobite poets had done before him) the barrenness of the landscape with the failure of Celtic heroic support for the Cause:

> Raise high the stones; collect the earth: preserve the
> name of Fear-comhraic.
> Blow, winds, from all your hills; sigh on the grave of
> Muirnin.
> The dark rock hangs, with all its wood, above the
> calm dwelling of the heroes.
> The sea, with its foam-headed billow, murmurs at
> their side.
> Why sigh the woods, why roar the waves; They have
> no cause to mourn.

The cairn of dead and unsuccessful heroes is a sign that the land has lost its chance of regeneration. It is now a barren place of sea, stones, and woods full of 'Moss and withered branches', ripe for the pathetic fallacy and the expositions of Romanticism. The time when heroes were 'chief of an hundred hills' whose 'deer drunk of a thousand streams' is over. The Highlands are grand, barren, and British:

> 'Thou art fallen, young tree', I said, 'with all thy beauty round thee.
> Thou art fallen on thy plains, and the field is bare. The winds come
> from the desert! there is no sound in thy leaves!'

After the heroes have fallen, a final death comes on the land and the land's identity:

> Autumn is dark on the mountains; grey mist rests on the hills. The
> whirlwind is heard on the heath. Dark rolls the river through the
> narrow plain. A tree stands alone on the hill, and marks the slumbering
> Connal. The leaves whirl round with the wind, and strew the grave of
> the dead. At times are seen here the ghosts of the departed.[14]

This is the fate of Scotland, shortly to be no longer a heroic culture, save in the grandeur of her landscapes.

The achievement of *Fingal* and *Temora* was the crown of Macpherson's career, which had earlier included some more overt if less symbolic Jacobite poems, such as 'The Highlander' and 'On the Death of Marshal Keith' (Field Marshal James Keith, brother of the Earl Marischal, is a German folk hero who died fighting for the Prussian forces in the 1750s). In his commemorative poem, written in 1758, Macpherson's lament for the lost world of the Stuarts clearly foreshadows his Ossian poems:

> But chief, as relics of a dying race,
> The Keiths command, in woe, the foremost place;
> A name for ages through the world revered,
> By Scotia loved, by all her en'mies feared;
> Now falling, dying, lost to all but fame,
> And only living in the hero's name.
> See! the proud halls they once possessed, decayed,
> The spiral tow'rs depend the lofty head;
> Wild ivy creeps along the mould'ring walls,
> And with each gust of wind a fragment falls;
> While birds obscene at noon of night deplore,
> Where mighty heroes kept the watch before.

Here can be seen the prototypical concepts of the Ossian poems.[15]

The note of departure and loss sounded by Macpherson was not unique. But Macpherson alone had cultural contact with the political realities of the Gaelic people, while having been educated in the world outside the Gaeltacht. Perhaps that is why his epic, despite or because of its emotional hyperbole, proved so effective. His patriotic view 'that the Irish Ossianic ballads were ultimately derived from Scotland' served only to underline the cultural nationalism of the whole enterprise. Even his sentimentalism had its roots in the post-Culloden experience of Jacobite culture, while his use of landscape derived from the fertility images (and their opposite) associated with the fate of the Stuart kings. Jacobite suffering paved the way for Romantic art. In the Jacobite song, landscape reflects the spiritual health of a nation. The pathetic fallacy was a feature of pro-Stuart literature long before *Fingal* (1761) and *Temora* (1763), Macpherson's major works.[16]

Macpherson was thought of as a 'notorious Jacobite'; but with the return of the Tories to power in 1762 and the end of half a century of Whig rule, such accusations tended to be taken less seriously, though Jacobite activity could still result in legal action. Despite the view of Macpherson's work 'as a piece of Scotch impertinence', and the cloud cast by early and enduring accusations of forgery, the poet's influence was considerable. In his prosperity, his political sympathies were still visible: for example, in 1784 he was significantly instrumental in restoring Cluny Macpherson's estate. Still retaining his local loyalties, internationally his books held sway over Europeans as distinguished as Goethe and Napoleon. Few were perhaps aware of the complex political codes and laments underlying his great work of fiction/adaptation. Macpherson ventured into remote antiquity to provide a new and more public language for the Stuart cause: but one which was also a confession of defeat.[17]

BURNS

Here Stewarts once in triumph reign'd,
And laws for Scotland's weal ordain'd;
But now unroof'd their Palace stands,
Their sceptre's fall'n to other hands;
Fallen indeed, and to the earth,
Whence grovelling reptiles take their birth.-
A Race outlandish fill their throne;
An idiot race, to honour lost;
Who know them best despise them most.

Burns[18]

Robert Burns is the subject of hagiography and celebration among a nation which usually accords neither kind of honour to its creative writers. Much of the Burns cult has directed itself towards an image of the poet as a couthie adjunct to the celebrations of the better-off, whether in Scotland or abroad. It is this kind of use or misuse of Burns's memory which has made some modern Scottish writers suspicious of the man himself, a 'sham bard' in the words of Edwin Muir, but it seems fairer to agree with MacDiarmid that the cult and not the poet is at fault.[19]

Burns's appeal lies in the fact that he seems, for an artist, crowningly unselfconscious – the ultimate common man, in fact, quite a strange role for a poet. That he is viewed in this light is to a great extent due to his use of the popular song, which he both reorganized and contributed to. In doing so, he became one of the few Jacobite poets we can name, and arguably the greatest among them. His approach to the oral tradition of vernacular Scots underlines his enduring popular appeal. Indebted to the Jacobite lyric and to the innovative work of (pro-Jacobite) predecessors such as Robert Fergusson, Burns was still a highly original writer.

His attitude to Jacobitism was broadly sympathetic, despite the political radicalism with which he is often associated. In fact, many Jacobites who did survive into the 1790s had almost equally radical views.[20] A century of dispossession had strengthened the revolutionary, and diluted the conservative aspects of Jacobitism. Indeed, as I shall later argue, this 'Jacobitism of the left' was to provide a potent account of Scotland's condition in the later struggles of the nineteenth and twentieth centuries.[21] In the context of the period of the French Revolution, the feeling that there was something rotten in the state of Scotland was common to Jacobite and Jacobin alike. Indeed, the French Revolution and the ideas associated with it certainly reinforced Republican nationalist feeling. Reactionary and radical politics converged, and the democratic instincts of Romanticism, which saw 'the popular art-song become the dominant literary form' in Scotland (on some levels, at least), renewed the voice of the Jacobite lyric. This advantaged Burns and the succeeding generation:

> There were . . . qualities latent in Jacobitism which made it attractive to a later generation of Scots moved by the first stirrings of Romantic nationalism, not least its aptness as a focus for anti-Union sentiment and as a symbol, therefore, for Scottish cultural and political distinctiveness.[22]

Romanticism's influence on Jacobitism was in the end to be a negative one, adopting Jacobite images on a symbolic level, but scorning them on a political one. Macpherson had prepared them to be only furniture for Romanticism, so much dead wood carved into interesting shapes. Of the important Scottish Romantic writers, only Hogg seems to have fully understood that the Clearances were a present-day political fulfilment of Jacobite prophetic ideology. In startling fashion they bore out the Jacobite view that the native polity (Scotland) was being destabilized or destroyed, and its inhabitants forced into internal or external exile. Hogg realized this; but too often the panoply of tartan and broadsword were sported by those very chiefs who were conducting these same Clearances. Romanticization of the Highlands which shared the sentiments but not the politics of Jacobitism bore out the decline in heroism those very politics lamented. The Jacobite critique suggested that money and the lure of English markets would destroy Scottish values. As far as the Clearances were concerned, this turned out to be too true.[23]

Burns stood only on the threshold of this period. What he did for the Jacobite song was to make it more respectable: after his time, Jacobite lyrics turn up more frequently in Scottish song collections. Making the Jacobite song respectable was a two-edged sword, however, since doing so undermined the subversiveness which gave its ideology a strength uncompromised by any participation in a British theatre of events. Burns, perhaps unconsciously, helped those who wished to render an image of Jacobitism as a glorious failure, touchingly elegized by sentiment. He cannot be blamed for this, for his own aim seems to have been to allow Scottish national culture a freer hearing, and to impose a pattern on its voice: 'to implant his version of the Jacobite tradition at the heart of the evolving Scottish national identity'.[24] The flaw in this aim was that it could be hijacked by a localized, sentimentalized version of this identity, which could regionalize and marginalize Scotland by removing the politics from its lyrics. Scotland began to think itself a Celtic country again, as Jacobite propaganda had affirmed; but it was to be largely a Celticism composed of echoes, the 'Tartan Curtain' that divided the new Scottish identity from the realities of both the national struggle of the eighteenth century, and the current tragedy of the Highlands.[25]

These cultural pressures undermined what may have been Burns's good intentions. But he nevertheless made a strong contribution to Jacobite ideology. His devotion to 'Liberty' can be seen as in the line of earlier radical Jacobites, in that it 'directly links the Wars of Independence with the Jacobite risings as heroic national struggles'. The idea of a heroic, traditional Scotland as having to wage perpetual war against English might and gold in order to secure its very existence was one central to Jacobite images of native heroism. Burns's 'Parcel of Rogues in a Nation' is a development of this traditional Jacobite critique. The degenerate present has sold out the heroic past.[26]

I have chosen two songs to emphasize this contribution to Jacobite ideas, which, while traditional, was innovative in that Burns acknowledged the end of any real political opportunity to restore the Stuarts, while insisting that the battle for liberty would continue. The message of Jacobitism to the Scottish polity would not die, though James and Charles were dead. It would henceforward be subsumed under the concerns of a larger struggle.

The two songs in question are 'Scots Wha Hae' and 'Ye Jacobites by Name'. The second appears to be an anti-Jacobite song. In fact it is far more complex. The last stanza reads:

> Then let your schemes alone, in the State, in the State,
> Then let your schemes alone in the State,
> Then let your schemes alone,
> Adore the rising sun,
> And leave a Man undone
> To his fate.

This stanza, and indeed the whole poem, might be read as anti-Jacobite verse were it not for the last two lines. The 'Man undone', we suddenly realize, is the speaker himself, who has done all the things he is now telling his fellow Jacobites not to do. It is too late for him, but not for others. The repetition of the word 'State' three times suggests the strength and established nature of the forces against which the Jacobites would now have to pit themselves. Earlier in the poem, Burns argues that the Jacobite appeal to ancient law is now outdated. New laws have compromised the indefeasible right of the Stuarts, who even if they were to return, could hardly repeal them all. No one can any longer say with confidence 'What is Right, and what is Wrang, by the law, by the law?' The argument from antiquity, beloved of the Stuarts, has been superseded: surely it can no longer be right to 'hunt a Parent's life/Wi' bludie war', when the Stuarts themselves are so long exiled as to be almost forgotten.

But again we are drawn back to the end of the poem. The 'rising sun' is an interesting image for Burns to choose as representative of the victorious side, as it primarily belonged to Jacobite propaganda. Its use here may be intended to remind the Jacobite preparing to change loyalties, who in fact was on the right side: James 'VIII' and 'III'. Thus although the Hanoverians are depicted as victorious and in the ascendant, they are so depicted in terms of an image which the Jacobite movement had long made its own: an interesting and ambivalent decision on Burns's part. The 'Man undone' who sings the song speaks of his defeat in the metaphor of victory. Moreover, his making reference to himself in the last two lines suggests that the audience for the song should not forget that one of the reasons the Hanoverian sun is rising is that it has 'undone' and abandoned to their fate men like the singer. Lurking perhaps behind the images of the doomed Jacobite and the rising sun is the idea that those who turn to adore that sun are blinded by its light, and forget those like the 'Man undone', whose suffering is a consequence of the Hanoverian (false) dawn.

'Ye Jacobites by Name' is a song which suggests acceptance of Jacobitism's final defeat, qualified through reservations and ambiguities. Burns did not want his audience to forget those who had been 'undone' by the Hanoverian state. The fact that the singer of this apparently anti-Jacobite song is a Jacobite himself is perhaps intended to show that Jacobitism remains an enduring belief, even though it may be pointless to rise in its support.[27]

'Scots Wha Hae' stands more clearly in a nationalist tradition (it has indeed in the twentieth century been adopted as Scotland's national anthem by the SNP). Burns himself acknowledged that it was a Jacobite song, though it fuses such ideas with more contemporary concepts of liberty born out of the French Revolution.[28] It also owes something to the language and sentiments of Barbour's *Bruce*. Burns was the first to combine the Jacobite analysis of Scotland's position as one long struggle for freedom with more current ideas of what constituted political liberty. In Barbour, the Declaration of Arbroath, the Community of the Realm of Scotland, and the Jacobite cause itself, Burns located concepts consonant with post-1789 usages of the term 'Liberty'.[29] Jacobite propaganda had, fifty years before, used such ideas to suggest a future of fecund renewal, political freedom, and religious toleration for the Scottish polity under a restored Stuart dynasty. Barbour and Blind Harry, authors of *The Bruce* and *The Wallace* respectively, had been republished as a patriotic act by eighteenth-century Jacobite antiquarians.[30] Burns used such amalgamations of the Wars of Independence and the Jacobite cause in the political parameters he adopted for 'Scots Wha Hae'.

The poem itself clearly combines traditionalism with a call to liberty. In the first stanza the address, in Bruce's voice, is to the nation as a whole, all 'Scots'. The first line mentions the talismanic Wallace, an icon held in common by Republican and Jacobite alike. The 'chains and slaverie' of the second stanza, a reference later reinforced in the phrase 'our sons in servile chains', is a metaphorical description of slavery. It is also one with a degree of literal accuracy if one considers the Jacobites who had been transported to the colonies as slaves, virtual or actual. Transportation and fetters were more an eighteenth- than a fourteenth-century problem. The method of delivery from slavery advocated in the song is fighting 'for Scotland's King and Law'. This was a Jacobite phrase, or at least a compound of Jacobite concepts: '. . . we are forced against our law/For want o' Royal Charlie' was a common complaint.[31] It implied that a struggle on the king's behalf was also one made on behalf of the law, and that therefore support for the Stuart monarchs was not, as their opponents claimed, support for tyranny and arbitrary power, but instead for true legality.

The last three stanzas make repeated reference to the idea of freedom, culminating in the reference to 'Liberty' in the penultimate line (a term with subversive connotations in the early 1790s, the time of the Terror). The ancient Scottish ideal of 'freedom', apostrophized by Barbour, is emphasized several times before adding the more contemporary ideological concept of 'Liberty'. Burns is uniting Jacobite and revolutionary traditions:

> Lay the proud usurpers low,
> Tyrants fall in every foe,
> Liberty's in every blow,
> Let us do or die!

This last stanza encapsulates the message of the song. The use of Jacobite analyses and Jacobite language in the earlier part of the poem is here combined with a call to future liberty. The call is ostensibly that made by Bruce, who is speaking the lines; but given the language of the earlier parts of the poem, and the contemporary reference implicit in the call to 'Liberty' rather than 'freedom', the audience are able to read into the poem a nationalist call to resistance against 'Tyrants' of every generation, including their own. 'Scots Wha Hae' is set in the fourteenth century; it uses Jacobite language and adopts, as Burns himself confessed, a Jacobite perspective. It also hints at relevance not only to the past, but to the present and future also, through the allying of the contemporary term 'Liberty' with older Scottish ideas of 'freedom'. Burns combines past and present to suggest a continuing relevance to Bruce's call in the poem.[32]

In these two poems, and indeed in his approach to Jacobitism generally, Burns seeks to do two things. First, he is in no doubt that 'Jacobitism' in its classical sense of revolutionary support for a Stuart claimant, is now politically dead. Yet he continues, in the poems discussed above and in others, the Jacobite critique. He aims to suggest a continuing validity for the Jacobite analysis. It is for him a nationalist understanding of the Scottish position which may have had to abandon its initial programme of a Stuart restoration, but which nevertheless will continue to be relevant in designing other political solutions intended to promote 'Liberty'.

Burns's work in the field of the popular song underlined its importance as a genre in both literary and ideological terms. The corpus of song he preserved, altered, or invented included a strongly Jacobite element. In this element (his element, perhaps), Burns was concerned to maintain the

Jacobite vision: one transmuted from active support for the Stuarts, but maintaining ideological consistency. In paying such attention to the Jacobite lyric, Burns acknowledged its continuing potential for patriotic utterance. It was, as perhaps he knew, one of the main resources of nationalist argument, a role it had fulfilled spectacularly well in the eighteenth century. To preserve Scottish nationalism, even at a cultural level, it was imperative that the Jacobite song culture be preserved also. Burns played a major role in this. It was not his fault that in doing so he helped make it respectable, and thus paved the way for nineteenth-century sentimental Jacobitism. Few who sing his most famous song, 'Auld Lang Syne', know that it was from the early eighteenth century often a statement of exilic Jacobitism, a longing for home on the part of those deprived of it by their politics:

> Though thou wert Rebell to the King
> and beat with Wind and Rain
> Assure thyself of welcome Love,
> for *Old lang sine*.

Burns married propaganda songs to folk culture.[33]

SCOTT THE INVENTOR

'Then the Cause is lost for EVER!'

Redgauntlet[34]

Few writers of a given nationality of any age can have been as aware of the dilemma between local and national patriotism as was Walter Scott. Although he was a Scottish patriot, he believed that Scotland's future lay in a Union which appeared to him to have healed what he believed to be otherwise incurable divisions in Scottish life: Highland and Lowland, Jacobite and Whig, Protestant and Catholic. Britain seemed to offer broader horizons than those hitherto encompassed by internecine strife.

In his novels, Scott set about presenting a version of history which reflected these beliefs. In doing so, he made extensive use of Jacobitism, making it 'the yeast of our national romance' rather than a serious political critique.[35] Scott himself expresses sympathy for Jacobitism, even to the extent of confessing that he would have fought in the Forty-Five. But he always presents this sympathy as one born out of the seductiveness of Stuart charisma rather than from any rational source. Dreamy characters like Edward Waverley and Darsie Latimer are drawn to the Jacobite cause: but in the end, good sense and the consideration of the rational benefits the Union has brought overcome this initial romantic appeal in the novels. In his characterization of Jacobitism, Scott takes a step beyond Macpherson. In Scott's view, Jacobitism is not only a lost cause, but it always had the makings of one, based, as he sees it, on emotion not fact. Scott's Jacobite lords, Ravenswood, Redgauntlet, Vich

Ian Vohr, are potent, overwhelming *Sturm und Drang* figures: they have no place in the peaceable interchange of civilized society. They are childlike in the extreme nature of their loyalties, resentment, and violence.[36] Scottish patriotism is childish, British patriotism adult: this is the equation offered.

Scott is himself a seductive historian. By rendering the clash of nationalist against Unionist (and Scott makes it clear that he equates Jacobitism and nationalism) as one of emotion versus reason, id against ego, he creates an idea of history as intellectual or personal development. As Scott's characters become more rational, they leave behind emotional responses to things. One of the premises of this development is that Scottish patriotism is emotive and therefore primitive, overtaken by the 'rational' decision to make Britain one nation. This idea has provided many damaging allegations about the backward-looking nature of Scottish patriotism.

Scott's view of Scotland emphasizes the beneficial necessity of change. In doing so, it promotes two ideas: the inadequacy of Scottish patriotism in coping with historical change, and the incompetence of Scots in ruling themselves (due to their historic divisions). In promoting these ideas, Scott created a powerful and popular view of Scottish history which emphasizes the conflict and poverty of the seventeenth and early eighteenth centuries (where most of Scott's great novels are set), at the expense of any more comprehensive understanding of Scottish history as a whole. Scott made nationalism seem old-fashioned, bigoted, and thus divisive.

He does this chiefly by making the Jacobite cause stand for Scottish national feeling as a whole. There is a case for doing this in the eighteenth century. However, Scott, perhaps deliberately, underestimated the radicalism of active Jacobitism and its association with ideas of freedom, all the more pertinent in the light of the repressive legislation of the previous century.[37] Scott stressed only its antiquarianism, and in his fiction made it the preserve of aristocratic misfits, apolitical dreamers, self-interested clan chiefs, and the criminal classes. In addition, he largely omitted mention of the brutality of the Hanoverian suppression of the Jacobite movement, Highland society, and the Episcopal church. When we read Scott's descriptions of government action, it is usually benevolent. He avoids the issue. In *Waverley*, Bradwardine is restored to his estate, despite having been 'out' in both the Fifteen and the Forty-Five. (His real-life model, Lord Pitsligo, spent sixteen years in hiding.) In *Redgauntlet*, an indulgent Hanoverian officer lets the Jacobites, Charles Edward and all, go home. In *Heart of Midlothian*, the Campbell chief and George II's wife obtain mercy for Effie Deans. The Jacobite figures in these novels, on the other hand, are portrayed as noble, but also quarrelsome, ridiculous, and out-of-date.[38] Scott's account of history and detailed knowledge of local circumstances has hardly ever been surpassed; but underneath his tempting claim to be writing history is a fictional slant which treats the past too elegiacally to allow the questions it raises to remain open. We know that Jacobitism was defeated; but Scott makes it appear doomed from the start by its churlish and stubborn clinging to a Scottish past rendered irrelevant by the sweet reason of the new British government. In blackening the one and exaggerating the merits of the other, Scott creates an impression of historical destiny which retains Jacobitism's charms while allowing us to feel them to be completely outgrown.

More seriously, his concentration on the creation of a fictional world which accomplished the delicate task of celebrating the Union while respecting Scotland's past (as long as its issues stayed in the past) led to Scott's neglect of contemporary issues, such as the Clearances. There is little evidence that Scott regarded them with the seriousness his contemporary, Hogg, did. Hogg understood how the Jacobite analysis might apply to the Clearances; it would not be unfair for us to speculate that Scott did not want to understand.[39] If the Jacobite analysis had contemporary relevance, Scott's attempt to render it a tableau of extinct heroics would fail. Scott preferred to make this pageant of the past Scotland's gift to the Empire: a way of showing Scottish distinctiveness while minimizing political threat. In doing this, he had to suppress in his fiction (and perhaps in his life) any message Jacobitism could give to the present.

Scott relied heavily on the idea that Scotland was a divided nation in his arguments in favour of the Union. His great fiction concentrates on the period 1638–1760, and his images of a divided Scotland nearly all relate to the historical experiences (as he presents them) of the seventeenth and early eighteenth centuries. In Chapter 1, I argued that the degree of political and religious division in Scotland during these periods was in large part due to the policies of successive governments. Scott makes it appear a tendency innate in the people. The Jacobite movement had taken account of the amount of division which existed in its stress on organic unity, political independence, and sacred kingship. Scott gives it no credit for its attempts (unsuccessful as they may have been) to unite Scottish opinion against the Union; but imitation is the sincerest form of flattery, and in his contribution to the cult of tartan, Scott accepts the Jacobite image of the Highlander as patriot. The 'garb of old Gaul' was to be the new national dress.[40]

Realizing perhaps that arguments in favour of a divided Scotland based on a narrow historical period are inadequate, Scott suggests a more deep-seated cause. He identifies the Scots as divided, more or less rigidly, into two racial groups: Celts and Teutons (Highlanders and Lowlanders). The clash between the politics of the two areas is thus explained in racial terms.

I shall argue in the next section that Hogg didn't identify these divisions at all, but, operating in the Jacobite tradition, viewed Scotland as a fundamentally Celtic country. This led him to a more unified understanding of Scottish history, with more potent political overtones than those Scott wished to cultivate. Scott's ethnic gulf allows him to introduce images of quarrelsomeness and division at many opportune points, such as between Highlander and Lowlander in *Waverley*, and Hector and Oldbuck in *The Antiquary*. It also allows him to suggest that the problem of internal strife in Scotland is endemic, rather than contingent on political differences.

In this as in so much else, Scott's history is not Scots history. While it is true that there was Saxon settlement in Lothian, the Borders, and south Galloway, the majority of Scots remained predominantly Celtic, with admixtures of Scandinavian, Norman, and other blood.[41] Scott confused linguistic and racial divides: a confusion still evident today, and abetted by the linguistic nationalism of the Gaeltacht (which has shrunk considerably since Scott's day). But the place-name evidence shows that Celtic Scotland extended far beyond the Highland line; and one might as well term the Irishman who cannot speak Irish a Saxon as say it of the average Scot. Nevertheless, the idea of a Scotland divided as decidedly along racial as political or linguistic lines is a potent one, and Scott did much to foster it.

It would be unfair to describe Scott's influence as predominantly negative. In popularizing an idea of Scotland, it was unparalleled. But it is that very idea which invented Scotland as a museum of history and culture, denuded of the political dynamic which must keep such culture alive and developing. Scott loved his country, but denied its contemporaneity. Macpherson had done likewise to an extent; but unlike Macpherson, Scott does not denigrate, by implication or otherwise, post-Union society. Rather he praises, indeed overpraises it.

Yet there lurks a revolutionary instinct in Scott. There is a sense that the happy and comforting conclusions he provides are forced endings, which forestall the possibility that the complex arguments of his fiction may conclude in a manner critical of the present establishment. There is undeniable sympathy with the Jacobites, even where they are portrayed as inadequate. Blake's comment on Milton, that he was of the Devil's party without knowing it, could be applied with some justice to Scott.[42] The more Scottish his subject matter, the more dynamically his fiction treats it.

Scott is therefore at his best writing Scots dialogue and at his weakest writing the stilted English by which he is unfortunately too often known. His work contains a desire for that victory it denies; and Scott's sensible heroes such as Reuben Butler, Argyll, and Morton are overshadowed in his fiction by the daring figures of Ravenswood, Redgauntlet, and Claverhouse. Scott's intelligence was phenomenal, and he may well have understood this division between his sympathies and his judgement. It was the misfortune of posterity that this division between 'emotional' nationalism and 'rational' Unionism was repeated in the minds of so many Scots. For this Scott was at least in some measure responsible. He offered a ratiocination for the dual vision of Scots who supported the idea of Britain.

Scott's arguments and historical misrepresentations serve to vitiate his sympathies: indeed, it is his British patriotic passion to prove his Scottish patriotic passion an inappropriate one. Although a Tory, he was of the Whig school of history, in that he believed in historical progression and irreversible trends. One of these trends, Scott decided, and underlined in his historical fiction, was that Scotland would be subsumed in the British state. In acting both as historian and novelist, Scott sought power over the imagination, while implying that the validity of this power rested on historical fact. This in itself was a brilliant fiction. Scott reinforced the idea that had surfaced at the time of the Union negotiations: that Scotland as an entity was doomed, and was possessed only of a past, not a future. The ideal medium in which to demonstrate this thesis was that of Jacobitism, the politically defeated creed which had served as the major vehicle for eighteenth-century nationalism. Scott made use of it in his fiction for precisely that reason: its defeat could be conveniently conflated with the defeat of Scotland as a whole. The past was to be buried with the full battle honours of Montrose, Claverhouse, and Charles Edward. But buried Scott was determined it must be.

The burial of Jacobite/nationalist sympathies with honours thick upon them was one Scott carried out throughout his fiction. He also carried it out in his life in a sequence of symbolic actions which directed the attention of the British establishment away from the radical dangers of Scotland's continuing history towards the pageantry of a safely deceased political struggle.

The event which enabled Scott to do this most effectively was the visit of George IV to Scotland in 1822. This was the first time a *de facto* monarch had been north of the Border since the seventeenth century. George, like his father, had a bit of a liking for the dynasty his own had defeated and its symbols: indeed, the future king wore tartan for the first time in 1789.[43] Scott was thus able to play on sympathies already awakened; and he was aided in this by a general desire to please the king. The choice of pageantry, tartan, and tradition helped to underline the picturesque distinction between England and Scotland, and to reassure the British government that there was now nothing to fear from it. In this context, Scott helped plan 'the transference of remaining Jacobite and nationalist sentiments to wider British imperial loyalties'.[44]

The Scotland thus presented was a Highland one, and sales of tartans in Edinburgh took off as a consequence of the king's visit (Scott neglected 'Teutonic' Scotland, which was useful when emphasizing Scottish division, but no use in giving Scotland a distinctive role in British unity). In his presentation, Scott chose rather to develop the legacy of Jacobite propaganda, which, unlike his novels, stressed the Celtic origins and cultural unity of the Scottish people, symbolized in the figure of the Highlander as patriot:

88

> King Malcolm's speech
> On the lips of our race
> Highland and Lowland,
> Both knew its grace:
> Highland and Lowland
> Ruled Kirk and State
> In the tongue of the Gael
> When Scotland was great.

It was this Jacobite voice, denigrated in his fiction, which Scott used to assert his country's identity to George IV.[45] This is a tribute to the power of Jacobite ideology in determining the nature of the Scottish identity.

The Jacobites had depicted their risings as national revolts against English rule. Posterity chose to agree with them. 'Sir Walter's Celtification of Scotland' was the romance that made this possible. Scott

> clearly wished to believe that the spiritual nature of a Stuart and therefore a Scottish monarchy, purified by exile and the blood of Culloden, had been made manifest in the fat form of the landlord of Brighton Pavilion.

It was not only Scott who adopted this position. At the time of the King's visit, the *Edinburgh Observer* suggested that:

> We are now all Jacobites, thorough-bred Jacobites, in acknowledging George IV. . . . This seems to be one of the feelings that stimulate the people here, at the present time, to make such exertions.

There were voices raised in disagreement. But 'the increasingly euphoric mood of resurgent Jacobitism' supported such assertions, and Scott's manipulation of them.[46]

Scott underlined the inheritance of the Stuart myth on which he drew when he altered a traditional Jacobite song, 'Carle, Now the King's Come', to a poem of welcome for George. Scott's pronouncements, most notably his statement that 'We are THE CLAN, and our King is THE CHIEF', support the view that he was transmuting Scottish Jacobite ideology into a British Hanoverian form. Although Scott would not countenance such a positive reading of Jacobitism in his fiction, for the purpose of spicing up the King's visit he was prepared to claim that it was still a strong ideological threat, saying that 'Jacobitism still survived "to a wonderful degree in Scotland"'. His use of its symbols as props for Unionism could be regarded as daring and dangerous, if the real thing was still a problem. No doubt Scott claimed that it was in order to add an extra dimension of excitement.[47]

Scott and Scotland displayed an almost pathetic eagerness to please during the King's visit. Yet the fact that his visit took place at all was a borderline decision. If George's own ministers had trusted him more, he might never have come to Scotland.[48] The enthusiastic welcome he received papered over some potentially dangerous political cracks. The Insurrection of 1820 had involved tens of thousands in a struggle for political rights, though few of these had risen in outright rebellion. Their slogan, 'Scotland Free or a Desert', still in use today, formed a sharp contrast to the pageant of the past being staged by Scott, although their use of tunes such as *'Hey Johnnie Cope!'* in their propaganda bore witness to the continuing influence of that past, an influence he neglected.[49] The Radicals had been severely punished; but even Patrick Walker's more moderate nationalist attempt to have King George fly the Scottish quartering on his visit went unregarded. Scott and his allies wanted the pageant they purveyed to be of the past entirely; and no current political events, not even the Clearances, were to jar the smooth progress of the expansive 'Celtic' play-acting which gripped Edinburgh in 1822.[50]

The transference of Jacobite symbols from the Stuart to the Hanoverian cause helped dull the radical edge of the Jacobite critique still further. Jacobite devotion to royalty was transferred from the sacred person of the nationalist Stuart kings to their opponents. Providing the Hanoverians sported the tartan and stressed their Scottish connections, the devotion of Jacobitical Tories to them was assured. Between 1820 and 1860, Jacobitism was turned into a tourist industry, a heritage trail into extinct history, the virtues of which could be patronized and the vices forgotten. Yet the radical edge remained, as we shall see, though in an altered form.

Meanwhile, Scott's synthetic romanticization of Scottish culture made an overwhelming appeal. On the Continent, it reinforced the images of Scotland created by Macpherson. But Scott's revolutionary sympathies did not go unnoticed either, and it is interesting to note that his texts were widely used by Hungarian nationalists in the 1840s. As for Jacobitism, he was determined to make of the 'sixty years since' the Forty-five a gulf which its nationalism could not cross:

> Scottish romance offered little or nothing in the way of a challenge or threat to the rationalism, moderation, or morality of enlightened modern society; it may present the reader with a vision of another, more dangerous, world of colour, excitement and high passion – but the location of that world is safely remote both in space and time.

Scott often changed the unsuccessful gestures of the past into futile ones. In doing so he intensified their romance while depoliticizing them. Hugh MacDiarmid, rightly, thought that Scott's defeatist interpretation had made of the Forty-Five a corrupt national symbol. It took a genius to manipulate the power of Jacobite ideology to his own purposes, as Scott did. His version of events became, and remains, highly influential. He was truly the Wizard of the North: a magician, but one who buried the Stuart myth of regenerative power.[51]

HOGG

Donald has foughten wi' rief and roguery;
Donald has dinner'd wi' banes and beggery:
Better it were for Whigs and Whiggery
Meeting the devil than Donald Macgillavry.

'Donald Macgillavry'[52]

If Scott did much to render Scotland's identity both primitive and respectable, Hogg cultivated the primitive as a disrespectable and forceful survivor from the past. As a writer 'of the Romantic age', but also 'of the folk and popular literature of lowland Scotland', he took it upon himself to combine innovative thought about the nature of his country and countrymen with the most stubborn duty to folk and history. But whereas Scott saw the past, in particular the Jacobite past, as an era of painful division to be superseded by one of imperial unity, Hogg both gave it more detailed respect and also remained unsure that its influence was not to be a continuing one.[53] He mentions, as Scott avoids doing, 'the disgrace of the British annals', the butchery after Culloden. When Hogg discusses Jacobitism's defeat in *The Three Perils of Woman*, he does so in terms which, while acknowledging the nature of that defeat, see it as a supernatural event rather than a result of the course of history. Hogg shows no interest in Scott's concern with the pressures of changing times; instead he postulates a Covenanter's curse as the cause of the fall of the House of Stuart: 'an old curse hanging over the race of STUART, and the drop of their cup of misery has fallen to our share.' This curse derives, according to the novel and tradition, from the sin of the so-called 'Killing Times' of the 1680s, when the royal authorities harried the Covenanters continually: 'These sufferers cried incessantly to the Almighty . . . until at last he sent out his angel, who pronounced the exterminating curse on the guilty race of Stuart, and a triple woe on all that should support their throne.' This suggestion, offered at the end of the novel after the defeat at Culloden, appears to dismiss the Jacobite past as accursed rather than picturesque. Sally, the heroine, prays to God: 'Lord, pardon my sins, and enable me to distinguish between the workings of thy righteous hand, and the doings of erring and guilty creatures!' This prayer seems to be offered up not only for herself and her relationships, but for an entire nation. 'God is just', says the defeated Jacobite Alexander Mackenzie: 'there is no contending with the lifted arm of an avenging God.'[54] The accursed status of Jacobitism appears to be confirmed by the absolute nature of its defeat. God's judgement appears unquestionable.

But Hogg's fiction often presents us with an apparent reality which turns out to be an unstable perception. Sally's prayer is superficially answered by the defeat of the Jacobite forces. But that defeat is accompanied by her death and the death of her child, who appeared to represent the only possibility of a renewing future. If the Jacobites are 'erring and guilty', God's 'righteous

THE INVENTION OF SCOTLAND·

hand' also appears to work through strange agencies. Although Sally and her child die, the survivors are her hypocritical Presbyterian employer, a perverted doctor, and the obsessive gravedigger Davie Duff, who displays a growing lust to cut off people's ears. This wretched and ridiculous crew are the Scots who survive, while Sally's prayer is answered by death. Hogg asks of her end, 'was it a retribution . . . for the guiltless blood shed . . . by the House of Stuart and their Highland host?' But this is a rhetorical question. Questions may be asked of God in the novel, but human beings do not see them answered. Sally's prayer, desperate though it is, is presumptuous. It is not for human beings (Hogg or his narrator included) to distinguish God's 'righteous hand' in action; nor can we tell from the defeat of a cause whether it was cursed from above. Indeed, the God postulated by the characters has, we are told, an 'arbitrary decree', a use of language which clearly echoes the Whig accusation concerning the 'arbitrary government' of the Stuarts. Those who see God as victor and avenger over the Jacobites are themselves viewing Him in terms which elsewhere they would use of their political opponents. Human beings put their own views on God, and in doing so help to absolve themselves of the suffering they have caused in the aftermath of the Forty-Five. Significantly, Hogg asks: 'Is there human sorrow on record like this that winded up the devastations of the Highlands?' The reference here seems to be to the continuing Clearances as well as to the aftermath of the Rising. Can this agony of 'human sorrow' be the result of what the characters think of as Divine justice? Hogg makes it clear that in conceptualizing that justice, the characters contradict each other. A Catholic priest informs the Jacobite Mackenzie that though he goes to fight in a righteous cause, the cause is doomed: 'thou fallest in the cause of Heaven, and thy soul shall be saved. Only be assured, that the hand of the Almighty is against thee.' This is strange. How can a cause be simultaneously righteous in God's eyes, and disliked by Him? And why does the Catholic priest accept the efficacy of the Covenanting curse, coming as it does from a heretical source? Hogg does not answer these questions, but allows the resulting uncertainties to compromise our belief in the righteousness of the victorious side. Although *The Three Perils of Woman* provides us with an argument for the 'absolute predestination' to disaster for the Jacobite cause, Hogg provides us with enough evidence to doubt this argument, as Scott would not have done.[55]

In *Confessions of a Justified Sinner*, Hogg goes further. This book, a classic analysis of the nature and problems of perception, has two narrators. One is Scott-like, a sensible modern; the other is Robert Wringhim, a fierce Presbyterian from Scotland's passionate past. Both these narrators have different approaches to the subject of the book, temptation and possession by the Devil. Significantly, neither narrative can ultimately be relied on. Both accounts have something to offer, but in neither case is the version of events proffered a definitive one. It is almost as if Hogg is symbolically pronouncing on Scott's efforts to make history seem progressive. In *Confessions*, past and present have differing perspectives on reality, but neither is objectively superior. In *Waverley*, the views of Colonel Talbot largely supplant those of Vich Ian Vohr, the Jacobite chief, but in Hogg, the old is not superseded by the new. Both have different perspectives; neither has a monopoly of the truth.

The bulk of Hogg's tale is set between the reign of James VII and II and the era of Union, that twenty-year period during which Scotland struggled in vain to retain constitutional sovereignty. The two families at the centre of the story, the Wringhims and the Colwans, are on opposite sides. Wringhim senior is 'blowing the coal of revolutionary principles', whereas the Colwans, young George in particular, are on the side of the Stuarts, associated with Jacobites and Episcopal jollity. George Colwan the elder 'leaned to the side of kingly prerogative', and later joins 'with the Cavalier party . . . in all their proceedings'. George the younger's friends 'were all of the Jacobite order; or, at all events, leaned to the Episcopal side'. (This was virtually the same thing, since few Episcopalians did other than support the Jacobites.) The sensible modern narrator equivocates over whether the Jacobites are or are not traitors (a Scott-like thing to do), but shortly after he does so, we learn of the murder of the younger Colwan at Wringhim's hands. Thereafter, Wringhim's disloyalty and unnaturalness are more evil and treacherous than anything else in the book. Wringhim destroys his family and his soul for the sake of an ideology.[56]

The destruction of the Colwans, Wringhim's relations, might be taken as a metaphor for the destruction of an organic, unified Scotland. There is something telling in the way Wringhim opposes himself so doggedly to natural ties and relationships in order to fulfil a barren, self-destructive ideology. That ideology is one of extreme Presbyterianism, which leads to his own damnation. He prefers it to all natural or patriotic ties (in 1706, the Church of Scotland agreed to Union providing its own established position was safeguarded). Wringhim loses his life and soul at the end, but *en route* he has destroyed the *status quo ante* of the Scottish life surrounding him, as it had existed at the marriage of George Colwan in 1687, two years before the Estates settled the crown on William (1689 – the year in which Wringhim was born). As Wringhim's life progresses, the gloom of the story deepens. Colwan and Wringhim are two kinds of Scottish character, two sides of the Scottish identity. The Jacobite side is murdered or dies; the scion of the anti-Jacobites is damned. Wringhim's own narrative serves to underline the horror of these events.

It is Wringhim's belief in predestination which does much to hasten his own doom, and this is significant when we examine Hogg's attitude to Jacobitism. It is to participate in Wringhim's error to suggest that the destruction of the Colwans/Jacobites was predestined, either in the theological sense, or through the no less influential idea of historical destiny, as espoused by Scott. We cannot trust the past, but nor can we trust the present's version of the past. Both attitudes can be found in Hogg's work.

In one theme, Hogg brought past and present together. In doing so, he centrally involved Jacobitism. Like Burns, he took advantage of the popular song in order to evoke the past, and/or to suggest something that was missing in the present. The Clearances proved ideal for this approach. As 'a professional sheep-farmer', Hogg was in a good position to notice them. The conclusion of *The Three Perils of Woman* appears to deal with the suffering of the Highlands both during the age of Culloden and contemporaneously. But it is in his poetry that Hogg makes the comparison between the Jacobite struggle and the Clearances most apparent. In his valedictory poem on the 'Stuarts of Appin', Hogg criticizes the Clearances in an unmistakably Jacobite context:

> And ne'er for the crown of the Stuarts was fought
>   One battle on vale, or on mountain deer-trodden
> But dearly to Appin the glory was bought,
>   And dearest of all on the field of Culloden!
> Lament, O, Glen-Creran, Glen-Durar, Ardshiel,
>   High offspring of heroes, who conquer'd were never,
> For the deeds of your fathers no bard shall reveal,
>   And the bold clan of Stuart must perish for ever!

'For the clan is no more;/And the Sassenach sings on the hills of green Appin', Hogg concludes. Not only is there the defeat of Culloden; there is the depopulation of the Clearances to contend with. This is clear from 'The Highlander's Farewell', another of Hogg's poems which places the Clearances in a Jacobite tradition:

> The glen that was my father's own,
>   Maun be by his forsaken;
> The house that was my father's home
>   Is levell'd with the bracken.

'The Highlander's Farewell' appears in Hogg's *Jacobite Relics*, commissioned by the Highland Society in 1818, and completed by 1821. In tandem with the work of Burns, the *Relics* were of paramount importance in preserving Jacobite song culture. The presence in the book, unacknowledged, of so many modern songs and those by Hogg indicated that the genre was not dead. In fact the ease with which Hogg could pass off his songs, such as 'Donald Macgillavry', as genuine suggests the power over the Scottish psyche Jacobite culture still possessed. Imitation could not have been so convincing if the consciousness motivating the originals had gone.[57]

Hogg's collection of songs in the *Relics* was not comprehensive (there is a marked dearth of sacred Episcopal songs, for example); but it was too comprehensive for its sponsors, who had wished for a more select and polite collection than the bold and fierce one they got. Jacobitism was still too hot a potato. It was said (by Francis Jeffrey in the *Edinburgh Review*) that Hogg's taste was 'coarse and vulgar', and wanted 'delicacy'.[58] The two important and still-underestimated volumes of the *Jacobite Relics* were insufficiently in tune with the contemporary taste for a sentimental Jacobitism, purged of political threat. The age wished to be assured that the claims and the political analysis of the Jacobites were consigned to oblivion by the now happy Union of imperial Britain. Some of Hogg's songs suggested otherwise:

> On Darien think, on dowie Glencoe,
> On Murray, traitor! coward!
> On Cumberland's blood-blushing hands,
> And think on Charlie Stuart.

Songs such as this draw parallels between ostensibly different betrayals and injustices to assure the listener of a common and continuing struggle by Scotland against England for political rights.[59] They stood in the Jacobite tradition of the literature of liberty, which articulated Scottish history as a struggle for freedom against a powerful neighbour. Darien, Glencoe, Bruce, Wallace, and Culloden are premises of one common grief, which views 1745 not as an obsolescent dynastic struggle, but the time when 'Scotland for freedom last stood . . . And sealed the true cause with . . . blood' (Hogg, 1819–21, II, 431). This is a very different reading from Scott's view of Jacobitism as a fading glory, the sunset of old Scottish honour.

Hogg's song collection was in a degree incompatible with such expectations. Jacobite literature *en masse* could not disguise its inheritance of a radical critique at odds with reactionary nostalgia. The songs Hogg collected attacked commercialism and hypocrisy; they suggested that the British government and the British state had neither legitimacy nor integrity. Such songs were unwelcome reminders of an age when Jacobitism was political action, not depoliticized nostalgia. Moreover, at a time when the divisions of Scottish society were being emphasized with a view to demonstrating how the Union had reconciled them, the Jacobite vision of unity and identity was an uncomfortable reminder of other versions of history. Hogg collected so many songs that they could not help but demonstrate the Jacobite challenge. In many of them, Scotland's history is encoded, not in the 'progressive' symbols of Scott, but in a typology of grief. The struggle is of honour against corruption, good against evil, liberty against gold, Moses against Pharaoh, Scotland against England. In this struggle, Highland and Lowland are seen as united, ethnically and politically. Bruce and Wallace are glorified as honorary Highlanders, and the dynastic struggle of the Stuarts is subsumed under an encompassing fight for freedom. Much of the Jacobite material Hogg collected made only too plain the correspondence between Jacobitism and nationalism. Dynamic, and often coarse and hostile, his lyrics made an impression inconsistent with the valetudinarian politics of Scott's pageant of regrets.[60]

Hogg himself was influenced by the tradition he did so much to preserve, as is demonstrated by his own poetry. In particular, he appears to have rejected the Celtic/Teutonic ethnic divide Scott had used to sharply distinguish Highlander from Lowlander. In 'Wallace', Hogg pictures the hero as at the head of a united people, both 'The Borderer in his homely gray' and 'The tartaned clans of every glen', 'Men of all colours':

> The green, the red, the pale, the blue . . .
> No force, no fraud, no strife they dread
> With doughty WALLACE at their head.

Wallace himself is described as one of the '. . . chiefs of worth/These heroes of the plaided north', thus at least obliquely suggesting that he is a Highlander. The Jacobite image of the Highlander as (true) patriot is being absorbed into Hogg's work as into Scott's pageantry, but in a more dynamic context. A similar process is going on in Hogg's famous song 'Lock the Door, Lariston', where the 'Saxon spears' are those of the English alone; Elliot and his allies, Borderers though they are, are Celts.[61]

On occasion, Hogg transfers his vision of unified Scottish sentiment to the Georges, as he does in 'Scotia's Glens' and 'Donald MacDonald'. In such poems, he comes closer to Scott. But more often, Hogg's patriotic sympathies appear purely Scottish. 'Caledon' is the 'Land of the Gael', oppressed by strangers; 'there is no day-spring for Scotland' following the defeat of the Stuart cause. Hogg often offers the Jacobite interpretation that all that Scotland truly is partakes of the patriotic spirit of the Highlands, and that anything else is un-Scottish:

> My country, farewell! for the murmurs of sorrow
>   Alone the dark mountains of Scotia become;
> Her sons condescend from new models to borrow,
>   And voices of strangers prevail in the hum.
> Before the smooth face of our Saxon invaders,
>   Is quench'd the last ray in the eye of the free . . .

The Saxons are the English, the Celts the inhabitants of 'Scotia', now in political eclipse.[62]

Elsewhere, careful study of Hogg's preface to the *Relics* suggests that he accepted the Lowland Jacobite songs as productions of a heroic culture shared in common with the Gaeltacht: 'the unmasked effusions of a bold and primitive race' (vii). His alignment of Highland and Lowland is clearly seen in his adoption of a Highland persona in his own Jacobite songs, such as 'Donald Macgillavry'.

'Donald Macgillavry' is one of Hogg's most famous songs. Donald is a radical Jacobite figure, opposed to Scottish self-interest in the Union, English gold and blandishments, and the suffocating nature of the new state born from both. Once again, we can identify the Clearances as a contemporary focus for Donald's economic wrath. The commercial self-interest of both Clearances and Union became one in the Jacobite critique. True to his older values of honour and faith, Donald cannot finally be 'blindit wi' blads o' property', but will, like Christ in the Temple, clear the 'gouk's nest' of pride and pelf with his righteous anger:

> Better it were for Whigs and Whiggery
> Meeting the devil than Donald Macgillavry.

Donald's integrity has cost him status: he has 'dinner'd wi' banes and beggery' in the wilderness to which his honesty has confined him, outwith the rich pastures of corruption. He is untouched by the lust for commercial gain of the post-Union Empire (Satan's last temptation to Christ in the wilderness was to offer all the kingdoms of the earth in return for homage). Donald declines the temptations of the 'towering pulpit of the Golden Calf', which felled 'the ancient oak of loyalty' to the Stuart cause:

> Donalds the callan that brooks nae tangleness;
> Whigging, and prigging, and a' newfangleness,
> They maun be gane: he winna be baukit, man;
> He maun hae justice, or faith he'll tak it, man.

Despite these brave words, Hogg was only too aware that it was 'Whigs and Whiggery' who had triumphed. Donald's clans were defeated, and doomed to exile:

> How could she [Scotland] expel from these mountains of heath,
> The clans who maintained them in danger and death!
> Who ever were ready the broadsword to draw,
> In defence of her honour, her freedom, and law.

In this poem, 'The Emigrant', the clans are the defenders of Scotland's laws, not their violators, as Scott suggests. The Highlanders, apostles of Scottish liberty, are doomed to exile by Culloden and the Clearances, experiences which conflate in the Jacobite analysis, as in the popular view we inherit, which represents the Clearances as directly resulting from the defeat of the Forty-Five. The clans are exiled because they stood up for Scotland's law: this account directly contradicts Scott's, which sees the clans as a threat to law.[63]

The songs of exile merged with the existing corpus of Jacobite literature. Exile from Scotland was seen as exile from the ideal country, the Camelot to which one day a Stuart Arthur might return, bringing 'day-spring for Scotland'. Besides discussing defeat and decay at home, Hogg's own lyrics reinforce the idea of an ideal Scotland, a 'Highland Elysium' such as that portrayed in 'The Maclean's Welcome':

We'll bring down the track deer, we'll bring down the black steer,
   The lamb from the bracken, and doe from the glen;
The salt sea we'll harry, and bring to our Charlie,
   The cream from the bothy, and curd from the pen.

This was Hogg's supposed translation of a Gaelic original. The idea of such freedom and power over the environment was now lost to many inhabitants of the Highlands. Hogg's song, ostensibly set in 1745, in fact contains the nostalgia of exile. This lifestyle and this autonomy cannot come again:

And you shall drink freely the dews of Glen-Sheerly,
   That stream in the star-light when kings do not ken

But now the Hanoverian kings 'kent' only too well the situation in the Highlands, which their governments had done so much to alter in the years after 1745.[64]

Hogg's own songs, as well as those he collected, demonstrate that Jacobite literature and ideology had outlived Jacobitism itself. They were tied to a positive, unified, and patriotic view of Scotland. Hogg inherited, selected, and adapted their tradition with this in mind. Politically, it was an interpretation of Scotland's position which was dynamite, and Hogg never committed himself to it. But he found it attractive, and though at times he claimed in his fiction that God's eternal justice was against it, Hogg as an author clearly suggests that human beings cannot successfully perceive what does or does not constitute divine intention. 'What is justice?' is the large, human, Socratic question; and if we confine it to ask 'What is justice for Scotland?', it appears that we cannot be certain that Hogg was certain of his answer. But his uncertainty contributed to his lack of popularity in comparison with the certainties of Scott. Hogg speaks of a great past, of 'The land where the strains of gray Ossian were framed – / The land of fair Selma, and reign of Fingal', but not to the exclusion of its relevance to the present:

No national calamity has ever given me so much pain as the total bereavement of the brave clans who stood to the last for the cause of the house of Stuart. It is a stain on the annals of our legislature which can never be blotted out.[65]

That 'never' sets Hogg and Scott apart.

4

Reality and romance

VICTORIANA

We were always in the habit of conversing with the Highlanders – with whom one comes so much in contact in the Highlands.

Queen Victoria

> Wha hasna heard of the year forty five
> When Charlie for Scotland sae nobly did strive
> And wha hasna sighed for the heroes sae brave
> Wha fought at Culloden a glorious grave . . .
>
> King Edward kens aye, kens braw and weel
> That his own kilty lads are as true as their steel

'The Bonnets o' Blue'

> The Lion of Scotland
>   has risen from his lair,
> Beware, Whigs! Beware!

Chartist rhyme[1]

The effect of the Victorian age on Scotland was at once simple and complex. Although many of the trappings of pageant and colour which served to render Scotland both picturesque and obsolete were in place before the Queen's accession, it was the years that followed which rendered them the convenient shorthand for the Scottish identity they were to remain. A Celticized Scotland of primitive and heroic images, drawing heavily if negatively on Jacobite ideology, was to develop to full flower in these years. As the images of a Celtic past were more and more adopted as the quaint insignia of present-day Scotland, they became emptied of political content. The kilt, the pipes, haggis, and the music-hall Scot became increasingly popular, but with little consciousness of the nationalist overtones the tartan had possessed in the eighteenth century.

Any political survival occurred only within the safe context of the British Army: hence a song like 'The Bonnets o' Blue' draws a direct parallel between the loyalty of Charles Edward's Highlanders and those who are now (the song deals with the Edwardian period) serving in the army. During the nineteenth century, the distinctive Scottish institutions which the Union had preserved, such as the Law, Education, and the Church, were becoming increasingly weakened by English influence or internal dissent (spectacularly, in the case of the 1843 Disruption).[2] But Scotland was not symbolized in the popular imagination through these institutions, which were truly a legacy of her history, but rather through the distorted pageantry of a Highland way of life which, ironically, was being destroyed by many of those who advertised it. Nothing could more clearly demonstrate how Scotland was only allowed to express its identity through its past. The Scottish church might defend the Scottish way of life and call for social reform. The Scottish educational system might give its students a distinctive cast of mind, and an education more progressive if less intense than that available at the great English universities; and Scots lawyers might oppose changes in Scottish society, breaches in the Union, or even the Union itself. All these institutions were current and contemporary, and might still exert a real if limited degree of political pressure against the intentions of the British government. Therefore they were most unsuitable as symbols of Scottish life. The Highlands provided much better symbols for a Scotland the authorities preferred quiescent. The Highland military challenge was defeated; the social system almost dismantled; the inhabitants of the Highlands exiled, poor, or serving in the British Army. It was safe to see Scotland in terms of a culture which hardly existed any longer, and was in any case in no condition to resist. Church, law, and education all had some power; in certain circumstances, they could provide rallying points for national identity. For that reason, they were unsuitable vehicles by which to express a Scottish sense of distinctiveness. Better the burns, broadswords, and tartans of a Jacobitism sentimentalized into Tory nostalgia than the industrial or institutional realities of the Lowlands. 'Pallid and shrouded', Gaelic culture 'could now be safely enjoyed by the curious upper-class'.[3]

Despite this sham Celtification, a radical undertow continued to exist in Scottish society which rejected this tartan drift. The Chartist rhyme quoted at the head of this section is an example of how quasi-nationalist sentiments continued to be expressed in radical quarters into the middle of the nineteenth century, which itself witnessed the birth of modern nationalism. Many surviving Jacobites adopted, in a Scottish context, a positive response to the libertarian ideas of the French Revolution, despite its killing of a sacred king, Louis XVI.[4] More right-wing Jacobitism of a vaguely committed kind survived surprisingly long: for example, the last Nonjuror (who denied the authority of William III and his successors) died in the 1870s.[5]

Burns had shown that Jacobitism and radicalism could meet. We remain unsure of their exact meeting place in the early years of Victoria's reign: but it is interesting to note how much genuine commitment remained amid the tinsel and boom of an imperial British version of the Scottish past.

Pageantry did, however, have its uses: 'Scotsmen often stress the gallantry of the '45 precisely to the degree they wish to obscure from themselves the shoddy, mercenary self-betrayal of the Union in 1707.'[6] The sentimentalization of Jacobite ideology depoliticized it. In doing so, its political purpose was obscured: opposition to Union in favour of liberty, integrity, and the native line of kings. In depoliticizing opposition to Union, the Union itself was depoliticized: if there was no serious opposition to it, it was not a politically controversial measure. Thus a comforting glow of politically meaningless Jacobite chivalry was cast over the eighteenth century, hiding the real controversies of that century out of the glamour of a factitious romanticism. Real Jacobite ideology still carried a hard-hitting political message which was uncomfortable. To make the Risings a fairy-tale of the children of the mist, a dream of Gaelic heroes, rather than the signs of a major European power struggle, was a priority for those who opposed that ideology. Perhaps to that end, one of Jacobite ideology's major vehicles, the popular song, was adapted and sentimentalized:

> The bathetic worst of Burns and his like was taken up and developed by music hall performers . . . and thereafter promulgated so powerfully by radio and television that to-day Scottish song still purveys a maudlin, drunken, swaggering and pseudo-patriotic ethos which . . . was the creation of a handful of influential composers and not the true song of the Scottish people.[7]

The influence of a sentimentalized, 'we-wuz-robbed' Jacobitism on the Scottish self-image continues to this day. As I suggested earlier, by beginning to make Jacobitism respectable, Burns unwittingly opened the door to its exploitation by those who did not truly respect it. Thus its radical message was endangered.

The Victorian age ratified an image of Scotland which was complex, in so far as it was delicately balanced between the ideas of Scottish and British patriotism, but simplistic also, in that its view of Scotland was partial, biased, and sentimental. The 1820s, 1830s, and 1840s were the decades which divided the Jacobite legacy and the myth of the Stuarts into two. On the one hand, there was the picture-book romance of the 'official' version; on the other, the still-surviving radicalism of Jacobitical nationalism, which re-emerged in the 1850s.[8] The belief that 'Charles Edward Stuart came to embody the salvation of the race' was not dead in Scotland. In Ireland also, where the church of the Stuarts was so much stronger, Jacobite feelings persisted well into the nineteenth century:

Long they pine in weary woe, the nobles of our land,
Long they wander to and fro, proscribed, alas! and banned,
Feastless, houseless, altarless, they bear the exile's brand;
But their hope is in the coming of Kathleen-Ny-Houlahan.
'If the King's son were living here with Kathleen-Ny-Houlahan.

In such fashion were the erotic Jacobite sentiments of lyrics such as 'The Blackbird' expressed in the nineteenth century.[9] In slightly differing form, they continued to be expressed by the Celtic Twilight, and by romantic Irish nationalism in the twentieth.[10]

Despite these and other survivals, it was 'the time-lagged perceptions' of a fake Celtic Scotland which dominated the Victorian consciousness regarding the northern kingdom. The 'wistful Jacobite songs' of Victoria's age not only reinforced that time-lagged identity, but also served to obscure the true force of what Jacobitism had to say. The problems posed by the genuine songs were as keen as when Hogg had published his *Relics*. Antiquarianism, which had become gradually detached from active political Jacobitism in the eighteenth century, now proved a factitious ally in the cause of inventing Scotland's picturesque past at the expense of its political implications. Only isolated areas of Jacobite and pre-Jacobite patriotism survived in unaltered form. One of these was the cult of 'loyal Wallace', a recrudescence of which in the middle years of the century caused mild embarrassment to the press and Establishment. The invention of Scotland could not altogether neutralize powerful historical icons, as we shall see. There were still 'sleeping echoes of Scottish resentment and aspirations ... Bannockburn, Flodden and Culloden with their doomed heroes'.[11] The neutralization of the political past could not suppress this kind of folk-memory, and it led to a popular historical understanding 'erected on the lost or betrayed cause'. Suppressed instincts of political struggle were vocalized in terms of betrayal. This continues to the present day, when both Scottish socialists and nationalists see themselves as inheritors and requiters 'of lost causes'.[12] The interpretation of Scottish society as doomed and defeated was manipulated by those who wished to present a picture of Scottish history as completed and irrelevant; but it also gripped those to whom that history was a continuing force, as manifest in the Clearances and exile, for example. The anachronistic patterns into which Scottish identity was thrust to keep it politically defused were belied by the economic changes of the nineteenth century, and the number of migrants and exiles they created. Yet the sense of a doomed nation factitiously created by the one group was only too bitterly experienced by the other.

Anachronistic images of Scotland were not rendered dominant by any conspiracy, but their effect was overwhelming. George IV's visit to Scotland had been a stupendously successful publicity stunt; but Queen Victoria's long affection for the country was more profound in its effects. To her is owed the final acceptance of the Jacobite song, which opened the floodgates of sentimentality. Burns and Scott had made the Jacobite song more respectable; but Victoria helped to enable its transformation into a cult, from the date of her public approval in 1842:

> When Queen Victoria, on her first visit [to Scotland] . . . in 1842, specially asked Mr. John Wilson to sing that exquisite song, 'Oh! wae's me for Prince Charlie' . . . that graceful act . . . finally removed any stigma of disloyalty that might be associated with the public rendering of the songs.[13]

This was the beginning of Victoria's captivation with Scotland, her 'dear Paradise', by which she inherited and reinforced the colourful, picturesque, and partial accounts of Scottish history fabricated by the previous generation's biased borrowing from Jacobite propaganda.[14]

Nostalgia was an artistic keynote of Victoria's reign in England as well as in Scotland. Not only was there a recrudescence in medievalism and such medieval activities as jousting; there was also the cult of Arthur and the connected idea of a unified British past. England was not immune from the fancy-dress school of history largely pioneered in Scotland.[15]

However it was in Scotland that a fundamentally escapist view of history most prevailed. Prince Albert, elsewhere and in other contexts a modernizer, was as backward-looking in his attitude to Scotland as his wife. He tried to live up to the *'beau idéal'* of the great hunters of the past: deer-hunters like Fionn, and salmon-hunters like Scott's Redgauntlet, who speared fish from horseback. Albert kept to this ancient way of hunting also, and was drawn poised above a stream, fishing spear in hand. As a deer-hunter he was not a success: 'from one day's deer-stalking, he brought back only a hare', and once got so frustrated that he shot 'a half-tame stag' from his host's window at breakfast. But despite his shortcomings as a latter-day Highland hero, both he and Victoria loved their adoptive country, a love which eventually led to the occupation of Balmoral in the heart of the Dee valley, near where Mar had raised the standard in 1715.[16]

Victoria was conscious of the Jacobite legacy, and laid claim herself (despite the German accent which persisted in the Royal Family to the time of Edward VII) to be a continuation of the Royal Stuart line: 'For Stuart blood is in my veins and I am now their representative and the people are as devoted and loyal to me, as they were to that unhappy Race.' In such terms, uttered by the Queen herself, did the Hanoverian dynasty finally accept the loyalty they had spent so long suppressing. This was the consummation Scott had sought from the 1822 visit. A climate was created in which Stuart and Hanoverian loyalties could be made one; and this was Victoria's intention. Unsympathetic to Episcopalianism, she 'gave great pleasure to her Scottish subjects' of a Presbyterian stamp 'by attending the services of the Church of

Scotland and thereby bridging the gulf "torn open by the madness of Laud and Charles I'".[17] The kirk was not a central part of the new popular image of Scotland as it was developing; but in attending its services the Queen helped to make herself popular.

Tartanry was nevertheless more important than Presbyterianism to the royal image. By the late 1850s, the dining-room at New Balmoral Castle had tartan everywhere. The passion for tartan in Scotland continued to swell. Both the Queen and her loyal subjects displayed their Scottishness and set the fashion simultaneously. Meanwhile, the economic suffering of those who had the greatest right to the plaid went on regardless.[18]

Before going on to discuss the Clearances, it is worth mentioning one of the strangest 'tartan events' of Victoria's reign: the appearance in Scotland of the Sobieski Stuarts, two brothers who claimed direct descent from the Royal Stuart line, and thus, by implication, to be heirs to the thrones of Britain far closer in line than was the Queen herself.

The two brothers, whose claim were almost certainly false, were a curious pair. The status they sought and opinions they expressed often fitted in far better with the tartan cult of the era than with any genuine Jacobitical feeling. Their politics, with the exception of their dislike of the Union, were nearly all sentimentally expressed; and when Lord Lovat 'built them an amazing Celtic Xanadu' on Eilean Aigas, they decorated it in a manner which exceeded the kitsch of Balmoral itself, 'combining a full-blown Romantic mediaevalism with the old heroic tradition, in a way that was to occur again and again'.[19] The job of the Sobieskis, as one hostile critic put it, was to persuade the gentlemen of the Highland societies that 'they have yet a *KING*!'[20] Mock it as some might, this was in no way regarded as a threat. In what the Sobieskis did and said, there was too much of the plangent note of dead romance to render them a political threat.

Nevertheless, their work is not without interest. *Lays of the Deer Forest*, which came out in 1848, is a typical production. It has more nationalist feeling than is found in many contemporary productions, but is still primarily a lament for times irrevocably past. 'The Exile's Farewell' speaks in a traditional manner of 'thy sons who sold/Their mother's glory for base Saxon gold', and of 'The base bribed Union's manacle', but real direction in the poems is seen to be lacking as soon as we come to descriptions of the Highlands:

> But in the lone black hut – the mountain cells,
> Where the deep Gaelic soul unbroken dwells,
> On the dark hill . . .

The sentimental idea of the Highlander as primitive is found in full force here, without the complexity or direct political reference of Ossian. Although the Sobieskis seem to understand the tragedy of those who can only find '. . . the bread/Of exile in a strange and distant land', their own view of the Highland way of life which is left behind seems romanticized. The heroic Gael, with his 'mantle of renown' is too mythological and unwieldy a figure when his presentation is not being put to active political use (as the Jacobites did), but is merely propping up a backward-looking idealism.[21]

It is possible to be too hard on the Sobieskis. Despite their play-acting, at times they seem to escape the saccharine world of sentimental pageant which enveloped them. Perhaps it was impossible to do so more than intermittently given the role they chose to play and the period in which they lived. Whatever their inconsistencies and limitations, they stood to a degree in the Jacobite tradition in that they were fiercely critical of Unionist trends in contemporary Scotland. In attacking the time-serving Scots who had lost the self-respect to be patriotic in their country's cause, the Sobieskis pulled few punches:

> Drop your cur-tails and snuff around the throne,
> Picking the bones and offal which may fall,
> Like dogs and beggars in Ulysses' hall.

Ulysses, Odysseus, eventually returned to his hall, and expelled those who had usurped it. The Sobieskis may have toyed with doing the same, but toying it of course remained. They were inconsistent and possibly consciously fraudulent: on that level, they were as factitious as much of the tartanry around them. But despite their participation in the nineteenth century's romanticization of the Stuart past, they attempted to express feelings of radical Jacobite protest unalloyed with any transference of loyalty to the ruling dynasty. In doing so they succeeded in commenting, albeit obliquely, on the contemporary political scene and the continuing problems and heartbreak of exile.[22]

THE CLEARANCES

Yet still the blood is strong, the heart is Highland . . .

> When the bold kindred, in the time long vanish'd,
> Conquer'd the soil and fortified the keep,—
> No seer foretold the children would be banish'd,
> That a degenerate Lord might boast his sheep.
>
> 'The Canadian Boat Song'

> Let them tear our bleeding bosoms,
> Let them drain our latest veins,
> In our hearts, is Charlie, Charlie,
> While a spark of life remains.
>
> Alexander MacDonald

105

In 1895, a Royal Commission found that some 1,700,000 acres under deer were fit for cultivation. Yet seventeen years later the area under deer had . . . increased by over a million acres.

Andrew Dewar Gibb[23]

The centralized government oppression to which the Highlands had been subject in the latter part of the eighteenth century involved the curtailment of the chief's powers, the banning of the tartan, and the suppression of the Episcopal church, as well as acts of overt barbarity. By the early 1780s, government attitudes were relaxing. Almost immediately, they were replaced by a more localized form of oppression: the Clearances.

The age of the Clearances continued until the end of the nineteenth century. The replacement of people by sheep, and the abolition of the ancient systems of land tenure, together with the resultant experiences of hardship and exile, are issues which remain emotive. The Clearances produced, directly in Gaelic and obliquely in English, a considerable and hostile literary response. The theme of exile was reinforced. Jacobite culture and the Clearances dovetailed into a single historical experience: the destruction of the Highlands.

It is still a popular misconception that the Clearances followed directly on the heels of Culloden. Recent historians have striven to point out they did not. Yet in one respect such efforts miss the point – Culloden and the Clearances go together because the latter even clarified and intensified the effects of the former. Implicit in the Jacobite critique was the idea that Scotland would be desolate if her rightful king were not restored. The Clearances appeared to many to exemplify that desolation. The clan system's privileges and powers had been rendered insecure by the laws passed after Culloden. In the circumstances, what could be more likely than that the leadership of the old system, their position undermined, would seek some measure of *rapprochement* or integration with the victorious structures of government? Such action, when it came, distanced them from those for whom they had previously been responsible: their clansmen.[24]

It is not the role of this book to attempt to discuss the Clearances in detail, a task much better undertaken elsewhere. What is of interest in terms of the Stuart myth is not the suffering of the Clearances alone, real and terrible as that was, but the way in which from an early stage the whole experience of the Clearances was associated with that of the Jacobites. 'The Canadian Boat Song' was an early and famous criticism of the Clearances, and the names of many well-known Scotsmen have been suggested as its author since its appearance in 1829. Its message, like that of Hogg in poems such as 'The Highlander's Farewell', is that the valiant clans are defeated both in battle and by economic forces: first vanquished at Culloden, then driven off the land by sheep. The plight of the exile is repeatedly stressed, as in earlier Jacobite lyrics; so is his longing for home. The conjunction of these themes has given the poem an enduring appeal which persists to this day; in recent years a television programme has been named after its most famous line. At the time when it was written, it summed up the growing reservations about the Clearances which had been earlier articulated, in different ways, by Hogg and Stewart of Garth, whose famous book on the Highlanders had appeared a decade earlier.[25] Highland society, 'crushed by the heavy hand of a vindictive conqueror', was now under pressure from 'the new system of statistical economy with its cold unrelenting spirit'.[26]

Garth's attack on this referred to the 1814–20 Clearances from Sutherland, which forced the departure of 15,000. These evictions, cruel as some of them were, served only to swell an already rising tide. By the end of the eighteenth century, up to a tenth of the population may have been lost through emigration. Between 1815 and 1838, 22,000 Scots emigrated to Nova Scotia alone. Evictions turned this tide into a flood. By 'the 1830s, the parlous condition of much of the Highland population' was acknowledged throughout Scotland. The agony was long-lasting: 'A century of Highland history is dominated by population clearances, forced evictions, and emigration under duress.'[27]

Some were worse than others, but few ruling families failed to implement evictions for economic advantage; and during the nineteenth century, these included chiefs from many formerly Jacobite families. Indeed, 'no family of chiefs who kept their lands in 1746 or had them restored . . . were innocent of Clearances except the Grants of Glen Urquhart and Glen Moriston'. The pressure to leave exerted on many inhabitants of the Highlands was irresistible. In 1750, more than a third of Scotland's population lived north of the Highland line; today, the proportion is 5 per cent. Barely half as many people live in the Highlands now as did at the time of the Fifteen Rising, and many of these are not Highlanders. Such stark depopulation, matched only in Ireland, is to be attributed to economic pressure and economic tyranny. In 1811, there were 250,000 sheep in the Highlands; in the 1840s, close on a million. The space for them was bought at the cost of human suffering. As the last survivors of Culloden were dying, the train of events begun by their defeat was gathering speed.[28]

The main argument in favour of the cruelties of the Clearances was an economic one, not a political one as seventy-five years earlier. As the *Economist* put it, 'The departure of the redundant part of the population is an indispensable preliminary to every kind of improvement.' This depressingly familiar argument, dominated by economic considerations, was vulnerable to the Jacobite critique, or a development of it. Since the Union, pro-Jacobite ideology had argued that if Scotland yielded to commercial priorities, she could expect only commercial exploitation, having abandoned the older values of nobility and liberty (to English or Irish commentators, like Pope or Swift, the post-1714 Whig state seemed obsessed with commercial values as a basis for social ones).[29] The Clearances sadly fulfilled the Jacobite prophecy. The oldest and noblest kind of Scot (the Highlander/Jacobite patriot) was being exiled from the land of his birth in the interests of a money-based (i.e. British) society in which Scotland was participating, having sold out to its corrupt values in 1707. To make it worse, whereas the Jacobites had created an idea of the Highlander as patriot to set against the image of a corrupt Lowland ruling class, tainted by the Union, it was now the Highlanders' own chiefs who were taking advantage of their position to impose the Clearances, an extension of pro-Union policy in Jacobite eyes. Things were going from bad to worse.

But not all of the Clearances even made unequivocal economic sense. The cult of the Highlands as containing a portion of defeated and primitive Scottish history which nevertheless in some sense encapsulated the Scottish identity was one popularized by Scott and adopted wholesale under Victoria. Its idea, that Scottish history was completed, and that Scotland had no continuing identity beyond that of a cute and safe relic, user-friendly to imperial Britain, was a dangerous one. It was a view which neglected present suffering in favour of the picturesque maintenance of anachronistic ideas.

Some of the Clearances were conducted as examples of just such anachronism, idealistic rather than primarily economic. What could be more picturesque and appropriate for a primitive land with a primitive history than to 'conserve' its primitivism, by turning populated and cultivated land back into wilderness? So that, 'By 1884 deer-forests covered 1,975,209 acres ... the vast majority of that area in the crofting counties.' In other words, almost 3,100 square miles, two-fifths of the area of Wales and a tenth of that of Scotland, was given over to deer. The figure was to go higher still.[30] Scotland could once again be the deer-hunting paradise of would-be ancient hunters, eager to follow in the remote steps of Fingal/Fionn, or the more recent ones of the Prince Consort:

> The reason for this sudden shift in the criteria for land-use was not of a socially-beneficial or indeed of a rational order. It was a product of a new set of images of the Highlands, created around the court of Queen Victoria through the 1830s and 40s, and elaborated on with increasing skill and fantastical removal from reality to this day [1986]. This was the image of the Highlands as a wild place full of kilt-wearing neo-brigands, and crooning lassies, where a man – well, a Very Important sort of Man – could rediscover the primitive blood-lust of the hunt.

This re-creation of the rural wilderness of the mythical noble savage cost the livelihoods and homes of many of the real inhabitants of the country. A pageant of fantasy, a British myth of Jacobitism-and-water, was used to undermine the very society Jacobitism proper had attempted to protect.[31] Recruitment to the British Army had been augmented by a more permanent kind of exile.

The Highlander's view of these events could be very different from that taken by the upper class, which increasingly found in Scotland the sporting and primitive paradise they had been led to expect. It had been created for them as one of the most select of heritage trails, though the heritage it proclaimed operated in destructive opposition to the reality of what it pretended to conserve. Visitors were largely ignorant of those still about them who might seek the return of their land:

> Ah then we would know exactly what to do –
> We'd drive out the keepers, and the English who come here,
> To ruin us and our land for their sport on the hill.
> We'd drive the deer that have taken over our ploughing-land
> Up, high on the top of the mountains –
> And down would come Nimrod.

Thus wrote John MacRae, 'leader of the Lochcarron Land League'. But active resistance of this sort came into its own only late in the day. At the height of the Victorian Scottish cult, its pageantry updated by Landseer's half-percipient, half-brutal Romanticism, the state of many of the people was worse than that of the Highland family in the painter's picture of a flood. Nor were their enemies the elements. Between 1850 and 1860, 4,000 were destitute in Kilmallie, Ardnamurchan, and Glenelg; 1,000 had their fares paid from Lewis to the colonies; 1,500 left Barra and South Uist; 400 families from Skye were given free passage to Australia (Skye lost huge numbers: 83,000 between 1840 and 1885); and 100 left Lochaber for the Antipodes in one sailing alone.[32] At the same time, many of the lairds in these areas were sporting to the full the dress of the tartan cult the age made so popular.

If there was something comforting in the factitious interpretation of the Highlands (and indeed all Scotland) made by many who stayed, what were the feelings of those who were under the threat of departure? The psychology of exile is a difficult area to probe with confidence, and it is cruel to make generalizations. Moreover, second-generation exiles often saw their homeland in the same factitious terms (as can be seen from the ideas American Scots frequently have about Scotland today). But it can be said that those who left often conformed to the Jacobite practice of speaking of the Scotland they had lost as a lost Elysium; a society once pure, now corrupt: fallen from the grace of autonomy to the degradation of dependence. The feelings expressed are very similar to those of Jacobite exile. The idea of a lost and desolated paradise is common to both: 'it clings tenaciously to the myth of the good life from which . . . ancestors were rudely expelled.'[33] This mood gained strength; but it was not based on a romanticized view of the past, but rather on the cruelties of compelling and present experience. The poetry of the Gaeltacht 'has not the strength for strong realism' found in the eighteenth century; it was substantially weakened as a cultural voice by the persistent attacks on Gaelic culture (and indeed on the use of Gaelic) made during the age of the Clearances. The 'Highland paradise' which Scotland had become in the eyes of the tartan cultists was not a paradise that extended to the Highlanders themselves, or to their way of life.[34]

Until the latter part of the century, one of the saddest features of the Clearances was the manner, reminiscent of the ghettoes a century later, in which those who were cleared off the land attempted little in the way of resistance. There was a passivity among those so many times defeated. In this way too, the Clearances seemed to fulfil Jacobite prophecy: they were yet another defeat, another piece of evidence that Scotland and traditional Scottish ways of life were doomed. Ironically, just as middle- and upper-class Victorians were celebrating Scotland in terms of ancient, inevitable, and colourful defeat, the terms of that defeat were being visited afresh on many who had suffered in the Jacobite cause a century before. But because the suffering was contemporary, and Scotland had no official contemporaneity, for a long time few outside those directly affected took much notice of it.[35]

It would be a great overstatement to claim that the nature of the politics of resistance to the Clearances was born out of the ideology of the Jacobite struggle. But what the Clearances did do was to reinforce and foreground the more radical terms of the Jacobite analysis, which had for so long laid emphasis on commercial corruption and imperial interest as agents of destruction in the life of the Scottish polity. The Clearances were like a long drawn-out Culloden; a continuing violation which validated Jacobite accusations of perfidy against the Anglo-British ruling class, and an experience which underlined the Jacobite theme of exile thousands of times. Feelings of loss, orchestrated by 1689 and 1707, were amplified by the noise of departure throughout the nineteenth century. The sense of defeat in Scottish culture was exaggerated by the plangent sentimentality of the tartan pageant; but it was nevertheless real, a response to the continuing loss of nationhood the pageant ignored, when it did not abet it. As Jacobitism was Scotland's defeat in the eighteenth century, so the Clearances in the north and industrialization in the south were the defeats of the nineteenth. The radical Jacobite analysis saw all these events in a similar light. Since the Union, it had suggested that all that remained for Scotland was deterioration and grief, if her ancient rights were not reasserted. It was a partial propagandist account; but the sufferings of the nineteenth century and the predominance of exile bore it out. James VII (or VI, depending on your point of view) was the first exile; would there ever be a last? Exile was the fate of evicted and successful Scot alike: some had to leave, some left to succeed. But the common denominator was departure from Scotland. James VII had supported the clan system against feudal superiors. He had to go into exile; now they had to go into exile, as they had been doing since the seventeenth century.[36] The absent Fionn/Fingal and the absent James remained in the memory of the people; but their kings did not come home at the hour of greatest need. Jacobite poets had long lamented the ruined might of the Scottish past: 'See! the proud halls they once possess'd decay'd.' Now this elegy on Scottish greatness was being rendered yet more appropriate through the depopulation of the Highlands. Had the Jacobites been right?

> Popular poetry and the Gaelic folk tradition are indebted to Jacobitism as one of their most potent and enduring sources of inspiration; indeed, for over two centuries they have enjoyed a tripartite, symbiotic relationship. What is striking . . . is the clarity with which a collective Gaelic consciousness emerges.

The source of inspiration was more than the romance of Jacobitism; it was the analysis it provided. In the light of the sufferings of Culloden and after, 'Charles Edward Stewart came to embody the salvation of the race'.[37]

In the 1880s, when the Clearances came to be resisted, the 'Celtic past' was utilized 'for intellectual and political purposes' with the support of Scottish nationalists like John Stuart Blackie, as well as more overt neo-Jacobite figures. The crofters, it was said, 'are going back on the ideas of a mythical age, and demanding their revival in an impossible present generated by "Patriotic bards and historians"'. These beliefs included the idea that crofters had had a perpetual tenure of their lands held in small communities, the idea of 'Celtic communism' which Hugh MacDiarmid was later to explicitly associate with Charles Edward. Jacobite ideas concerning the unity of the people and the land, and the centrality of the well-being of the land to that of the nation, were powerfully opposed to the kinds of changes in land use which had gone on. The opposition of Stuart politicians to enclosure has been adduced by opponents of the Clearances in recent times.[38] The Duchess of Sutherland's appropriation of 794,000 acres of clan land in the 1814–20 period would have brought strong condemnation under any serious Jacobite critique.

Ideas of traditional land use associated with Jacobitism were ideologically important in the 1880s, and neo-Jacobites certainly supported the crofters' struggle. The victory the crofters won at the Napier Commission and the success in getting crofting MPs elected to Parliament bore the marks of a radical movement, but one with traditional roots, such as land-based radical agitation can often possess. The crofters' victory, and indeed their campaign, corresponded with the growth of a more wide-ranging interest in Scottish nationalism, which itself took root in the Jacobite analysis, as we shall see. The leaders of the SHRA (Scottish Home Rule Association) in the 1880s included John Stuart Blackie (Celtic revivalist), Cunninghame Graham, and Dr G. B. Clark, a crofting MP. Scottish Home Rule had diverse support, Lowland and Highland, radical and conservative, from the very start. Gladstone promised Home Rule All Round (for Scotland, Ireland, and Wales) on his famous speaking tour in Midlothian. It did not arrive.[39]

The Crofting Act did. The radicalism (with strong traditionalist overtones) which had secured at least partial victory for crofters' rights was matched further south in Scotland by the agitation which resulted in the restoration

111

of the office of Scottish Secretary after 140 years' abeyance. Highland and Lowland, it seemed, had awakened together.

PATRIOT STIRRINGS

Round the plinth [of Wallace's statue] are written quotations from his speeches to the Army of the Commons of Scotland; lounging upon the plinth, yawning and bored (even in the sleet) are the tired and old and the unemployed of Aberdeen in great number. Wallace fascinates them, you would say. He belongs to a past they dare not achieve, they have come to such horrific future as he never visioned.

Lewis Grassic Gibbon

The Scottish Highlands, once the home and glory of the White Rose, became the most utterly Bal-moralized portion of the realm.

The Royalist, November 1903

Despite their proximity, there are no other two peoples in the world so different from each other as the Scots and the English.

R. L. Stevenson[40]

As I suggested earlier, radical Jacobitism did not die out. Indeed the creation of the past as a sequence of sentimental icons so assiduously practised by tartan cultists kept alive some of the ideas of that past which those who propagated it might have preferred people to forget.[41] In particular, the figure of Wallace (albeit a Jacobitized 'loyal Wallace', a populist iconic counterweight to the royal prestige of Bruce) continued to carry overtones which the Scott-like view of patriotism as emotion was unable to suppress. It is significant that it was the Jacobite vision of Scottish history as struggle for liberty rather than journey to defeat which resurfaced as the basis for a revived Scottish national movement in the middle of the nineteenth century.[42]

The symbols of the patriotic past (history as liberty) had continued in use to some degree by radicals in the earlier nineteenth century. The traditional Highland means of communication in wartime, the Fiery Cross, was used in political action as late as 1820 (it continued to be used, in less savoury circumstances, by the Ku Klux Klan in the US). The United Scotsmen and similar groups of radicals in the 1790–1820 period showed some consciousness of this radical side to Jacobite historical theory.[43]

After 1822, the symbols of the past became for a time largely the property of those who had taken them over in the interests of preserving Scotland as a distinct but compliant partner in Empire. Chartism possessed nationalist undertones, and these were occasionally voiced through the traditional symbols of Scottish nationhood.[44] During the Disruption of 1843, 'both political and nationalistic' opinions were voiced. The Free Church dissenters

grounded part of their case in the Act of Union. The consent of the

Scottish nation was necessary to authorise changes in religious affairs, and the will of the British Parliament was patently not the same as the will of the Scottish people.

This argument, potentially one with dynamic political consequences, was not applied beyond the immediate circumstances of the dissenters' position. Some individual Free Church ministers did, however, carry it further.[45] Moreover, the Free Church as a whole was to display, particularly in the Highlands, a greater autonomy than the Church of Scotland in its actions.

In the 1840s, the sense of Scotland as a contemporary polity was limited to clerics and radicals. Explicit political nationalism did not emerge till the next decade. When it did, there were in the main three kinds of supporters it attracted: the literary coterie, the reformist businessmen, and the radicals. There was also the odd Free Church minister, James Begg being the most prominent.

The literary coterie was composed of a variety of conservative and radical writers, many with Irish nationalist sympathies, frequently attracted not only to Jacobite ideas, but to Jacobitism itself (though none seems to have contemplated the actual return of a Stuart monarch – that was to come later). The second group's support was found among Glasgow reformers and businessmen, who felt that not enough time was being devoted to Scottish affairs. The radicals, with their motto 'Scotland arise!', could perhaps trace their ancestry back to the 1820 Insurrectionists and beyond to the French Revolution, if not to the radical side of Jacobitism itself.

These interests came together to form the short-lived but influential National Association for the Vindication of Scottish Rights (NAVSR), which, 'supported by both Dr. Begg and the Radical Duncan McLaren on one wing, and by the Tory romantics on the other . . . had for a time the makings of a great national crusade'. The Association was launched in November 1853, with a meeting of 2,000 at Edinburgh; there were 5,000 in Glasgow the following month. Its aims were based on the negotiation of a better deal for Scotland (probably within the framework of the Union), and its language and political programme were heavily biased towards a traditional, even a deliberately antiquarian, view of the nature of the Scottish polity. But this antiquarianism was active and vital, not passive and defeatist – the first time the past had been used in a politically creative way for many years.[46]

James Grant is a typical literary nationalist of the period. A novelist with strong Jacobite sympathies, he launched an attack on England's role in the Union in 1852. His arguments were among the chief catalysts which led to the formation of the Association:

Grant aroused the interests of the Scottish public by his campaign against the irregularities in the Royal Arms. Such symbolic protests have played an important part in nationalism . . . because of the interest and sympathy they arouse in Scotland.

Grant's criticism of the English misuse of the Royal Arms was similar to that made by Walker on the occasion of George IV's visit in 1822. This protest, and its success in striking a chord in the hearts of many Scots, was a sign of the fundamentally traditionalist nature of the nationalism which was being awakened. The important part the symbols of the past were to play in validating its continuing vitality was as material a rebuke as could be given to those who proclaimed the past extinct. Resurgent Jacobite nationalism set out to cock a snook at those who 'adored the rising sun'.[47]

Grant's fiction allied Jacobite and patriotic issues. His *Scottish Cavalier* (1851) is a typical example of the execution of this aim. In this and other novels, 'his best heroes were Jacobites'. He wrote for adolescents, attempting to recreate a Jacobite mood in order to nourish the nationalism he was promoting, with its emphasis on the ancient traditions and rights of Scotland. As 'a staunch admirer and adherent of the House of Stuart', he transferred its politics to the Scotland of the nineteenth century in his role as joint Secretary of the Association.[48]

The value set on tradition and the past by Grant and others was not null, like the 'official' version of Scottish history. It went hand in hand with a commitment to restore national traditions and Scotland's political voice. These patriots subscribed to the ideology of history as liberty, and saw Scotland's potential for intellectual and political growth stunted by the sheer weight of English political domination inherent in the Treaty of Union, as the Jacobites had done. Nor was the conservative wing of nationalism alone in being attracted to the Stuarts: right into the present century, left-wing nationalists have also admired the Jacobite cause and some of its leaders. The idea of Scottish history as struggle and the Jacobite reading of the Clearances were ideological positions of potentially universal appeal. The Jacobite analysis was a consistent thread binding together nationalists of 1700 and 1850 in their common concern over social and cultural disasters resulting from Union. The covenanting dynamic was almost exhausted, either through clerical infighting, or the compromises of the established church. Even in the eighteenth century, many Presbyterian nationalists had agreed with the Jacobites.[49] In the post-1843 climate, the Free Church reasserted some of the old values of Presbyterian nationalism: but the Church of the Disruption could not claim the same degree of continuous history as could Jacobite ideology. Nor was it associated with resistance through armed struggle since Culloden was already seen as a national battle and a national tragedy, a time when 'Scotland for freedom last stood'.[50]

For all these reasons, the Jacobite interpretation possessed a continuing appeal. It hardly mattered that the only Stuarts who could be brought back were remote mid-European royalty (Francis V of Modena, to be exact), since the Jacobite cause stood, as it always had after 1707, for more than the cause of the Stuart kings alone: it stood for Scotland, traditional and free. Even the great eighteenth-century Jacobite, the Earl Marischal, had been virtually a Scottish Republican; and the Roman Republican iconography the Stuarts themselves adopted was suggestive of the diverse nature of their support. Radical Jacobites concentrated on liberty and struggle; more conservative ones identified the Stuarts with a cultural corpus of tradition and authority, the loss of which had been the beginning of the end for Scottish independence. Symbolic political gestures, drawn from the great examples of the past (those neglected by the Union faction of 1707), suited both.[51]

James Grant's protest to the Lord Lyon, concerning irregular quarterings and the improper flags on the new florin coins, was a sign of these feelings, as was his desire to restore the Scottish Secretaryship, abrogated since the time of the Forty-Five. Other members of the Association, most notably its leader W. E. Aytoun, were even more politically rooted in Jacobitism. Aytoun's *Lays of the Scottish Cavaliers* is heavily biased towards Jacobite ideology, with its iconography of heroism set against the more sordid and limited values of the modern world. Aytoun combines Romantic attitudes to landscape (though some of these were originally Jacobite) with a keen sense of sympathy for the Highlander as Scottish hero:

> On the heights of Killiecrankie
> Yester-morn our army lay:
> Slowly rose the mist in columns
> From the river's broken way,
> Hoarsely roared the swollen torrent,
> And the Pass was wrapt in gloom,
> When the clansmen rose together
> From their lair amidst the broom.

Dundee's army are ironically compared to the 'stately deer' being hunted by the government forces. But these deer are not those who are now idly pursued by Victorian plutocrats; instead it is they who do the hunting, sweeping aside those who had chased them into the mountains:

> Like a tempest down the ridges
> Swept the hurricane of steel
> Rose the slogan of Macdonald –
> Flashed the broadsword of Locheill!

The Highland heroes turn on their tormentors. Aytoun's 'Burial March of Dundee' may be both a lament for ancient heroism and a comment on modern political circumstances.[52]

The National Association collapsed under the jingoistic pressure exerted by the Crimean War (1854) and the Indian Mutiny (1857). But the spirit which had animated it was not to be obscured, surfacing in the Gaelic revival of the 1860s (the Gaelic Society of Inverness was founded in 1871), and in the Home Rule and neo-Jacobite movements which followed. The reaction in favour of positive rather than negative readings of the Scottish past grew in these decades.[53]

The most immediate aim of those who had worked for the Association was to secure a monument to Wallace on the Abbey Craig at Stirling. 'Either Scotland has no history at all, or that history finds its centre in Wallace' was the motivation behind this campaign, which (to English disapproval) attracted the attention of some supporters of the Young Ireland movement. The emerging cult of Wallace, for long a submerged but not forgotten icon, was a sign of a new and positive approach to Scotland's past. Beginning in Scotland, enthusiasm for the celebration of Wallace as liberator spread to Scots exiled in the colonies. Such celebration expressed itself most frequently and forcefully in the erection of statues and monuments, sometimes covered in anti-English sentiments, like the Aberdeen statue; and sometimes grandiose in size and situation, portraying the hero as almost a classical deity:

> Wallace monuments became a symbol of Scottish patriotism all over the world. . . . Perhaps the most famous was at Ballarat in Victoria, Australia, . . . unveiled . . . in 1889 . . . [which] cost £1000.

The Ballarat statue was subsequently to be a focal point for Scottish nationalism in Australia.[54]

The Wallace Monument went up on the Abbey Craig in 1856. It was a symbol of renewed optimism in Scottish nationhood. This was seen most clearly in the reaction of the English press. One might think that the extreme cultivation of historical pageantry in Scotland would have led to the Wallace Monument being accepted by commentators as just another antique curio, expressing a struggle for liberty long since safely accommodated in the parliamentary Union of the two countries. This was far from the case. The English papers recognized that the Monument was a focal point for renewed national feeling, not the mere icon of an extinct past. *The Times* tried to make it the latter, calling 'Wallace . . . the merest myth', and acidly commenting that 'Scotchmen . . . seem to do nothing but masquerade in the garments of their grandfathers'. It was even suggested that the Monument signified the growth of a provincial mentality in Scotland! Demonstrations of renewed national identity could thenceforward be stigmatized with the label of 'provincialism' (they still are). The only way in which Scotland could demonstrate it was not provincial was to remain a province: this was the clear implication of such an approach.[55]

In England at this time, the Oxford Movement was reviving the ecclesiastical politics of Laud's seventeenth-century Anglo-Catholicism, and concomitantly evincing its sympathy for the Stuart kings. In Scotland, such moves were identified by the now sadly depleted Episcopal church with their own 'Scottish non-juring tradition'. The Episcopalians were at last being reconciled to the Anglican church, a process facilitated by the Jacobitical overtones of the Oxford Movement. They were recognized as a province of the Anglican communion from 1867 onwards, and their rehabilitation provided another sign of Scotland's growing reassertion of its own traditions, a sign confirmed by the (eventually successful) battle for the use of the Scottish Prayer Book rather than the Book of Common Prayer.[56]

Duncan McLaren, the leading light of the NAVSR (National Association for the Vindication of Scottish Rights), was meanwhile championing Scottish causes as MP for Edinburgh, 'winning for himself the title of "M.P. for Scotland"'. Nationalism was clearly reawakening; and Unionists attempted briefly to tar it with the 'popish plot' brush as they were doing in Ireland. This was ineffective, although there was a limited connection between the two movements, as the crofters certainly learnt from Irish land agitation in their own campaigns. The campaign for a Scottish Secretaryship, perhaps a relic of what has been dubbed the 'aristocratic localism' of Jacobitism, proved eventually successful in 1885.[57] A strong reliance on the traditions of Scotland, particularly those highlighted by the Jacobites, continued to be evinced: 'Patriotic agitation tended to give a continuing legitimacy to groups on the fringes of the Scottish establishment: Jacobite, Gaelic enthusiasts'.[58] These enthusiasts for the traditional past had to differentiate themselves from those for whom the past was merely a sentimental construct of defeats. Nationalist or pro-crofter action made this differentiation public, visible, and resented. Sometimes, what appeared to be relatively trivial points were elevated into controversial issues. William Burns, who published *The Scottish War of Independence* in 1874, was 'the first man to bring home to Scots the enormity of allowing Great Britain to be referred to as "England".' As with the Wallace Monument and the Royal Arms, symbolic issues of apparently little intrinsic importance could whip up a great deal of nationalist feeling.[59]

Symbolic politics had of course played a central part in the self-projection of the Stuart cause. The complex iconography of Jacobite patriotism had used embedded codes and symbols for a century. Symbolic gestures such as wearing the tartan and giving the toast over water, to say nothing of white roses and whistled airs, had long been the day-to-day discourse of Jacobitism. The methods of expression adopted by Scottish nationalism in the latter part of the nineteenth century owed much to the deliberate manner in which earlier nationalists had made themselves plain through symbols, codes, and tokens. The special status of Scotland and the Stuarts had been the hidden message of eighteenth-century Jacobitism; now nineteenth-century patriotism claimed back that special status for the nation in related terms. Symbolic politics was nothing new, but its capacity, then and now, to stir Scottish sentiment did and does emphasize how long-standing a means of patriotic expression it has been. The political language of traditional symbols was one which had endured as an encoded record of anti-Union sympathies in the eighteenth century. It continued as a patriotic language into the nineteenth and twentieth. Symbols were the only form in which patriotism had found it safe to express itself; and their centrality is attested by the very manner in which they were usurped by the tartan cultists. It was owing to the traditionalist approach of Jacobite nationalism that the icons of Scottish history were of such symbolic importance, part of an allegorical reading of history as liberty, Scotland's perpetual struggle. The Jacobite portrayal of the Stuart cause as not merely a dynastic struggle, but rather the latest in a long line of battles for liberty, had led in the eighteenth century to a strong identification of the Wars of Independence with the Jacobite Risings.[60] This continued after Culloden. Charles is not infrequently described as a 'second Bruce', most notably by Robert Louis Stevenson, and his landing in the West, almost alone, paralleled that of Bruce in 1307.[61]

If the Royal Stuarts were the inheritors of Bruce, the liberty of the people they fought for was the inheritance of Wallace in the Jacobite account, which balanced one against the other. The powerful recrudescence of pro-Wallace feeling and of a Wallace cult in the nineteenth and early twentieth century (the Elderslie memorial went up in 1912) was an indication of the endurance of the interpretation of Scottish history as a battle for liberty. The survival of such an interpretation, which might replicate its message to each succeeding generation, was a matter of some concern to those who wished Scottish history to be pictorial and quiescent.[62]

Nationalist feeling continued among radical, business, and Jacobitical groupings. The Earl of Bute, caricatured by Disraeli as Lothair, was a good example of the last type. Interestingly, the role of Wallace and the Wars of Independence in nationalist thought often took the form of subsuming the working and business classes into a picture of the nation based on the patriotic Highlander's struggle for liberty in the eighteenth century. In Charles Waddie's 'Is Scotland to get Home Rule?', although the Lowland industrial towns are included in the patriotic resistance, a dominant image is that of the Highlands and the Highland charge:

> From distant isle, from hill and dale,
> From mountain hoar, and lowly vale,
> From barren glen and fertile strath,
> By metalled road or mountain path
> From teeming workshop, mart, or street,
> Let all the sons of Scotland meet,
> A true, a loyal, a patriot band,
> And sweep all traitors from the land.

The idea of the 'patriot band' is one closely related to eighteenth-century propaganda song, and the preponderance of Highland and rural scenery reinforces the idea that the concept of Highlander as patriot is the one in Waddie's mind as he conjures up the band of patriots to resist the 'traitors' of the 'land'. These, presumably, are Unionists. The image of true-Scot and traitor-Scot had a strongly Jacobite ancestry.[63]

It would be wrong to suggest that Jacobitism, even symbolic Jacobitism, was the dominant element in renewed national feeling. Yet even nationalists of a radical school, such as John Morrison Davidson, showed considerable interest in the message of the past based on Wallace and the anti-Unionists of the eighteenth century. Jacobitism, in its full sense of support for the Stuart claimant, was a fringe belief (though shortly to undergo a surprising resurgence); in the sense, however, that nineteenth-century nationalism was the beneficiary of a patriotic cultural heritage, Jacobitism was the chief testator.[64]

The association of Home Rule with the crofting question further emphasized the link between the Clearances and the national struggle (as it was now often seen) of Culloden. 'John Murdoch told the Crofting Commissioners in 1883 that it had been a disaster to tell the Highlander that his culture was valueless and his language a barbarism.'[65] Such complaints went right back to the Disclothing Act of 1747 and beyond (that they were also complaints relevant to the policies of *some* of the Stuart kings was by this time often forgotten). The attempt to renew the self-respect of the Highlands after so long in the shadow of Culloden and the Clearances was one which brought aspects of Jacobitism and the Jacobite period to the fore. There were strong attempts to rehabilitate Macpherson's reputation; and publications such as *The Celtic Magazine* showed some signs of restored confidence in and about the Highlands. Radicalism on the ground was joined by limited sympathy from the Scottish (in particular) establishment.[66]

As I mentioned earlier, aspects of Highland radicalism idealized a glorified Celtic (and quasi-Jacobite) past of wealth and valour. The implication was that such a past had come to an end at Culloden. The political significance of the battle was underlined anew in the Highlands, as it had been by renewed patriotic feeling in the Lowlands. It is strange to think that a battle over in less than an hour, fought out between 5,000 Scots, French, and Irish (half of whom were never engaged in combat) and 9,000 English, Anglo-Germans, and Highlanders, the last and one of the most strategically incompetent battles ever fought on British soil, should have had such an effect on a national psyche. The decisive battles of the Civil War and the Wars of the Roses are nothing to it. At Towton in 1461, ten times as many died; at Naseby in 1645, Charles's defeat set him on the route to ignominy and death. No king died as a result of Culloden, nor was the status quo in any way altered; but the three-quarter truth that it was the last battle for Scottish liberty endured and grew. On the monument erected on the moor in 1881 by Duncan Forbes were put words in memory of the 'Brave Clans/who fought for/SCOTLAND AND PRINCE CHARLIE'. They stand there to this day as evidence of the belief that Culloden was a battle for Scotland as well as a crown.[67] And in a sense it was. The Jacobite claim to be the true nationalists, though consciously challenged by some, has passed unchallenged into the national consciousness.

If the Clearances and the Crofting Commission were at the sharp end of the Home Rule question, Jacobite ideology was also receiving support from the lusher pastures of the South. The leaders of the Oxford Movement had shown sympathy for the Stuarts, and their sympathy was echoed by writers like Algernon Charles Swinburne and many lesser artists towards the close of the century.[68] Most notable perhaps was the support of John Ruskin, who combined his Stuart sympathies with a radical political agenda which had much in common with the intellectual legacy of radical Jacobitism in its opposition to the imperialism of commerce. His support for Scottish Home Rule (under a Scottish monarch) was displayed in an interesting article in the *Pall Mall Gazette* for 16 January 1887. Subsequently he was widely quoted as a supporter of Home Rule and neo-Jacobitism.[69]

In Scotland too, there was a marked increase in literary interest in the Jacobite cause. The Jacobite song, both in original and sentimentalized format, experienced increased popularity. Novels, plays, and poems all dealt increasingly with the politics and history of Jacobitism. The most important writer to participate in this boom was Robert Louis Stevenson, the most able Scottish novelist of the period. In *Kidnapped*, *Catriona*, and *The Master of Ballantrae*, as well as in some shorter fragments, he deals in differing ways with the enduring problems bequeathed by Jacobitism. The end of the century felt less secure in its response to history than did those who welcomed George IV to Edinburgh a lifetime before.[70]

NEO-JACOBITES AND HOME RULERS

Within the last few years, however ... a new Stuart literature has come into being: there is scarcely a magazine or review but has had its say upon some detail of the subject, from the Casket Letters to the death of the Cardinal who was king *non desideriis hominum sed voluntate Dei*.

The Royalist, 16 April 1890

The hero ... of an unknown romance, the dweller upon unknown memories.

R. L. Stevenson

'Theid an dutheas an agaidh nan creag' (Hereditary right will withstand the rocks) ... What they fought for, we will work for!

Theodore Napier[71]

The end of the nineteenth century witnessed a reaction by the artistic and literary classes against the values of material progress, and the burgeoning worlds of imperial and industrial power. Encapsulated in the phrase '*épater les bourgeois*', an attack was launched against the comfortable and materialistic values of an expanding middle class. Part of the structure of this attack was political. Those artists who launched or participated in these hostilities found allied ideas among the anarchists and emergent left, or, more commonly, in a politics of nostalgia, whose 'dreams of more comely ages' glorified an aristocratic, artistic past.[72]

In England, this took the shape of a strong predilection for pre-1688 society (the Glorious Revolution being linked to the rise of the middle classes). The cult of the Stuarts was revived. Strong returning interest in the Stuart kings was evident throughout the 1870s and 1880s, culminating in the Stuart Exhibition of 1889–90, where thousands of important items from the Stuart period were displayed under the patronage of figures like Edward Burne-Jones, Lawrence Alma-Tadema, and Holman Hunt. Stuart memorabilia boomed at auction, and an entire neo-Jacobite movement was launched, which speedily subdivided itself into antiquarian and political wings. The latter clamoured, noisily but ineffectively, for an actual Stuart restoration – the first political group to do so for over a century.[73]

Those members of the artistic community in England who sympathized with the renewed interest in an aristocratic and courtly past, such as Herbert Horne, who called for the restoration of a 'Carolean age of manners and beauty', identified their middle-class enemies as the new Puritans.[74] This was developed from Arnold's negative view of the middle classes in *Culture and Anarchy*, but extended in its remit so as to suggest that the Cavalier/Puritan dichotomy in society was still dangerously alive. Their case was supported by the rehabilitation of Cromwell which had occurred during the nineteenth century, a rehabilitation which had shadowed and echoed the pro-Stuart articulations of the Oxford Movement:

> For nearly half a century the worship of an idealized Cromwell has been the favourite cult of those Radicals who preached the fake gospel of Revolution and yearned for a Republic. The new religion called for a new revelation; what the book of Mormon was to the followers of Joe Smith, Carlyle's *Letters and Speeches of Oliver Cromwell* became to such latter-day saints as these. On all sides the cry arose: – 'There is no hero but Cromwell, and Carlyle is his prophet.'

Such was the kind of vituperative review which appeared in *The Royalist*, the chief among the neo-Jacobite papers.[75]

In Scotland (and to some extent Ireland), the pro-Stuart reaction was a different one. Instead of *'épater les bourgeois'* the same spirit manifested itself through the so-called Celtic Twilight, a revival not of aristocratic so much as of national and nationalistic identities. The Celtic Twilight has come in for a bad press: it is said that it misrepresented Scotland and Ireland as dying Celtic nations with no future.[76] This is only partly true. Some of the writers and artists of the period undoubtedly fed the imperial myth of a moribund Gaeldom whose great achievements were all in the past. Others, however, were the custodians and helpmeets of renewed national feeling. Ireland's own independence was to a degree born out of the Celtic Twilight, in the persons of such as its ideological inheritor, Pearse: 'When he [Pearse] opened Scoil Eanna in September 1908, he put . . . a large mural of the young Cu Chulainn taking arms . . . [in] the main hall.' This kind of iconography of the Irish past is found in Republican circles and areas to the present day. Pearse's aim was 'to recreate and perpetuate in Eire the knightly tradition of the . . . Emain Macha . . . the high tradition of Cuchulainn . . . the noble tradition of the Fianna . . . the Christlike tradition of Colum Cille'. These heroic episodes were revivified in the literature of the Celtic Twilight in Ireland, and eventually led Pearse 'inexorably to live out a myth of redemptive self-sacrifice in the G.P.O.'[77]

This renewed interest in the mythology and heroes of the past was less fatally marked in a Scottish context; but there also the Celtic Twilight accommodated the promise of a new dawn. Out of history and myth came, as so often, the identity of dispossessed nations – renewed interest was a sign of restored consciousness.

In the last section, I argued that the connection between Jacobite and nationalist values was once more being made explicit in Scotland. In 1887, Theodore Napier, arguably the most prominent political figure of the Scottish Celtic Twilight, instituted an annual pilgrimage to Culloden, where Forbes's monument had been raised six years before. Napier, whose achievement will be discussed in detail in the next section, was one of the first to once again make Jacobitism and nationalism explicitly one cause. Napier drew conclusions from the always implicit premises of their relationship, and in doing so foreshadowed many of the Jacobitical elements in twentieth-century Scottish nationalism. He was one of the first nationalists to readopt the Highland dress as an anti-Union symbol rather than a quaint relic. Napier deliberately emphasized the nature of the tradition he was reviving by dressing in the manner of a pre-1688 Highlander, thus also perhaps attempting to avoid the factitiousness of Victorian tartanry.[78]

Likewise the factitiousness of much Victorian interest in Jacobitism, dependent as it was on sentimentalism, was exposed by the surprising commitment of the neo-Jacobite organizations. The Order of the White Rose, founded on 10 June 1886, saw itself as a successor to the famous Jacobite Cycle Club, while its mission was to exemplify the spirit of Jacobitism. In this, it confessed Jacobitism to have a political and moral agenda far beyond that contingent on the return of the Stuart monarchs: the kind of agenda, in fact, which has been argued throughout this book.

But for some, the spirit of Jacobitism was not enough. In 1891, the Legitimist Jacobite League was formed, committed to the actual restoration of the Stuarts as well as to a Jacobite political programme. It was that programme, however, which made an impact on public debate during the last years of Victoria. James McNeill Whistler, MacGregor Mathers (Count Glenstrae in the Jacobite peerage), Marmaduke Langdale, and the poet and Irish nationalist Lionel Johnson were among those dedicated to 'the principles of the Order of the White Rose', a political programme based on support for aristocratic values, the removal of remaining religious disabilities, and greater recognition of the separate identities of Scotland and Ireland. Jacobite values even reached the House of Commons: when Gladstone's Bill to remove remaining disabilities from Roman Catholics was put forward in 1891, Sir John Pope-Hennessey wished to see the legislation extended to include the Royal Family.[79]

Jacobite candidates attempted to get elected to Parliament. Gilbert Baird Fraser, Herbert Vivian, and W. Clifford Mellor were all involved in standing or considered standing for Parliament as Jacobites in 1891. Public meetings were held in support of the Stuarts, and a pilgrimage organized to the statue of King Charles at Charing Cross, for which a well-known poem was written.[80] At first, the authorities attempted to suppress such activity, and there were clashes with police. But by 1893, Jacobite supporters had won the right to lay an annual wreath at the statue, a right which the Royal Stuart Society continue to exercise to this day.[81]

Such symbolic and substantial political action won the neo-Jacobites sustained publicity. Questions were asked in the Commons; viciously anti-Jacobite letters appeared in the press, and MPs were quizzed by querulous constituents regarding secret Jacobite sympathies.[82] Jacobite societies grew up everywhere: in East Anglia, Devon, Glasgow, Great Grimsby, Oxford, St Ives, the Thames Valley, Wishaw, and Aberdeen. Requiem masses were held for those who fell at Culloden, and for as many Stuart martyr-monarchs as opportunity offered. The hopes of the restorationist neo-Jacobites must have seemed rewarded when HRH Prince Robert (*de jure* Prince of Wales, and Duke of Albany and Cornwall) arrived at Victoria Station in 1897. Lady Helen Clifford Mellor greeted him with a bouquet of white roses. Unfortunately, the bold Pretender (the Bavarian prince) had come to London to celebrate the Diamond Jubilee of Queen Victoria. He was to prove even more of an equivocal asset when he appeared in arms and high rank for the Kaiser in 1914, an event which effectively put a stop to restorationist neo-Jacobitism.[83]

The neo-Jacobites of the hardline Legitimist League, who went as far as to produce and distribute anti-Hanoverian propaganda on the accession of Edward VII, were mostly oddball aristocrats or dilettantes on private incomes. Theodore Napier was one of the few talented political activists who supported actual restoration. On the other hand, the members of the Order (about 500) were frequently artists or other persons of consequence, such as the infamous Marquess of Queensberry, or the writer Andrew Lang.[84]

Lang expressed the potency of ancient Jacobite images of restoration and renewal in poems such as 'The Tenth of June 1715', which makes use of the story of Iseult in its suggestive symbolism of the returning sail:

Day of the flower and the King!'
When shall the sails of white
Shine on the seas and bring
In the day, in the dawn, in the night
The King to his land and his right?

To Lang, famous collector of fairy-tales, Jacobitism was a fairy-tale, perhaps the greatest one of all.[85] To other writers of the Celtic Twilight, such as Bernard Kelly and W. Blaikie Murdoch, the Jacobite heritage was a spiritual one, a lasting protest of elegance against utility, art against materialism, heroism against commerce:

> But if the white rose of the Stuarts had faded forever in blood, the lost race, in him, their last and greatest hero [Charles], had reached its immortality – enshrined for ever in the pages of romance, endeared to all generous hearts in the realms of song.[86]

Blaikie Murdoch combined the patriotic interpretation of Jacobitism found in Scotland with the more widespread *fin de siècle* interpretation of Jacobitism as a defence of art and aristocracy against 'the Cromwellian herd' who 'hated literature and painting'. Cromwell's status as the representative hero of bourgeois revolution, combined with the Puritans' well-reputed dislike for art, made both excellent political and artistic targets. Murdoch and those who thought, like him, that 'the execution of Charles I dealt a terrible blow to artistic activity in England [*sic*]', created a politics out of the exercise of their own literary gifts, and turned their energies towards renewing the cult of Charles the Martyr. This led to a revival in the iconic images of the Stuart kings which had been so carefully cultivated in the seventeenth century. During the 1890s, Sickert and Mallarmé were only two of the artists contributing to Jacobite publications. The personal cult of Charles was revived not only through poems and memorabilia, but also through the foundation of the Society for King Charles the Martyr (4 April 1894), and by the scores of little hymns and poems which came out in praise of the king, in defiance of the crusty colonels who wrote disapprovingly to the press concerning the reawakening of Stuart enthusiasm.[87]

Statues of Charles played a considerable role in the symbolic political gestures of the neo-Jacobites. The marches to decorate them, and the occasional anti-Jacobite reaction of spoilation, formed the centre of a political protest made in terms of public works of art. Throughout the 1890s, statues of the Stuarts and Cromwell were praised or abused, decorated or removed, throughout Britain. When a statue of Oliver Cromwell was erected to mark his tercentenary (1899) the anti-Jacobite Frederic Harrison could hardly contain his delight:

> At last, after two centuries and a half, London has a statue of the greatest ruler who ever governed the three kingdoms. The hatred

of his memory, which so long kept him in exile from the Palace of Westminster, has at length fizzled out in the whining of a handful of Ritualists, Jew financiers, and Jacobites.

Harrison goes on to suggest, as his part in the strategy of the war of the statues, that Charles I's statue should be removed from Charing Cross, and replaced there by Cromwell:

Let Oliver stand in Charing Cross hard by the very spot where some of his bravest Ironsides shed their blood.[88]

Such attempts to recreate the spirit and feuds of the Stuart era were common. A statue of Charles II was destroyed at Salisbury; 'another image of the regicidal ruffian' (i.e. Cromwell) was erected at St Ives, where the neo-Jacobites had considered themselves strong; and 'London politicians' laid wreaths 'on the graves of Ludlow and Broughton, leaders of the rebels'. The neo-Jacobites were paying dearly for their right to venerate Charles I. The crowning insult was perhaps the removal of the statue of James II from Whitehall in 1897, which the neo-Jacobites seemed to read, perhaps correctly, as a snub in the year of the Diamond Jubilee. They planned a demonstration against it. The last flurry of this and similar protests probably occurred in 1902, when an Assertion proclaiming Queen Mary (the Stuart claimant) was 'affixed to hoardings . . . in London on June 20'. This was the last major symbolic protest made by the English neo-Jacobites.[89]

It was also the most notorious. A minor writer called Allen Upward wrote an anti-Jacobite novel, *Treason*, which professed to show 'how a Roman Catholic, Mary III, was proclaimed (on the Walls of Saint James's Palace) Queen of Great Britain'. Upward regarded the protests of 1901–2, which culminated in the one above-mentioned, as serious threats. His book, which went through several editions, is able to scaremonger effectively by raising the spectre of popery. The Roman Church is described as 'crowned mother of a hundred Pagan temples, the Egyptian Isis', and in the sequel to *Treason*, *The Fourth Conquest of England*, 'papal troops' as well as 'Roman and Anglican volunteers', aid a German invasion in restoring the Stuarts, in a finale which brings together all the diverse strands of xenophobia and paranoia native to the British imperial psyche.[90]

Upward's scaremongering was laughable. By 1905, neo-Jacobitism in England was largely a spent force, though a movement of sorts continued up to the First World War. Despite the Order of the White Rose's adoption of Jacobitism as a political programme, there was little it had to offer a successful imperial state. Kaiser Wilhelm's suggestion to King Edward that he should shoot those who questioned his title was understandably ignored, though the hasty reaction of the authorities and police to the early manifestations of Jacobite protest showed that support for the Stuarts could still touch a raw nerve. Tolerance or neglect arrived when the neo-Jacobites had satisfactorily displayed their amateurishness for all to see. Murdoch's idea of the Stuarts as 'the family of artists scorned by a nation of shopkeepers' was one insulting to the latter, but it did nothing to restore the fortunes of the former. Henceforward English neo-Jacobitism would be little more threatening than a scholarly hobby.[91]

In Scotland, matters stood somewhat differently. The revival of a more explicit Jacobitism did much to stimulate the awakening of long-dormant political arguments which were freed from hibernation. Theodore Napier's *Appeal to Loyal Scotsmen*, published in 1899, revives the idea of a federal rather than an incorporating Union, advanced by Andrew Fletcher of Saltoun and his allies in the last Scottish parliament. Napier displays a commitment to 'the old Royal Stuart line', but his emphasis is on the 'restoration . . . to Scotland of her long-lost Parliament', and he bemoans the fact that his country seems '*content to lick her chains*'.[92]

Napier's arguments were more than straws in the wind of contemporary opinion. G. W. T. Omond's work on the Union question showed a revival of interest in a less decided form. James Mackinnon, in *The Union of England and Scotland* (1896), developed an early version of a modern Home Rule position. Significantly, Mackinnon considered that the origins of growing support for Home Rule lay in awareness of a 'growing intensity . . . of the past and its claims', an awareness later to be manifest in the nationalism of such as Compton Mackenzie and Ruaridh Erskine of Mar.[93]

This sense of the past was visible in Scottish art and letters. But in Scotland, so much depended on the version of the past adopted. The defeat of the Jacobite cause was now so psychologically merged with the destruction of Scottish independence that those concerned with the state and future of Scotland returned to it again and again, trying to find in the age of Jacobite struggle the nature of Scottish identity, and the validity or desirability of a Scottish polity. It was still difficult (and is so now) 'to approach the subject without feeling something of party heat and something of party bias'.[94] But the unease with which it was approached by writers like Stevenson contrasted with the brisk surface certainties of Scott. The Jacobite effect could no longer be simply consigned into the jumble of a colourful past. It was once again an agent for change, or at least an unease which contributed to a broader perspective on Scotland's future than had hitherto been taken. 'Home Rule All Round', the promise of the Liberals from 1894, was a manifestation of the political pressures which had been building up inside Scotland for forty years.[95]

There were, of course, still those like Wilmott Dixon, who held to the view that 'Sir Walter Scott first roused English [*sic*] people to the conviction that Jacobitism was a harmless memory of the past' (and Dixon considered this the correct view). The Kailyard school excluded the new national questioning as they had also excluded new social developments. J. M. Barrie's Captain Hook, dark Stuart pirate and nursery Redgauntlet, is an example of the limited and old-fashioned approach even the most talented of the Kailyard writers took. In *Peter Pan*, Jacobitism is merely a matter of bogeymen.[96]

High Victorian Jacobite romanticism also remained strong. Pittendrigh Macgillavray's address to the '45 Club in 1911 is typical of the dying fall of the Walter Scott school of Jacobitism: 'The Gael . . . had gone forth in the quest of a dream . . . spoilt children of the mist . . . were they not indeed Romance personified!' Macgillavray's description of the Celts as having been 'born with the fairies' gift of second sight, and a little handful of gladness wherewith to outweigh the evil of things' is typical of the sentimental view which had dominated the previous ninety years. The 'legacy of sweet and bitter memories' of which Macgillavray spoke was indeed a legacy of Jacobitism, but it was one of more than memory. The pageant was not over, nor had the mist closed for ever on the Celtic fringe.[97]

THEODORE NAPIER

HIS MAJESTY, King Robert, returned to Edinburgh this morning . . . King Robert the Fourth – whom God preserve.

'Scotland in A.D. 1950'
The Fiery Cross 32:7 (1909)

The constitutional recovery of the rights, honours, and dignities lost to our nation in its past history, and more especially since the Revolution of 1689.

Objectives of *The Fiery Cross*

When you parted with your ancient royal Stuart line in 1689 . . . you virtually paved the way for the passing of the infamous Act of Union, whereby Scotland's political liberty was bartered for 'thirty pieces of silver'!

Theodore Napier[98]

Theodore Napier, like the Scottish patriots of the next two generations, Ruaridh Erskine and Wendy Wood, was born outwith Scotland. The May 1921 issue of *The Jacobite*, which proudly styled itself 'the only Jacobite paper in New Zealand', records that he was born in Melbourne in 1845. On his return to Scotland, the land of his ancestors, he plunged himself into ancestral politics, appearing to sincerely believe that the restoration of the Stuarts must accompany any Scottish parliament. Although he was secretary in Scotland of the London-based Legitimist Jacobite League, he became in effect an increasingly independent operator. His methods were not their methods. While they busied themselves with statues, debates, and demonstrations, Napier devoted himself with single-mindedness to the cause of Scottish nationalism, a by-line of English Jacobite interest, but central to his creed.[99]

The 1890s were a fruitful period for Napier. The flagship achievements of the 1880s, the Crofting Acts and the restoration of the Scottish Secretaryship, were increasingly backed by demands for Home Rule. The Liberals were being chivvied along by the newly-formed Scottish Home Rule Association (SHRA). On the more radical left, early Labourite politicians showed, as the ILP were to later, a marked inclination towards Home Rule. Keir Hardie in particular was strongly sympathetic. At this time, there was, as may be imagined, little use of Jacobite-descended imagery on the further left. The Liberals and the SHRA had stronger associations, especially in the area of the crofting question, discussed above.[100] However, the true heir of Aytoun and James Grant was undoubtedly Napier, though he was to be more extreme than they.

For the moment, the SHRA, which 'was to confirm in their Home Rule sympathies many of the Radical leaders in the Highlands and many of the leaders of the Labour movement', was the most powerful force. Home Rule was associated with the crofting question; and the success of the crofters in the 1880s provided a firm base for a wider Home Rule campaign, whose success was manifested in the support gained from the Liberal Party and formalized in 1894. Three years later, Napier was the first to foreshadow the more thoroughgoing campaigns of petition, straw poll, and Covenant, which otherwise belong to the twentieth century.[101] He 'almost single-handedly obtained 104,000 signatures to a diamond jubilee petition to Queen Victoria protesting against the misuse of the national names.'[102] Like the campaigns of the 1850s, this nationalism was largely symbolic: but it showed, like those, how Scots could be aroused by the misuse of the term 'England' to describe Great Britain.

The petition was a sign of Napier's ability to take political protest seriously in a manner neo-Jacobites in England failed to do. Throughout his career, he was able to maintain a serious and often forward-looking approach to the constitutional reform of Scottish affairs, while still believing in the restoration of the Stuarts. Despite the practical side of his patriotic activity, Napier's Jacobitism was a living entity rather than a political programme. He still wanted the queen over the water to come home.

The years after 1900 saw significant developments in Scottish affairs. In that year, the Young Scots Society was formed to press for Home Rule. Within three years, it had 1,580 members in twenty-seven branches. In 1901, Theodore Napier launched his own paper, *The Fiery Cross*, a title with deliberate reference to the method by which the Highlands had been raised in the era of the Jacobite risings. The cover portrayed a heavily armed clansman, with the legend 'Woe to the Wretch who fails to rear/At this dread sign the ready spear!' The image and language clearly drew on the old idea of the Highlander as patriot, and the threatening address, as the contents of the paper made clear, was directed at those who failed to support Scottish independence.[103]

Napier made his journal as Jacobite in spirit as it could be without actually rendering it a neo-Jacobite organ. It was intended to be the political voice of outright nationalism, speaking from a point on the spectrum far beyond that of the Home Rulers. In this it was innovative. The *Celtic Magazine* was responding to the new political climate by making more nationalist noise than it had done in the early days of the 1870s, but it and other publications continued to reflect a Home Rule rather than nationalist position. Despite his revival of federalist views, Napier's policies could only be compatible with the achievement of complete political autonomy for Scotland. The twelve original Articles of the *Fiery Cross* were as follows:

1 Restoration of the Stuarts.
2 Restoration of Parliament.
3 Restoration of the Mint.
4 Restoration of Privy Council.
5 Restoration of Court of Admiralty.
6 Restoration of Stone of Destiny. (Briefly done 1950)
7 Restoration of Royal Arms in Scottish quarters in Scotland.
8 Deletion of St George and the Dragon from British coinage.
9 'England' not to 'be used in an Imperial sense'.
10 Restoration of the clan system and of the people to the land.
11 Multiple voting.
12 Opposition to '*Jingo-Imperialism*' and '*Militarism*'.

Clearly some of these aims were more trivial than others. For example, the achievement of 1 and 2 would deliver all the rest. In practice, Napier gave differing priorities to those aims he felt were more or less achievable.[104]

The criticism of militarism was pursued at great length in the pages of Napier's journal. At the height of the age of Empire, it echoed the traditional Jacobite opposition to foreign wars and imperial adventures. It also emphasized the radical edge to what was otherwise (save for the 'restoration . . . of the people to the land') a traditionalist programme. Radical and conservative Jacobite elements once again appeared together.[105]

The Articles formed an ideological backdrop to the contents of *The Fiery Cross*, but the journal did not dwell on them in the obsessive way found elsewhere in the neo-Jacobite press. Its scope was wider. The first number called for the establishment of a National Party in Scotland, and criticized Home Rule Unionists in a manner which would be familiar to nationalists of today, asking of the Scottish MPs 'who among your amiable 72 have stood up to protest?', their first loyalty being to Westminster. In another article, addressed to the Highlanders, much is made of the common Stuart heritage of Scottish patriotism.[106]

The accession of Edward VII brought Jacobite protests in England, as discussed above. In Ireland, nationalist opinion to 'new commonness upon the throne' was hostile. In Scotland, protests centred on the symbolic question of regnal numbers, one that was to surface again in the attacks on 'EIIR' pillar-boxes, half a century later. Edward's adoption of the title 'Edward VII' rather than 'Edward I of Great Britain' (Edward VI had ruled England from 1547 to 1531) was regarded as a hostile act by some nationalists. The Scottish Patriotic Association (SPA) objected to 'renewed Edwardian aggression' (the first three English Edwards had been among the most hostile of kings towards Scotland). In response, the Bannockburn Day demonstration was begun, a rally still carried on to this day by the SNP. The first rally in 1901 saw David Macrae, SPA President, argue that Edward's adoption of the higher numeral was a symbolic sign of English overlordship, which implicitly claimed suzerainty over Scotland for his English predecessors. This argument dated back to at least the 1690s. Theodore Napier, in his customary pre-Revolution Highland dress, addressed the gathering, kissing his dirk and denying his allegiance to Edward. Subsequently, 1,100 people signed a written protest.

It may be hard to take such theatricals seriously, but they undoubtedly had an effect. The rallies at Bannockburn continued, drawing as many as 15,000 in 1912. The question of regnal numbers, though symbolic, continued to feed the strength of nationalist feeling. The foundation of the Scottish National League, by John Wilson in 1904, was the first effective step towards the National Party for which Napier's journal had called.[107]

The Fiery Cross laid stress on the importance of the Culloden Day commemoration, which Napier had himself instituted. His motto, 'What they fought for, we will work for!' underlined the way in which his nationalism was committed to the Jacobite analysis and experience, a point also made by the publication of mocking songs like 'Our Anglo-German King' in the journal. Napier was not, however, unaware of more realistic contemporary politics, reporting on the First Pan-Celtic Congress in Dublin in August 1901, and expressing with other Scottish patriots his dislike of the Boer War. The Boers were another small nation oppressed by England, as suggested in Napier's equation 'Scotland in 1746=Transvaal in 1901'. He was successful in creating and contributing to an atmosphere where even symbolic political criticisms were taken seriously by a wider group in Scottish society than had hitherto been the case. For example, the Convention of Royal Burghs went so far as to hold a vote on the correctness of the King's title, and although it was upheld by sixty-five votes to six on a division, the act itself was a significant one.[108] The attempt made during Edward's reign to abolish the 'Celtic garb' on active service in the army lent further credence to the nationalist view of him as anti-Scottish, as the wiping out of the last privileges of the Auld Alliance through the Entente Cordiale must also have done. Napier sent a document called 'The Assertion' to the press: a protest concerning the right of 'her Royal and Imperial Highness [Mary IV of Scots] as Heiress of the Houses of Plantagenet and Stuart'. It was no doubt intended merely as an irritant, but Napier also meant it seriously. One of his supporters,

Ida Marie Browne, wrote and released at the same time 'An Open Letter to my Countrymen', which called on the Scots to 'wake again from your indifference into the spirit that animated the brave hearts of 1745'. The ultimate aim of Napier and his supporters might be the restoration of the Stuarts, but in the meantime they lost no time in reiterating what else the Stuart cause meant to Scotland – self-respect and independence. In this they stood in a long line of Jacobite sympathizers, who had emphasized the political aims of the movement at least as much as the interests of the dynasty they supported.[109]

For example, the article by 'Strathgarry' in a 1903 edition of *The Fiery Cross*, while arguing that 'our braw Scottish Thistle . . . has been crushed to the earth by the hoofs of the detestable "House of Hanover"', uses this as a premise, not for agitation on behalf of the Stuarts, but for the establishment of 'A Scottish National Party'. Neo-Jacobitism and nationalism were becoming fused, as Jacobitism and nationalism once had been. As 'Dr Wylie' wrote in the twelfth number of *The Fiery Cross*, 'The past is . . . a vast reservoir of moral force'.[110]

Napier and his colleagues displayed the effects of that force in terms which were to foreshadow many later nationalist complaints. It appears to have been Napier who first understood the connection between Scottish football and transferred nationalist emotions. In an editorial of 1902, he criticizes the neglect of a Scottish Home Rule Bill by Scots who are given 'to swell with pride over a SCOTTISH VICTORY . . . at football'. His journal was also concerned with anti-imperialism and the rights of small European nations, concerns which were to absorb future generations of nationalists in Scotland and abroad. An interest is shown in pacifism, and demand of *The Fiery Cross* for 'The Teaching of Scottish History in Schools' is one still being made in the 1990s. The journal also contains evidence of tension between Scottish and Irish nationalism; then as now, some Irish nationalists regarded Scotland as an exploiting, rather than exploited, nation. As one said of the Scots in a 1905 issue, 'they have won an ignoble peace by acquiescing in the rule of England'.[111]

A more modern understanding of nationalism, shared with the Scottish Patriotic Association, continued to be accompanied by overt Jacobitism. Napier writes of the current Stuart heir, Mary, that she

> had never yet demanded their allegiance. . . . If she did demand her
> right by sword and rifle these would be forthcoming; but they hoped
> that peacefully she might come to the throne of her forefathers.

If not Mary, there would always be others; as the columnist 'Jacobus' (!) remarked, there were 858 members of European royal families closer by blood to the throne than was Edward.[112]

Sacred Jacobite argument and feeling also find a place in the pages of *The Fiery Cross*. In issue 20 (1906), Gavin Scott's article, 'Why I am a Jacobite', is placed next to an extract from the writings of George Lockhart of Carnwath, which compares Scotland's fate to that suffered by the Jews for resisting the Lord's Anointed. At the end of the era of the Clearances, the Jacobite prophecy of perpetual suffering for a disobedient Scotland was confirmed in continuing force. Napier, for all his struggles, which he abandoned to return to Australia in 1912, must have felt that the present was degenerate compared with the past when he saw how small was the band of Jacobites which surrounded him, and how at first not one Clan Society sent a wreath for his annual pilgrimage to Culloden.[113]

He nevertheless achieved much. Notwithstanding his eccentricity and extremism, he successfully introduced an uncompromisingly nationalist note into Scottish political discourse, one firmly linked to the Jacobite inheritance. *The Fiery Cross* probably had a circulation of less than 1,000, and comparable journals were equally small (such as *The Scottish Nationalist* and *The Scottish Patriot*). But though only a few thousand may have read them, many more were involved in or saw reports of Napier's petitions and protests. These had not been carried out as petitionary Home Rule ventures: they were the articulations of a full-blown nationalism which for the first time in a century directly and bitterly criticized the British state. Napier's politics were impossible to realize; but his impossibilist tactics gave nationalism a higher profile. The great sat up and took notice of the SHRA and those such as Napier. As Winston Churchill carefully put it in a speech in Dundee in 1911: 'There is nothing which conflicts with the integration of the United Kingdom in the setting up of a Scottish parliament for the discharge of Scottish business.' It is just possible that at this time one might have been set up, for the Scottish Bill of 1913 passed its second reading in August 1914, 'but then had to be abandoned', for obvious reasons. The same fate befell Irish Home Rule proposals, but in Ireland there was greater demand and greater distrust, and the 1916 Rising ensued.[114]

Many Scots who had been part of the Home Rule movement died in the First World War, which, ironically, was supposed to be about Britain's concern for the rights of small nations. By this time Napier had left the country. His place was taken by the Hon. Stuart Erskine, a fellow neo-Jacobite of the 1890s period, who had been born in Brighton in 1869. After 1900, Erskine 'became passionately absorbed in the Gaelic revival', and owned the paper *Guth na Bliadhna* from 1904 to 1925. Described by one recent historian as a 'Jacobite Catholic Aristocrat', Erskine tried, more intensely perhaps than Napier had done, 'to fuse nationalism to the cause of revolutionary politics'.[115] He is thought to have been behind the 'Scottish Party' programme of 1907. Like other political theorists who accepted the Jacobite analysis, Erskine was both pro-Gaelic and intent on emphasizing the Celtic nature of the Lowlander, 'the English-speaking Celt of the plains', who was to be included in the politics of the patriot Highlander. Erskine had a discernibly stronger pro-Celtic bias than Napier, which appeared in his programme for 'complete national independence, and the restoration to Scotland of her Celtic system of Government and her Celtic culture'. For Erskine, the cultural side of Jacobitism was more important than the restoration of the Stuarts. Like Napier, however, he saw his patriotism bound up with the traditional images of king and nation articulated so skilfully by the Stuart propagandists of an earlier age.[116]

Erskine was one of the few who kept the Home Rule issue alive through the strife of 1914–18, when nearly one in six Scottish servicemen lost their lives. When the new world of 1918 emerged, he was in the forefront of those who carried the national question forward on to the shaky political ground of the 1920s. These years themselves were also to see a renaissance in Scottish literature, which gave a voice to new perceptions of the old traditions of Scottish culture campaigned for by Erskine and Napier.[117]

5

A nation once again?
Scotland since 1918

THE SCOTTISH RENAISSANCE

So long as Scottish literature remained parochial and confined itself to the romantic image of Scotland originating from the work of Robert Burns and Sir Walter Scott; so long as it was seen as an unimportant regional appendage to English literature, it aroused no opposition and little interest.

Duncan Glen

I have no concern with, nor interest in, Charles' faults and failings as an individual. They have not impaired his efficacy as a symbol of the Gaelic Commonwealth Restored.

Hugh MacDiarmid

We must not be deceived by the ridiculous trappings with which our enemies have covered the great tale of the '45. It is a living issue and not a mere dead-end. The coming men will study it and its great men as the real Scotland.

F. W. Robertson

Gregor was taen; Pearse was shot
I' the cauld dawn frae prison;
Wallace they hackit an hung on yetts ...

Jist as aince their sib betrayed
Charles Edward prince o' a cheated race;
Had sold ere this their people's traist
For the Union's faithless peace.

Sydney Goodsir Smith[1]

Hugh MacDiarmid and Wendy Wood, two of twentieth-century Scotland's most prominent nationalist figures, were both born in 1892. One was an innovative radical, and Scotland's most important poet since Burns; the other was a largely traditionalist patriot. Yet in their very different ways both typified Scottish nationalism of the post-1918 era: prickly, individualistic,

134

and given to a continuing reliance on symbolic political gestures in the absence of consistent electoral support. Both supported but ultimately left the SNP, and in this too they were not untypical: the only realistic nationalist political party has often proved an unhappy home for intellectuals with cultural nationalist priorities. Wendy Wood and MacDiarmid both stressed the values of the past, but in different ways. While Wendy Wood was a nationalist of the Napier school with strong neo-Jacobite leanings, Chris Grieve (Hugh MacDiarmid) brought Scotland's historical dilemmas into the twentieth century.[2] He gave a strong alternative voice to a literature which had been long content in large part to echo the cultural agenda set for it by Scott, or else to depart entirely into the realm of fantasy, as in Barrie's plays or MacDonald's novels. MacDiarmid's part in turning this tide remains paramount because of his rehabilitation of Scots as a modern artistic medium.[3]

MacDiarmid was a friend of Erskine's, in whose views the revolutionary John Maclean was also interested. As the Labour Party became increasingly established in British politics, its interest in the smaller theatre of Scottish Home Rule declined. Both Maclean and the ILP were to use the interests of this neglected area, the former spectacularly through revolutionary activity which made him a folk hero to many who never shared his views. In *All Hail, the Scottish Workers' Republic!* (1920), Maclean called for the implementation of ideals which properly belonged to the ideological baggage of Jacobite sympathizers like the aristocratic Erskine, manifested in their modern form during the crofters' struggles of the 1880s. Maclean argues that 'the communism of the clans must be re-established on a modern basis', and that Scots should be 'carrying forward the tradition and instincts of the Celtic race'. Thus was the image of the Highlander as patriot, living in an ideal society opposed to the British world of class and commerce, resurrected in the thought of the modern left.[4]

The heritage of the Jacobite idea of a radical community struggling for liberty against a moneyed oppressor was taken on board in the twentieth century as it had been by Burns at the end of the eighteenth. The nationalist left elaborated it in order to create the idea of the clan system as a specifically Communist one. This undoubtedly grew from the earlier Jacobite view of the clan as a patriotic community of oppressed equals.[5] Nor were those on the left who adopted it unaware of its origins, as Hugh MacDiarmid himself clearly shows in his 1945 article, 'A Scots Communist looks at Bonny Prince Charlie'. Here he criticizes Scottish cultural thinkers who dismiss 'the Forty-Five as a Romantic Dream and Charles as a False Hero'. Instead, and quite remarkably, MacDiarmid suggests that:

There can be no minimising the high significance of a Cause (however romantic and unreal it may seem to those 'practical people' who have brought us to so sorry a pass) which retains such unexhausted evolutionary momentum as to reappear with renewed vitality after being suppressed for a couple of centuries of unparalleled change.

This idea, rightly italicized, is the fruit of the radical reinterpretation of Jacobitism made by some on the nationalist left. In August 1945, Jacobitism was being described as having *'unexhausted evolutionary momentum'*: MacDiarmid was identifying it with what was progressive and radical in Scottish patriotism. He saw it not only as bearing political fruits of loyalty, co-operation, and democratic social organization within a patriotic community, but also as a catalyst for creative artists, 'men like Alasdair MacMhaighstir Alasdair and Iain Ruadh Stiubhairt'. Poetry and politics went together, and MacDiarmid's positive interest in the traditions of the one are matched by the value he gives to the other. A positive interpretation of the past succours the present.[6]

MacDiarmid was to have plenty of opportunity to display this interpretation in the years following 1920. In 1921, a Scottish National League was formed by William Gillies and Angus Clark, in conjunction with Erskine; the Scottish National Convention followed in 1926.[7] At this time, MacDiarmid was publishing *A Drunk Man Looks at the Thistle*, his intense philosophical attempt to provide a modern vehicle for the Scottish vernacular. *A Drunk Man* is suggestive of the kind of Scottish psyche posited by Gregory Smith in 1919, with his famous mention of the 'Caledonian Antisyzygy': an obsession with the past manifested in the present through divisions of judgement between the head and the heart:

> Hauf his soul a Scot maun use
> Indulgin' in illusions
> And hauf in gettin rid o' them
> And comin' to conclusions
> Wi' the demoralisin' dearth
> O' anything worth while on Earth

This is the sterile conflict in which the Scottish past tied to a British present must exist.[8] MacDiarmid's metaphor here is one which connects strongly with the fiction of Scott, who gave expression to this conflict while positing that its results would be fruitful ones. It was Scott who combined in his books the idea of devotion to past illusions, and the necessity of thinking through the consequences of such devotion, eventually discarding it in so far as it was politicized or of contemporary relevance. To Scott, the 'conclusions' were not necessarily demoralizing: they were the historically inevitable partnership of Scotland in the British state. A hundred years later, MacDiarmid is pointing out that Scotland as a psychological entity has not dropped out of existence, and that the conflict Scott assumed would be resolved, in fact continues. In so far as Scotland remains self-consciously Scottish, it experiences a 'demoralisin' dearth' born out of the conflict of past glories and present failures, at the heart of which lies the political question of the Thistle: is Scotland to be perpetually torn in the dialectic of two loyalties, Scottish and British? It cannot abandon its past, as Scott thought it could. But unless that past becomes an *'evolutionary momentum'*, as MacDiarmid characterized Jacobite ideology, it remains barren nostalgia. Only in renewed participation in the developing present can what is past be fertile and potent anew.[9]

MacDiarmid's contribution to that renewed participation was twofold: through his restoration of the potentials of the vernacular, and in his use of the past and its images to describe ways of loosening Scotland from the grip of self-conscious impotence brought on by a celebration of the past which failed to find in it implications for the present. In a poem like 'Separatism', he makes use of the ancient image of the sword as the agency which delivers Scotland from the bondage of (Unionist) worldliness ('a' the warld beside'), and the kind of Unionist prudence eighteenth-century Jacobites had characterized as corruption:

> If there's a sword-like sang
> That can cut Scotland clear
> O' a' the warld beside
> Rax me the hilt o't here,
>
> For there's nae jewel till
> Frae the rest o' earth it's free
> Wi' the starry separateness
> I'd fain to Scotland gie

MacDiarmid attempts to find this 'starry separateness' in himself, so that he can divorce his voice from the role of mere complaint and celebrate the potentialities of Scotland. One of the methods he adopts in this is to locate poetic voices of the past, and write as if through their understanding, compounded with his own. These voices can be Jacobite ones:

> I was a bard in Alba and Eire
> Two hundred years ago.
> Michael Comyn was one of my friends
> Who was two men, you know,
> A Protestant buck outside
> And a Jacobite at heart, . . .
> And I wish I had half his skill
> In the poet's art,
> Yet I treat the way that he trod . . .
>
> At every Cross in Scotland I pause,
> Crying (in Scots) like O'Heffernan

The situation of being 'A Protestant buck outside/And a Jacobite at heart' was one forced on many Scots in the eighteenth century, as MacDiarmid knew.[10] The tradition he is adopting here is one which can free the experiences of the past to teach the present. O'Heffernan, to whom MacDiarmid compares himself, was an Irish Jacobite poet of the eighteenth century. Together with another poet, O'Sullivan, he was used by Yeats to form the basis of his character Red Hanrahan. Here MacDiarmid is following Yeats's practice of using the past (particularly the myths of the Celtic past and the poetry of the Irish Jacobites) as a voice to express the nationalist concerns of the present.[11] To Yeats, the deposition of James II saw the end of Celtic civilization in Ireland;[12] as a poet, MacDiarmid on occasion followed this lead when discussing Scotland. His reference to Jacobite poems of exile, like 'The Wandering Hawk', and his habit of quoting and translating Scottish Jacobite verse shows his fascination with the topic.[13]

The story of Jacobitism had long since convinced its hearers that the Forty-Five was a brilliant flash of national patriotism, cruelly smothered at Culloden. The romanticization in the early nineteenth century had helped also to suggest that the Rising was the last such manifestation. On the other hand, for those who had inherited the older Jacobite tradition and its analysis, the possibility of reawakening the spirit of the Forty-Five was always there, and this was to be explicitly shown by the use of the Rising as a positive symbol during the early development of the SNP. Such a thing was romantic nonsense to those who accepted the version of Jacobitism so brilliantly popularized by Scott, but it continued to be vital to those who did not. MacDiarmid was aware of the inheritance of both traditions: that of the nationalists of left and right, and that of the sterile tartanry which comprised the power of the Stuart myth to many people, to whom distance lent the only legitimate enchantment to the Jacobite cause:

> And Charlie o' the gowden heid
> Won little support till he was deid
> And maist that's left's frae folks wha'd tak'
> The ither side gin he cam' back.

The poet is well aware how far the images of the Forty-Five are now the sentimental preserve of Tory Unionism. Such 'Jacobites', MacDiarmid says, replace patriotism for their country's present with an exaggerated and false devotion to its past, a past which, they have assured themselves, cannot repeat itself:

> A isna gowd that glitters
> And weel I mind ane came
> And kindled in oor lyart hills
> What look't like livin' flame.
>
> Tho' a's no' gowd that glitters
> He keeps his meed o' fame.

> It's easier to lo'e Prince Chairlie
> Than Scotland – mair's the shame![14]

Gold is of course what Scotland preferred to the Stuarts in the Jacobite analysis. Charlie's metaphorical gold did not glitter because his countrymen preferred the real thing. Elsewhere, MacDiarmid opposes to this lifeless commercialism a more fertile and enduring symbol of the Jacobite cause to express his feeling of being 'companioned by an irrecoverable past,/By a mystical sense of such a destiny foregone':

> The rose of all the world is not for me.
> I want for my part
> Only the little white rose of Scotland
> That smells sharp and sweet – and breaks the heart.

The white rose is an unequivocally Jacobite symbol, and the association of that Jacobite symbol with the identity of the country as a whole ('the little white rose of Scotland') is one which stands foursquare in the tradition of the propagandists, poets, and singers of the eighteenth century.[15] MacDiarmid and Compton Mackenzie, otherwise nationalists of very different beliefs, shared interest in and respect for this central symbol, as did Wendy Wood, who grew in her back garden a cutting from the white rose Charles Edward picked a flower from at Fassifern. MacDiarmid saw the classless Scottish spirit as deriving from the clan structure iconically opposed by the Jacobites to the class-based structure of the British state. Mackenzie's understanding was a more aristocratic and patriarchal one, yet both men could use the party symbol of Jacobite loyalty as a metaphor for Scotland as a whole. Indeed, Jacobite ideas were in the air in the 1920s and 1930s as they had not been for many years. Even Lewis Grassic Gibbon, himself no nationalist, was able to say, 'I like the thought of a Scots Catholic Kingdom with Mr. Compton Mackenzie Prime Minister to some disinterred Jacobite royalty.'[16] Grassic Gibbon, though he had generally little time for Jacobitism, regarded Charles Edward as a Scottish patriot. The images of the eighteenth century continued to have their effect.

It is noteworthy that as renewed Jacobite interest manifested itself in nationalistic terms, the 'official' version of Jacobitism began to retreat from the romanticizations of the nineteenth century, and Charles began to be increasingly evaluated to his discredit by those unwilling or unable to read Jacobitism positively.[17] It is hard to resist the thought that modern attempts (now perhaps on the decline) to discredit the Jacobites and the leadership of the Forty-Five were perhaps in part an ideological reaction to the fact that Charles Edward was once again being taken politically seriously. Jacobitism had long before adjusted its symbols to national feeling so well that any renewed interest in nationalism was bound to take note of it, and perhaps even to understand the national question in part through its eyes. This was especially true given the role Jacobite ideology had had in the development of the myths of Bruce and Wallace.

The idea of a Jacobite kingdom as 'Catholic', mentioned by Grassic Gibbon, sheds an interesting light on another way in which the Scottish renaissance, many of whose writers were more involved in the mythopoeic past than MacDiarmid, shared the Jacobite world-view. The idea that the Reformation had been bad for art and bad for Scottish independence (since the reformers of the sixteenth century looked to England rather than the Auld Alliance, France of course remaining Catholic) became widespread at this time (the 1920s and 1930s) and remains current to this day. Criticism had been made of Calvinism in the past, but seldom (save by the Jacobites) so localized and defined in political terms. This kind of view was bound to be sympathetic towards the Stuarts. Mary had resisted the Reformation's progress; James VI had tried to dilute its effects; Charles I, Charles II, and James VII had all sought a religious settlement hostile to the interests of Presbyterian Calvinism. In exile, the Stuart kings had taken refuge in France and then Italy. The Stuarts were Catholics and Scottish patriots, inimical to Calvinism and in favour of the Auld Alliance. Renewed sympathy with their cause was an obvious concomitant of hostility towards the Scottish Reformation, intensified by the fact that they had also been a dynasty supremely favourable to the arts.[18]

Edwin Muir, the poet who was MacDiarmid's contemporary and nearest rival in stature, is one of the writers most closely associated with the anti-Reformation point of view, most pithily expressed in the modern nationalist sentiment of strangling the last minister with the last copy of the *Sunday Post*. Muir, although in most respects a nationalist, could never escape from the Redgauntlet-like feeling that the Cause was lost for ever – Scotland's, as well as that of the Stuarts.[19] As he himself wrote of Redgauntlet in *Scott and Scotland* (1936):

> Redgauntlet . . . seems to incarnate, against his will, Scott's conviction that Scotland was bound to lose its nationality, and that Scottish manners and character must unavoidably melt and dissolve into those of England.[20]

This view is close to Muir's own. In his largely fatalistic poetry, Muir accuses the Reformation of having for ever destroyed Scotland's ability to be 'a tribe, a family, a people'; he declares that the divisions it brought to Scotland helped to 'fell the ancient oak of loyalty' (the Stuart cause and badge), and replace it with the 'Golden Calf' of Presbyterian mercantilism which put money before independence. A similar position is put forward in Muir's *John Knox: Portrait of a Calvinist*; but it is in his poetry, particularly in poems like 'Scotland 1941', 'The Incarnate One', and 'Scotland's Winter', that the heart of his argument lies. For Muir, the victory of Calvinism/commercialism has crucified Scotland – and there may be no resurrection. Though distinguished by a twentieth-century sensibility and a Modernist sense of crisis, Muir's case is in essence that which would have been made by a Jacobite apologist of two centuries before. Like Napier and the Jacobite anti-imperialists, Muir links Scotland's fate with the fate of small nations everywhere, as in his famous poem, 'The Combat'. It is the 'kingdom lost/Sleeping with folded wings', like Fionn and the Fianna in the mountains near Inverness, an image of a heroic past which may never be found again.[21]

Few writers of this or later periods were prepared to adopt such a definitively elegiac note as did Muir. But those who sought in the past the answers to the problems of the present frequently shared his hostile attitude to the Reformation, as did William Soutar and Fionn MacColla, the latter of whom thought 'that the effects of the Reformation in Scotland have been wholly catastrophic'. MacColla was sympathetic to a view emerging among Scottish historians: that in the Wars of Independence, Scotland owed her freedom to the Catholic clergy.[22] But he was scathing towards the established historical views about Jacobitism, attacking historians who 'wrote with arrogant finality (and in total error) about the aims of the Jacobites without taking the trouble to learn a single word of the language in which these aims were clearly set forth [Gaelic]'.[23]

John Lorne Campbell's *Highland Songs of the Forty-Five* attempted to remedy this kind of deficiency when it appeared in 1933. Campbell chose a selection of Gaelic songs and poems from the prominent poets of the Forty-Five period with a view to rebutting the long-standing Whig argument (still alive then – and now) that the Highlanders had been unaware of the cause in which they were fighting, and had gone with Charles as much for plunder or under pressure as for any reasons connected with Jacobite belief.[24] In choosing a selection of poems which rebutted this argument, Campbell became one of the first modern anthologists to use the Jacobite song for ideological statement, and to recognize its political potential. Although the field of Jacobite song was still largely dominated by sentimentalists like Harold Boulton (who wrote the words to the Skye Boat song), Campbell's attempt to make Jacobite literature speak for itself once again was significant in the sympathetic context of the renaissance period.

Campbell's demonstration of the purity of purpose of the Jacobite Gaels implicitly aligns itself with Muir and MacColla's view, (and, indeed, the traditional view) of the Lowlands as a corrupt seat of commerce and cash interests. As Alan Bold later put it, 'Lowland commercial interests . . . betray the concept of one Scottish nation'. Thus the ideological understanding of Union made available by the Jacobites 225 years earlier continues to develop (in tandem with the radical idea of the Highlander as the patriot of an egalitarian Republican society, itself a Jacobite image) up to the present day.[25] John McGrath's *The Cheviot, the Stag, and the Black, Black Oil* is only one of the more spectacular evolutions of this view, though McGrath, as might be expected, concentrates more on the corruptions of capitalism than those of Calvinism. Yet many writers (Max Weber not least) in Scotland and elsewhere have seen these as linked. The Jacobite association of commerce with the Presbyterian central belt which had betrayed the nation in 1707 was one revived in the twentieth century by economic historian, nationalist, and socialist alike. The Clearances had reinforced this case, and economic exile was still continuing – 630,000 Scots left Scotland between 1911 and 1921, besides those killed in the War.[26] The Jacobites had prophesied a Scotland drained and impoverished to pay for English imperialism. They mourned and celebrated the theme of exile, political or economic, which underlined this prophecy. These themes, of exile and commercialism, passed into the Jacobite heritage, conjoined with a sense of overwhelming loss, reinforced by the exile of the Stuarts and their supporters, the Union, the Clearances, and last but not least the oppressiveness of a Victorian sentimentalism which chose to emphasize the lost nature of all Scottish causes for its own cultural purposes.[27] Its propaganda was pervasive. In the twentieth century, even the politicians ostensibly committed to Scottish Home Rule acted as if that commitment was a sentimental one, an item always on the agenda, but implemented only in the dying fall of its own non-performance, a non-performance in which many Scots acquiesced.

But the 'Scots Renaissance is/Pro-tartan and pro-Catholic', and as such was able to recapture the symbols of the sentimentalists to use as icons of renewal.[28] However much the anti-Union symbolism of the tartan was debased, the power of such symbols was never quite extinct. Nor by the 1920s and 1930s was the interest of a Jacobite understanding of Scotland's situation limited to oddball enthusiasts, or eccentric campaigners like Theodore Napier. MacDiarmid aligned the Union with the demands of capitalism, as the Jacobites had done:

> International Finance is bent upon destroying the sub-conscious (the race memory) of all peoples and making them incapable of creative reaction against the Zeitgeist. Everything is to be sacrificed to the illusion of Progress.

This is what had happened in Scotland; this article, 'Wider aspects of Scottish nationalism', appeared in the November 1927 issue of the new *Scots Independent*.

Other early issues of this paper commented favourably on Jacobitism and Episcopalianism as patriotic movements, and contained some of the earliest articles to display an understanding of the malign influence of the sentimental cult of the nineteenth century on Scots' understanding of themselves:

> This 'Highland' cult is amusing, and it is exasperating. Like British Israelism it gives no heed to history, anthropology, or philology. Originating about a century ago, fathered by Sir Walter Scott and

Stewart of Garth (mother unknown), it has been fostered ever since by our military and feudal caste, tartan kilt-makers, sellers of souvenirs and advertisers of whisky.[29]

In contrast to such critical comment is other discussion as to whether a united front of Jacobites and nationalist Whigs would have been possible, and rhetorical questions which display strong sympathy for the Jacobites:

What inscription was on so many of the flashing swords that greeted the raising of the standard? 'Prosperity to Scotland and *No Union*!'

Other articles at this period include 'The great marquess', an attempt to claim Montrose as a nationalist, and 'The white rose of Scotland', which urges the adoption of the Jacobite badge as national symbol: 'Who will dare to laugh at Scotland of the White Rose?'[30] This was very much the line adopted by MacDiarmid and Compton Mackenzie. In his symptomatic *Prince Charlie*, published in 1932, the year after he was elected nationalist Lord Rector of Glasgow University, Mackenzie argues a utopian Jacobite position. Should Charles have won, he suggests,

The American colonies would never have been lost. The French Revolution might never have happened, for it is not outside possibility that Charles would have become in fact as he still was in theory King of France too. The long martyrdom of Ireland would have been averted. The decline of Scotland into a provincial appendage would have been avoided. Religious toleration would have been achieved long before it was. There might have been no exploitation of the poor by cynical industrialism.

This kind of Jacobite triumphalism is as remarkable as it was not untypical of nationalist sympathizers in the 1930s: 'the loss of the White Cockade must bring ruin upon Scotland', and in their view it had done. As one reviewer remarked, 'such ardent admiration as Mr. Mackenzie's will help to fan the fascination again to a red glow'.[31] Mackenzie's admiration was certainly ardent, but he was only one enthusiast among many. William Power, F. W. Robertson, and D. H. MacNeill were only a few of those who wrote in sympathy with the Jacobites. William Power in particular was influential, being of those who associated Scotland's fate with the success of the Reformation. With others he attempted (in some degree successfully) to roll back the stifling influence of sentimentality on Scottish culture and identity. What he replaced it with was also rooted in the past:

writers, such as William Power . . . [were] an important social influence in Scotland, because under their guidance a whole generation grew up which took for granted as their cultural milieu a sort of romantic Scottish patriotism based on dialect stories, the cult of Bonnie Prince Charlie, Burns [etc.] . . . .[32]

143

Like Napier, however, Power was at times politically shrewd, and up with, and even ahead of the times. His 1947 article in *Scottish Opinion* argued for 'A United States of Europe with Scotland taking a leading role in the championing of smaller nations', a theme which was to be the subject of much discussion within the SNP over the next fifteen years.[33]

F. W. Robertson, a research student at Edinburgh University in the late 1920s and an expert on Jacobite literature, was perhaps the most outspoken of these writers in his conflation of Jacobitism and nationalism:

> The blether about the romance of the '45 obscures the real movement, which demanded a free Scotland. . . . We must not be deceived by the ridiculous trappings with which our enemies have covered the great tale of the '45.

Robertson followed on from Napier and Erskine in making a positive reading of Jacobitism central to Scottish patriotism.[34]

The influence of writers and artists on non-Communist western society has been increasingly doubted and diminished in the twentieth century. It is hard to evaluate the impact of the Scottish renaissance on Scottish society, but to the question 'How much?' we can answer 'More as time went on'. But what is perhaps more important than the extent of its influence is the cultural prestige it returned to a Scottish identity under pressure from reductive sentimentalism. Moreover, writers like MacDiarmid were far more confident of articulating identities in ideological terms than earlier poets or novelists had been. Scotland's literary awakening after 1918 helped to compensate for the political failures of pre-1914 Home Rule agitation. It provided a more coherent view of Scotland's role in the modern world than had been available from the NAVSR, the SHRA, or the neo-Jacobites. Yet despite this new articulateness and complexity, the Jacobite analysis remained vital to the political statements of the Scottish renaissance. The developing understanding, on both left and right, of Scotland's political position still had room for the old nostrum, even as it found itself a more modern form of political expression in the first major vehicle for independence since the Jacobites, the Scottish National Party.

THE RISE OF THE SNP TO 1945

> The aim of the Prince's men in 1745 is still our aim in 1946 – a free Scotland.
>
> F. W. Robertson

> We do not want to be, like the Greeks, powerful and prosperous wherever we settle, but with a dead Greece behind us. We do not

want to be like the Jews of the Dispersion – a potent force everywhere
on the globe, but with no Jerusalem.

John Buchan, 1932

Now is the time when we should stop and turn, look upon our land
with affection and devotion, with a warm promise without either
boasting or threats, and unsheathe the blade of our hot spirit.

George Campbell Hay, 'Feachd a' Phrionnsa' ('The Prince's Army')[35]

Throughout the 1920s, the political scene was rapidly changing. Ireland
became a Free State, the Liberal Party collapsed, and Labour formed its
first, minority, governments, forgetting its commitment to Scottish Home
Rule in the process. In Scotland, an increasingly separate political culture
was being articulated by artists, nationalists, and journals like the *Scottish
Review* and *Guth na Bliadhna*, which had survived the First World War.
Post-war activity led to the foundation of Lewis Spence's Scottish Nationalist
Movement of 1926. Two years later, on 23 June 1928 (Bannockburn Day)
the National Party of Scotland (NPS) was inaugurated at Stirling. Napier's
dream was at length realized.[36]

Nationalism in Scotland had been less affected by the Irish struggle of
1916–21 than might be supposed. Those who were influenced generally belonged to the ranks of the artistic cultural nationalists, men like
MacDiarmid and Neil Gunn, who wrote articles on Pearse for the *Scots
Independent*, which emphasized that the Irish patriot had had 'to go back
through the centuries to find its [Ireland's] golden age'. Pearse's use of the
past in the politics of the present did not go unnoticed by those with similar
aims in Scotland.[37] His cult of Cuchulain, and the mythologizing of Yeats and
others, were refracted in the pattern of mythopoeic explorations undertaken
by the writers of the Scottish renaissance. Naturally a dispossessed nation
would look to its past for validation; but the mystic, mythic understanding
of the past evident in some of the work of Muir, Gunn, Goodsir Smith, and
Mitchison among others was and is evidence of a particular way of looking
at the past, one not unrelated to that made available in the period of the
Celtic Twilight, which itself had proved so influential on Irish nationalism.[38]
In a Scottish context, this mythic viewpoint frequently incorporated the
anti-Presbyterian (and by implication pro-Jacobite) nationalist view. When
Eric Linklater stood as the National Party candidate in the East Fife
by-election of February 1933, he

> devised a policy for Scotland based upon a model combining the Court
> of King James IV with Edinburgh in the eighteenth century, incor-
> porating certain Norse and Celtic values, and ignoring 'the cultural
> blight of Presbyterianism and the industrial revolution'. . . . During his
> discussions . . . he had found himself more than once quoting a dictum

of the German critic and poet Herder: 'Study the superstitions and the sagas of the forefathers.' That was what Yeats and Synge had done.[39]

Linklater later turned against nationalism because of what he felt to be the incompetence of its leaders. Perhaps, however, his disenchantment reflected a more deep-seated reaction among the artists and writers who had supported nationalist points of view in the 1920s. Their disparate vision, heavily dependent upon history, could have no central place in the political programme of a modern small party of respectable intentions, which was what nationalism was to evolve into during the 1930s. MacDiarmid himself scorned the NPS as a mere secretariat, and remained suspicious of bourgeois nationalist priorities.

This may have been an over-reaction, but there is little doubt that the Scottish National Party, which grew out of the NPS and the more culturally nationalist Scottish Party in a 1934 merger, has long remained suspicious of the cultural nationalism of which it was the inheritor. Indeed, one modern historian has gone so far as to say that 'So far as the S.N.P. is concerned the Scottish renaissance might never have occurred.' This view finds an echo among Scottish writers to the present day: 'Certainly in the past, the SNP's neglect of the Scottish heritage has been shameful. The party has tended to adopt purely political arguments, which ... is a spiritually bankrupt approach.'[40] Neo-Jacobitism, anti-Presbyterianism, and traditionally-based cultural nationalism, which had begun the agitation for Scottish liberties, appear to have been regarded as political liabilities by the centrist, provincial middle-class party to which they gave birth. Subsequently, the SNP had proved jittery in the face of any recrudescence of the Theodore Napier spirit, whether in the guise of Wendy Wood's Patriots, the 1320 Club, or more recently, Siol Nan Gaidheal.[41] No matter how small or ineffective such organizations may be, proscription is a course not infrequently adopted. The concern displayed at the annual conference in 1979 over a tiny group known as 'The White Rose' is only one of the more recent signs of hostility shown by the SNP to that strain in nationalism which dates to the Jacobite era. As Lewis Spence remarked after the Midlothian by-election of 1929, some of the nationalists harked back to 'a Jacobite restoration', while others wanted to restore the Auld Alliance and turn the clock back to before the Reformation. Such apparent eccentrics were a potential embarrassment; the strange thing was that so many intellectuals were of their number. The Jacobite analysis was still a potent force, reinforced by the the domination of the past in Irish nationalism and by the concerns of the Scottish renaissance.[42] Nor was it even in the twentieth century entirely divorced from the surviving Stuart dynasty. At the end of the 1970s, members of both Siol Nan Gaidheal and the Scottish Patriots were fêting a Jacobite pretender, who claimed to be the legitimate descendant of Charles Edward Stuart. At a soirée held on 16 June 1979, and attended by Wendy Wood and Lady Compton Mackenzie among others, he was introduced as 'seventh Count of Albany and head of the House of Stewart'. After initial social success here and elsewhere, he was eventually suspected of fraudulence by a history student at Glasgow University, and appeared to vanish from the scene.[43]

Literary nationalism came under attack in the 1920s and 1930s, and the cry that the nationalists were 'simply irresponsible poets and papists' gained ground. The National Party, 'committed to tackling the Scottish heartland rather than the Celtic fringe', felt it could not afford to be seen to grant too much credence to such elements. At the end of the 1920s, Erskine had seen which way the wind was blowing. For him, the literary and cultural nationalists were at the heart of nationalism. Like Wendy Wood, he did not believe that Scotland would ever achieve independence through fighting to get MPs elected to Westminster. He left Scotland for France in 1930, never to return.[44]

Though many little magazines came and went, the Scots Independent remained at the heart of the cultural nationalist argument in the pre-war years. W. G. Blaikie Murdoch, a veteran neo-Jacobite and president of the Edinburgh branch of the Scots National League in 1925–6, helped to found the paper. When a majority of the League subsequently agreed to join the National Party, the paper went with them. During the 1930s and 1940s, it continued to contain many articles from the messianic school of Jacobitism:

> We feel as if it were yesterday that the prince passed; that he was at Prestonpans, invaded England . . . the glamour of his presence is with us still. Loyal Highlanders support him, children strew his way with flowers . . . the tax gatherer looks askance at the passing of heroes.[45]

The last line echoes both the sacred and anti-commercial strains in Jacobite ideology. The entrance of Charles into Edinburgh is likened to that of Christ into Jerusalem.

Nationalism of this kind continued to flourish throughout the 1930s. Although somewhat bereft of a detailed cultural agenda, organizations like Clan Scotland, the 'Youth Section of the National Party of Scotland', reflected the persistent ideal of the Highlander as patriot: 'Clan Scotland wishes to train clansmen how to LIVE FOR THEIR COUNTRY'. Clan Scotland disavowed any comparison between itself and the militant street politicians of Italy or Germany, though some analogies could doubtless be drawn. Unlike these, however, it was fairly ineffective, and does not appear to have equalled the 40,000 members of the Welsh Youth Movement, despite its boast to be 'the Political Army of the National Party', sporting as its insignia two crossed broadswords and a targe. Jacobite symbolism had not been forgotten.[46]

The influence of the Jacobite period could be seen in a different way in John MacCormick's arguments for a 'New National Covenant', which began in around 1930. The idea of patriotic Scots forming a compact to disassociate themselves from the policies imposed by an English government was one which dated back to 1638, and various supportive articles in the

Scots Independent emphasized the nationalist aspects of the Covenant-ers. MacCormick was in part successful, his Covenant of 1950–2 which demanded Home Rule being a symbol of the seventeenth century dragged into the twentieth. (MacCormick's ancestors, incidentally, were Jacobites who fought at Killiecrankie and Sherriffmuir, on what his son describes as 'our side'.)[47] The Covenant idea was perhaps the reply of a moderate centrist like MacCormick to the more vociferous extremists of cultural nationalism. The militancy of 1936, when Welsh nationalists made an arson attack on an RAF base, and the Wallace sword was removed from Stirling by masked men (this happened again in 1971), could seem a diversion from the serious attempt to gain Home Rule. Such symbolic nationalist actions, though still psychologically powerful, could be seen by the SNP as belonging to a past which in the long term would have to be abandoned if serious electoral progress was to be made.[48]

It was being made at this time, albeit slowly. Although Linklater got barely 1,000 votes in Fife, the NPS took a sixth of the vote in Kilmarnock, and in 1936 Andrew Dewar Gibb, standing as the SNP candidate for the Scottish Universities, got 14 per cent. In 1931, the NPS had 8,000 members, and throughout the 1930s, it and the successor SNP continued successfully. Government response was limited but tangible. In 1939 the Scottish Office was moved to Edinburgh, while nationalist successes continued throughout the war, culminating in victory at the Motherwell by-election of 1945, which marked the highpoint and the end of the 1930s surge.[49]

Votes cast apart, the SNP were also successful in attracting moderate opinion towards some degree of Home Rule, as John MacCormick hoped. Straw polls indicated a majority in favour of greater Scottish autonomy, and middle-class opinion was instrumental in setting up the National Trust for Scotland (1931) and the Saltire Society (1936), as well as other similar bodies. These organizations displayed a degree of interest in the past traditions of Scotland greater than that now to be evinced by the National Party proper. Mythopoeic renditions of interpretations dependent on or similar to the Jacobite analysis remained popular among artists and writers. The idea of 'Reformation as a surrender of the idea of community', adopted by Neil Gunn, Edwin Muir, and others, was one major aspect of the intellectualization of a fundamentally traditionalist Jacobite position. Neil Gunn remained loyal to the SNP, being Vice-Chair of the party in 1942, and a contributor to its funds till 1970. He thought that defeat for the nationalists would be 'Scotland's final Culloden'.[50] But the SNP continued to move away from the mythopoeic cultural nationalist tradition, even when parallels could be drawn with the success of similar ideologies in Ireland: 'As Cuchulain, single-handedly, defended the marches of ancient Uladh, so Wallace . . . defended his native land.' Hugh MacDiarmid's reaction to the SNP's continuing drift away from the images of the Scottish Renaissance was a strong one:

> In all other countries I know of where independence has been gained
> or regained the necessary impulse came from poets or other artists. . . .
> I have no use for any Scottish Nationalist movement that is not above
> all concerned with the position of Scottish culture.

This reaction was shared among both traditionalist and radical intellectuals.[51]

It might be expected that those who were marginalized by the political
drift of the SNP should adopt these arguments, but less obviously partial
commentators have also made the same points:

> The most significant single feature of the new S.N.P. policy [in 1946]
> was the total omission of a section on Scottish culture. The S.N.P.
> was to be a party fighting for the small man. . . . By shunning
> intellectuals . . . the party is forced to rely upon men who are by
> definition hostile to the state and incapable of understanding how it
> is run . . . as town councillors or parliamentary candidates they are
> often incredibly inept.

This damning assessment of the SNP's failure to address the issues of
traditionalist nationalism is a reflection of a direction effectively taken in
the 1930s: to repudiate the neo-Jacobites and Gaelic Communists, often able
people, in favour of a respectability which has often proved chimerical in
terms of political advantage.[52]

The early stages of modern Scottish nationalism were built on the foun-
dations of an understanding of the past which owed much to the Jacobite
analysis. The activities of men such as Aytoun and Napier, combined with
those of the crofting activists, the SHRA, and even of radicals such as
Maclean and MacDiarmid, had been of a kind which sought at least some of
the answers for Scotland's present in Scotland's past. This was less facile than
blaming the English, and less transient than arguments primarily economic
in scope, or based on temporary and often illusory political advantage. The
ideologies of the seventeenth and eighteenth centuries remained alive. As
Compton Mackenzie put it in 1931, 'The Cavalier spirit and ideals can
never die.' The idea of Gaelic communism was only one of the many
strange ways in which the twentieth century adopted these ideals to suit
itself.[53]

A STRANGE SURVIVAL

In the armed Risings of 1715 and 1745 a great part of the following
achieved in Scotland by the Stuart claimants to the throne came from
the Jacobite Party's appeal to Scottish patriotism and their definite
pledge to abrogate the Treaty of Union of 1707.
Scottish Claim of Right to the United Nations, 1947

To all ... Jacobites ... may be applied the ancient words: – 'They were stoned, they were sawn asunder, were tempted, were slain with the sword, they wandered about in sheep-skins and goat-skins, being destitute, afflicted, tormented. They wandered in deserts and in mountains, and in dens and caves of the earth. Of whom this world was not worthy ...' But we must be worthy of them ... shoulder to shoulder, sons of the Gael.

Scots Independent, 16 January 1965

The dizzying snow blossomed against his face.
He was the ghost so powder-white and dumb.
Iain Crichton Smith, 'Prince Charles'[54]

The Second World War was a momentous crisis in international affairs. The issues raised following its conclusion were hardly less momentous. The atom bomb had been dropped; Europe was divided between power blocs with non-European power bases; and the British Empire, of which Scotland was so much art and part, began a process of dissolution signalled by the independence of India in 1947. The Britishness of Scotland was increasingly less of a proud boast to be able to make: and in the 1960s, Scots began to demonstrate electoral discontent with the state in which they were bound as junior partners.[55]

More wonderful than this was the persistence of the Stuart myth in Scottish literature and the productions of the Scottish consciousness. Much of its manifestation demonstrated that the divisions of the seventeenth century were still alive. Prince Charles Edward was portrayed as would-be hero or drunken villain, depending on the writer's own political point of view. Even serious historians were locked in partisan judgements.[56] Jacobitism continued to be a talismanic subject in literature, history, and popular culture. In the very month the war ended, Hugh MacDiarmid's leading article on Charles Edward spread over the entire front page of the *Scots Independent*, recalling not the end of six years' war in Europe, but the two hundredth anniversary of the Raising of the Standard at Glenfinnan.[57]

The continued use of Jacobite symbolism in commercial contexts showed not only its power in the marketplace, but also the degree to which it had been conflated with the Scottish identity. Like that identity, it was a source of fascination. Historians and laymen alike continued to argue over whether Charles would have been successful had he marched on from Derby; and, more recently, the radical side of Jacobitism has attracted attention also.[58]

These interests were not limited in any way to the antiquarianism of a professional intelligentsia. Books on the Jacobites did not drip unevenly into the marketplace, to be read by students and intellectuals. Rather they sold fiercely; so fiercely, that they were written and published at a pace

150

which far outstripped new discoveries or understandings of the Prince and his period. He was still a cult, still an icon, still a dream forgone, or a false lure in the eyes of those who saw him as a failure and his cause as inadequate. But whatever was said in praise or dispraise of the Jacobites, there were always sharp answers which tended the other way: and the very controversy of the subject reflected its endurance in the Scottish psyche. The myth was powerful, and even in the interwar period, Episcopalian children were still brought up to think of Charles as their rightful king. Even in the 1980s, anti-Home Rule books such as *Is There a Scottish Solution?* (1988) take pains to rebut what are seen as the nationalist pretensions of the Jacobites.[59]

There have, of course, been two sides to Jacobitism since the early nineteenth century. Scott's idea of Jacobitism as the quintessentially lost cause has led many to adopt a *post hoc ergo propter hoc* diagnosis which emphasizes the inevitability of Jacobitism's defeat. This is still common today.[60] But such a point of view underestimates the strength of the Jacobites in the eighteenth century, and the diverse nature of their support. Most importantly, it neglects the ideology of Jacobitism, which offered a continuingly relevant critique concerning the position of Scotland within the post-1707 state, as well as being a potent myth-creator and 'myth-kitty' for the Scottish identity.[61]

The constitutional strength of the Revolution Settlement generated its own imperial British myths which long obscured through mockery or neglect the positive critique offered by Jacobite ideology. We are all inheritors of the constitutional upheavals of 1688–1707, and the highly-centralized state, inimical to religious (at first) and political autonomy, which the victors of these upheavals generated. Dedicated to Empire and the fight against France, post-Revolution Britain drifted towards imperialist war and power. History is always written by the winners in the first instance; and the idea that Jacobitism was a fruitless and sentimental reactionary struggle which at best displayed only wrong-headed loyalty among Scots who would have been better off being killed by the French is a typical invention of the constitutional victors in the post-1688 era.[62] The increasing religious freedom James had given, in Ireland and elsewhere, was dismantled after 1690; the Scottish Estates abolished in 1707; and the Cornish parliament lost after 1714, though Cornwall retained more parliamentary representation than Scotland. The centralizing nature of the post-1688 settlement is clear. Combined with a battery of repressive religious and secular legislation, it could be seen to make a mockery of the Revolution's claim to be establishing a freer and more tolerant society. Freer for whom, when millions suffered from religious disabilities (some extreme), and when there were 200 capital offences in English law?[63]

As a critique of these victors, Jacobite ideology had much to offer. The settlement to which it objected still raises controversial issues in our lives today. Even the language of the eighteenth century on occasion persists. The radical writer Tom Nairn recalls a man leaving the cinema after a showing of *Kind Hearts and Coronets* while the National Anthem was still playing. He answered a remonstrance in his broad Scots accent with the words, 'Damned if I'll stand still for *the Electress of Hanover*'.[64]

But Scott's evaluation of Jacobitism has also remained strong. The quotation from Iain Crichton Smith which heads this section is indicative of the dual, divided way in which the Stuart legacy can be viewed, both positively and negatively. The contradictory images of snow and blossom, ghost and living man, can be seen as displaying this division. Is, or was, Jacobitism a life-force and source of renewal for Scotland? Or a dangerous, dead myth? Yet the very fact that this uncertainty continues, and conflicting views are still expressed, shows a vitality in the Stuart myth's power over the Scottish imagination. In Naomi Mitchison's novel, *The Bull Calves*, the author's image of 'the Prince is . . . based on . . . the year-king'. She writes of Prince Charles Edward as 'the king who dies for his people; the Frazerian figure who enshrines . . . the solidarity of the defeated and the oppressed, and the persistence of the values of love and imagination which history has spurned'.[65] Although reservations emerge concerning this view, the reappearance of eighteenth-century Jacobite mythic propaganda in the twentieth century is significant: 'the old symbols and their regenerating forms remain potent.'[66] The sense of loss around which so much Scottish art and thought foregathers is one in which the loss of the Stuarts, and, as importantly, the Scotland they represented in Jacobite propaganda, is as central as Union itself. The recreation of the mentalities of the past, and the adoption and inheritance of traditional iconographies and discourses, reinforce that sense. Even names can carry ancient dynastic echoes. As George MacBeth writes in 'My Christian Name':

> To be George? . . . I dislike it, a hint of *Georgic*, rustic as bees. Too stupid, bumbling, to be a firm name. And too redolent of the Georges, the end of the Jacobite expectations in the white noise of the '45. I hear the death rattle of cockades. . . . Even now, [from the site of Culloden] the tourists will walk away dejected, as if defeated.

The idea that the Stuarts were tempted to take up the English throne and then betrayed by England, ahistorical though it is, is also found, for example in Tom Scott's 'Fergus II: Scotland 1967':

> A Stewart capital aa thae years afore
> England tempit their House to suicide
> In yon fell trap they set aside the Thames

Scott goes on to link the betrayal of Scotland by England with a radical view related to the Jacobite analysis of the eighteenth century:

> The English landlord squats upon the neck
> That English kings could never bow for long

But Union has condemned Scotland to the economic tyranny of English capital and imperialism.[67]

On occasion the Jacobite legacy is symbolically appropriated by the modern left. Ailie Munro, in *The Folk Music Revival in Scotland*, tells us that 'The Glasgow Socialist Singers and the Young Communist League . . . made a recording of "The Red Flag" to the tune of "The White Cockade".' After 1950, folk-songs and popular songs of the protesting left merged to an extent with the growing number of nationalist songs. 'We dinna want Polaris', along with other non-nuclear songs of the 1960s, is an example of this trend. Alastair MacDonald's 'Scotland First' album shows both kinds of song as closely interrelated in the pro-nationalist propaganda of the late 1960s.[68] Such songs, remote as they may be from overtly Jacobite subject matter, frequently follow the 'parcel of rogues in a nation' thesis, and make definite their link with this aspect of their inheritance in the manner in which they deal with commercial exploitation and the Clearances. The nature of these protests and their continuing relevance (for example, on the question of Scottish land ownership) ensures that the terms of the Jacobite analysis they inherit are uncontaminated with the kitsch of sentimental Jacobitism. As in the period of the French Revolution, traditional ideas emerge in new contexts.[69]

An example of how left- and right-wing radical nationalism can combine in accepting Jacobite interpretations of Scotland's situation can be found in the speech given by Hugh MacDiarmid at a 1320 Club Symposium at Glasgow University on 6 April 1968. The Club, subsequently expelled from the SNP, was sympathetic to the kind of right-wing nationalism put forward by groups like the Scottish Legitimists (a neo-Jacobite kind of organization still active in the early 1960s), and by Wendy Wood's Patriots. The Club's leading light, Ronald MacDonald Douglas, was not averse to writing of 'The Idiot Race', Burns's term for the Hanoverians.[70] In his address, MacDiarmid, from a very different political background, spoke of the Scottish classless spirit as deriving from the clan structure, thus reiterating his long-standing case that Celtic Scotland was opposed in its more radical nature to the demands of the British state, and that Charles Edward had been a revolutionary leader. This address was perhaps symptomatic of a new generation of cultural nationalist thought, one which synthesized the radical and traditionalist sides of the Jacobite analysis, and made possible a new understanding of a 'Jacobitism of the left':

> We can trace a surprisingly similar frame of mind [to that devoted to the Jacobites] in some modern views of the Highland clearances and Red Clydeside. In its essential structure, such historical understanding as exists in to-day's Scotland is erected on the lost or betrayed cause.

The Jacobite cause continues to renew itself as a national obsession, both directly, and as a metaphor of loss used for ostensibly differing causes of complaint. This had long been the case. In the 'Radical War' of 1820

> it was said that Etienne MacDonald, duke of Taranto, who had been one of Napoleon's marshals and was the son of a Jacobite exile, was in the hills with a body of French troops sent to liberate Scotland.

The story of Taranto in the hills is like the story of Fionn or Charles, waiting like a Scottish Arthur, to return in the hour of need. The hero must return to free his people. In Scotland, however, the simultaneous demand for and distrust of heroes has been a paralysing force.[71]

Yet the metaphors remain enchanted ground. The mythopoeic impulses of the Scottish Renaissance have helped to clarify them. The terms of the Jacobite analysis which appeal to both left and right seem at last again to have found their common ground in the cultural nationalism of the twentieth century. Poets such as Sydney Goodsir Smith can write on a wide range of mythological and traditional figures and subjects, while never abandoning the modern radical statement as an acknowledgement of their merit and force:

> Wi brides and swickerie and idle promits
> Till the recreant lords of Scotia Meretrix,
> And nou, the lords defunct, rules,
> Great Hure o' Gowd that ruled the lords
> Scotland's plebs alike
> In selvin utter thirldom, happilie.
> Heirs of Wallace, Saltoun, John MacLean
> – Gif some there be –

The thirteenth, seventeenth, eighteenth, and twentieth centuries are placed here in a single metaphor.[72]

As Tom Crawford has pointed out, every revival of Scottish literature has gone hand in hand with a revival of the traditions of the past.[73] The call of the past and its typologies is strong. Folk literature and culture survives powerfully in the work of generations of Scottish writers who are otherwise divorced from its context. Indeed, some writers have claimed that Scotland's inability to grasp opportunities such as that provided by the 1979 referendum stems directly from the depths of this very historical consciousness: 'how could a romantic, tragic nation do anything else, when it had been nurtured on a diet of romantic, tragic history, based largely on myths?' This is a bleak if not infrequent accusation, rather like Edwin Muir's, in that it assumes that the dominance of Scotland's historical typologies in the determination of any native psyche is bound to be a negative one. In this, it is but one step removed from Scott's view of history. But, tempting though it may be on occasion to accept such catch-all readings, the analyses of the Jacobite past have proved more than a tragic nuisance in the history of Scotland. The metaphor of loss can be a dangerous one, but it has been a vital one also, just like the dual interpretation of Jacobitism itself. Whether its analyses are positive or negative forces depends largely on those who adopt them, and whether they believe in the Jacobite metaphor of history as liberty, marred by loss, or the propaganda of Tory nostalgia, history as loss, and liberty lost for good.[74] The Jacobite metaphor has shifted into many shapes in Scottish history.

One of its more recent appearances, heavily disguised, is in John McGrath's play *The Cheviot, the Stag, and the Black, Black Oil*, which was performed both in Scotland and Ireland during the SNP surge of 1974. McGrath is determined to reject a negative reading of the past. As he writes in the preface:

> One thing I had insisted on was that we broke out of the 'Lament' syndrome. Ever since Culloden, Gaelic culture has been one of lament – for exile, for death, for the past, even for the future. Beautiful, haunting lament. And in telling the story of the Highlands since 1745, there are many defeats, much sadness to relate. But I resolved that in the play, for every defeat, we would also celebrate a victory. . . . At the end, the audience left knowing they must choose . . . they must have confidence in their ability to unite and win.

This was clearly an ideologically committed reading of Highland history, and one apparently suitable for the more optimistic 1970s.[75]

McGrath uses the traditional medium of the popular song, adopting particularly the habit of the Jacobites, setting new words to old tunes to express his dissatisfaction with Scotland's colonial position. 'Bonny Dundee' is used in this way to satirize the aims of Improvement, and 'I Will Go' is presented as even more than usually indicative of the experience of the Clearances:

> Oh the Laird
> Had the law
> And the police were his servants
> But we'll fight
> Once again
> For this country is the people's
> Yes we'll fight, once again.

McGrath blends twentieth-century socialism with crofter radicalism and the old reading of the Highlander as patriot (symptomatic of true Scottishness) in a play which, though partial and didactic as history, is a prime example of the way the experiences of the past were being rewritten and restated in the 1970s. In his more recent *Border Warfare*, McGrath also encompasses the idea of history as liberty, implicitly present in *Cheviot*, where he repudiates the reading of Scotland's history as doom and lamentation. He is especially caustic towards Victorian sentimentalism:

And Fingal's Cave
The Chieftain Brave
We are the Monarchs of the Glen

Such verse parodies the tartanization of the Victorian age in a way still relevant today. In arguing that false sentimentality had acted as a cover and even an excuse for perpetuated exploitation, *Cheviot* sought to render the true past a radical dynamic to destabilize the present. Its comforting assertions of tartanry and Highland heritage were to be displayed as fraudulent in the eyes and ears of those it claimed to speak for.[76] *Cheviot* recognized the roles of Culloden and the Clearances as acts of damage to the Scottish psyche, and attempted to reinterpret their suffering and oppression in positive terms. Its view was that 'the tragedy of the Highlands has become a saleable commodity': another distant echo of the Jacobite interpretation of events. Honour and community have been replaced by commercial interests, Anglo-Scots and American. Such is McGrath's case, in which a Highland metaphor for the Scottish experience is uppermost.[77]

The Cheviot, the Stag, and the Black, Black Oil was only one of many positive assertions of Scottishness after 1970. That so many of these continue to draw on the symbolism of Jacobite propaganda and the episodes of the Jacobite period is evidence that 'the rising struck a historical chord that is still ringing'. The fact that as recently as 17 September 1989, an article in *Scotland on Sunday*, discussing the country's situation, could opine that it was Prince Charles's retreat from Derby which doomed Scotland to English domination, shows how far the Jacobite cause can become a focus of challenge to all the arguments that supported the Union. No longer a political threat, it nevertheless sums up manifold dimensions of loss, struggle, community, and identity. It is a strange survival, posing questions which have never fully been answered. They were being asked again in the 1960s, in a different way.[78]

THE SNP SINCE 1945

Raise your eyes
And mobilise
The race of the Gael.

'Scotland the Brave' (New Set)

Hear now, freedom's call,
We'll make a solemn vow,
Vow by the roses o' Prince Charlie.

The Corries

This is one of the rare moments when the real voice of the Palace is heard.

Neal Ascherson on the Queen on devolution, 1977 [79]

Robert MacIntyre won Motherwell for the SNP in 1945, during a wartime truce between the major parties. He lost it at the subsequent general election, after which the victorious Labour government neglected to implement the Home Rule they had promised. In opposition, Churchill made some positive noises on the subject, but these were rapidly forgotten after the Conservative victory of 1951. Indeed, some socialists opposed Home Rule in the 1950s on the grounds that it would deliver a permanent Tory majority in Scotland: times change.[80]

During this period the SNP were unable to exert any electoral pressure. Like the Liberals, they were badly squeezed in the 1950s, the decade which saw the apogee of the two-party state. John MacCormick's Covenant had attracted up to two million signatures in favour of Home Rule: but these signatures did not become votes for the SNP, and like the Chartists before them, the new Covenanters failed to make petitions count with government.

The persistent importance of a symbolic politics rooted in history was again displayed in the removal of the Stone of Scone to Scotland in 1950, and in the disrespect with which EIIR pillar-boxes were treated after the accession of Elizabeth in 1952, on the same grounds that half a century before had led Napier to protest at the title of Edward VII – the adoption of an incorrect regnal numeral. In the case of Elizabeth, the protesters carried their point, and there are no EIIR pillar-boxes in Scotland today – surely one of the paltriest political victories of all time. The lesson was learnt; and twenty years later the Scottish Post Office emphatically advised against the use of EIIR on the Silver Wedding stamps and envelope.[81]

Despite these flurries, the SNP proper achieved little. The cultural nationalists no longer clearly had an abiding city within the party, and after the failure of the Covenant, its political direction seemed uncertain. Then in the early 1960s, like the Liberals in England, it began to benefit from more fluid political conditions. At the time of the Bridgeton by-election in 1962 there were perhaps only a couple of thousand members, perhaps fewer; by the end of 1967, there were 60,000. The SNP's victory at Hamilton that year showed that it was capable of defeating Labour in a Labour stronghold; which was a task the Liberals found nearly impossible. Success appeared to grow rapidly in a wave of nationalist hysteria – the SNP have always been able to confer more hype on by-election victories than any other party. As in the 1930s, the nationalist wave had been preceded by victory in a Glasgow University rectorial contest (1965), and young people continued to be attracted by the party throughout the 1970s. But in the first flush of victory at Hamilton, it appeared that the party's new support would be almost limitless. Taking themselves seriously perhaps led in part to the banning of the 1320 Club in March 1968, ostensibly because of the 'right-wing militarists' in control.[82]

Victory at Hamilton appeared to have its effects. In January 1968, the 'first sub-committee of any House of Commons committee sat in Edinburgh'. By March, the SNP were registering opinion poll scores in the high thirties, with figures of 61 per cent favouring Home Rule and 26 per cent independence. In the municipal elections in May, the SNP gained a hundred seats, with 36 per cent of the vote in Glasgow (a figure never seen again). In June, a freak poll in the *Daily Record* suggested that 80 per cent favoured independence. The SNP won eighteen from twenty-one seats in Cumbernauld, with 46 per cent of the vote. The polls showed them at 43 per cent nationally, their highest reading ever. By the end of July, this had fallen back to 25 per cent. Despite holding this level of support into 1969, their performance at that year's local elections led many to think that the bubble had burst. Twenty-four losses in the municipal elections of 1970 were followed by a general election in which the SNP took only 11 per cent. But they gained their first seat ever at a general election: the Western Isles.[83]

Oil was the main issue which renewed mass support in the early 1970s, enabling the SNP to maintain high poll readings for several years, and to become the second party in Scotland at the October 1974 general election. From 1974 to 1978 it looked as if nationalism was finally taking off, and in the process marking out a new political destiny for Scotland. But the wrangle over the Labour government's resulting devolution bill was the basis of a war of attrition by members of both major parties against the issue, which bored the public. The SNP also, like all third parties, had to keep winning to keep support high, and the lack of any by-elections in Scotland until 1978 made this difficult to do. When one finally came, in Glasgow Garscadden, the campaign was bungled, and Donald Dewar, a formidable Labour candidate, won comfortably. At Westminster, there was a lack of discipline among the party's MPs, and a lack of understanding of the political spotlight they were under. As at other times before and since, the SNP showed that it could initiate success, but found it almost impossible to capitalize on it. There were nationalist waves, but never nationalist tides.[84]

One reason for this was and is that the SNP is too dependent on the political issues of the day for its support. The oil campaign lost its freshness in the late 1970s; the civil disobedience campaign of the early 1980s was based on a low level of support and was an immature mimic of anti-Thatcher protests carried on better by Labour; and in 1988–9 the anti-poll tax campaign failed to live up to the targets set for it by the SNP. The party seems perpetually on the look-out for a single issue which will deliver independence; none ever does, because issue politics are pressure-group politics and therefore marginal politics. To an extent, these opportunistic campaigns are a substitute for the broader-based traditionalism which the SNP has largely jettisoned. As each issue in turn fails to deliver enduring political support, the sense of disappointment contributes to a backwash which lowers the party's popularity and threatens its internal unity.

The chief thing to notice about such campaigns is their concentration on economic circumstances which may be transient, and their neglect of underlying questions of cultural and national identity. The SNP's concentration on economic matters is often in danger of rendering it a regionalist pressure-group rather than a nationalist party. Concern with the issues of Scotland's history and their legacy often appears minimal. In this, the SNP are at a disadvantage compared to nationalist-inclined members of the radical left (the Communist Party said that 'the 45 was *not* a dynastic adventure' as long ago as the 1930s). Among these, the SNP is suspected of aiming for a Scotland fit for shopkeepers and the small-town bourgeoisie. The nationalist-inclined left's understanding of Scotland's past is probably more complex and interesting than that of the nationalist party itself.[85]

In the 1979 general election, the SNP's support almost halved in the wake of the devolution referendum fiasco. During the ensuing three years, received opinion turned towards the view held on the left of the party, who argued for concentration on Central Belt urban seats, and for a more aggressive campaigning strategy. Although the first part of the policy received some tardy vindication through the victory of Jim Sillars at Govan in 1988, it was attempting to replace Labour while Labour were the only party who could replace the Conservatives at Westminster. This was unrealistic, and the SNP vote suffered in the 1983 and 1987 elections.

Since 1987, the SNP have shown more aggression in the Commons, and a greater readiness to use spoiling tactics. This is in part perhaps a recognition of the validity of Erskine and Wendy Wood's opinion that independence could never be won by playing Westminster at its own game (Wendy Wood herself had taken this point of view, arguing that Scotland's Estates should reconvene to repeal the Union).

The successes of cultural and traditionalist nationalists had been limited, but by rejecting their methods and ethos in favour of more narrow political opportunism, the SNP did itself a disservice. Despite more aggressive tactics in Parliament, the SNP's refusal to participate in the Constitutional Convention in 1989, compromise- and Labour-oriented body as it was, was a sign that a sectarian and partisan political outlook continued to obscure broader cultural priorities. An older generation of cultural nationalists would have acted differently.[86] The SNP's search for political opportunities, from Scottish steel to the poll tax, lead to temporary victories but few permanent advances. Each favoured issue or by-election success is greeted by an 'independence tomorrow' cry of burgeoning triumphalism. But such issues and successes are transient, and tomorrow never comes.

Few, if any, modern European nationalist parties have been successful without cultural nationalist priorities. In Scotland, the Jacobite analysis has been a unifying theme in subsequent cultural analyses, as this book argues. In the last section I will deal with the manner in which it has been voiced since 1970, and the continuingly ambivalent nature of that voicing. Both on left and right, in worlds as divergent as those of commerce and symbolic politics, the Jacobite analysis survives. The Stuart myth remains at the heart of questions of definition. Its positive readings are seen in much of Scottish culture, political and otherwise, this century; its negative, sentimental reading is still heavily used to sell images of Scotland. The pageant of a discontinued past is strongest in the cash registers of the Royal Mile, the views across what is now Highland wilderness, and the Englishman's home which is his castle. Scott's idea that the past is over sells well in the present.[87]

THE FACT OF THE MYTH

The myths we have created of our homeland have not been atemporal myths that can be applied to any specific historical situation (as, say, Yeats's myth of Cuchulain can be applied and reapplied by him to Ireland throughout his life) but myths of the end of the very culture whose being they are supposed to express ... the living imagination emigrates, the fixities of reminiscent memory stay at home; the imagination returns in foreign garb, our memories are exported as the essence of ourselves.

Cairns Craig, 1983

Too long we have waited our hero's return

The Corries

The Queen ... as head of a country in opposition to ourselves ... was 'fair game' and should not be exempt from the campaign of aggression, criticism and insult. Especially as we had our own Prince, HRH Michael James Stewart, the ... direct and lawful heir, resident in Scotland and present at the meeting.

Minutes of the Scottish Patriots Group Meeting, 8 July 1979

'Bonnie' Prince Charles Edward Stuart: a divisive symbol of the Highland past who was opposed as a reactionary by most Scots even 250 years ago.

Mick Hume and Derek Owen [88]

Whatever the fluctuations in fortune of political parties since 1970, Scottish history, literature, and culture are now much more widely discussed. One of the facets of this discussion has been an examination of the Jacobite inheritance. Scathing appraisals of nineteenth-century tartanry and sentiment have emerged, and the damage these have caused in the Scottish consciousness has been assessed. Unfortunately, attacks on sentimental Jacobitism have too often conflated the positive and negative aspects of the Stuart legacy. While blaming nineteenth-century imperial culture for cultivating Jacobitism and its symbolic adjuncts as a fashionable and decorative lost cause, such attacks nevertheless still often presume that the cause was a lost one to start with. Such assessments are often made by those who are themselves inheritors of positive features of the Jacobite analysis, and who yet are forming conclusions about Jacobitism which belong to the sentimental history they are trying to disparage.[89] Their own debts to the radical side of Jacobite ideology are disconnected in their arguments from the view that the truth about the Stuarts is to be found in the words of those they claim did not tell it.

Positive readings of Jacobitism can often appear unconscious ones. A play like McGrath's *Border Warfare* draws heavily on the Jacobite interpretation of Scotland's history as a struggle for liberty, but it has little time for Jacobitism itself. Its ideological legacy is present, unacknowledged, perhaps because decades of sentimental misreading have emptied the historical events of Jacobitism of real political content. Yet the idea of Scottish history as a struggle for liberty is one articulated through the neglected ideology of eighteenth-century Jacobitism.

In recent years, historians have begun to show considerable interest in Jacobitism, having found evidence both of the seriousness of its ideology and its radical edge. In particular, studies of popular Jacobitism have revealed widespread lower-middle- and working-class support. The idea of a 'Jacobitism of the left', with the Jacobite leaders as revolutionary figures able to appeal to the urban lower classes, has gained ground. Such an argument, while radical in scholarly terms, only embodies what is already evident from the legacy of radical Jacobitism to Burns and MacDiarmid. 'Gaelic Communism', with its adjunct ideas and philosophies, is only one example of the continuing contribution 'Jacobitism of the left' has made to modern culture.[90]

Popular culture still remains very interested in Jacobitism. Charles Edward remains the iconic messianic figure (or devilish fraud and tempter, or doomed irrelevance, depending on your point of view) he has always been. Book succeeds book – and still there are never enough to adequately lionize, denigrate, or calmly assess the leader of the Forty-Five. The fact that such a remote historical figure can still attract the kind of venom evident throughout books like Susan Maclean Kybett's 1988 biography is evidence of Charles's enduring appeal to so many, that he should continue such an irritant to some. The great 'near miss' of Jacobitism is a source of endless fascination. The question, 'What if Charles had advanced from Derby?' is reiterated again and again by serious and popular historian alike, even to the point of fantasizing.[91] The commercial and sentimental exploitation of Jacobitism evident throughout the Victorian period still continues in tandem with a more serious fascination with the Year of the Prince. The defeat was the victory of the Forty-Five, and this contradiction has left the Scottish psyche an enduring legacy. In its negative form, this heritage is one of fatalism and readiness to accept defeat; in its positive form, it manifests itself in ideas connected with the ideology of history as liberty which synthesize apparently diverse figures and events in patriotic self-definition. Wallace and Charles, radicalism and traditionalism, football and politics, are the kinds of people and subjects yoked together in this synthesis. Yet the positive and negative sides are sides of the same coin, which made the latter a tempting analysis to make. As the goalposts were being torn down at Wembley in 1977 after the 2–1 defeat of England, the Scottish fans chanted 'Gie us an Assembly and we'll gie ye back your Wembley.' Victory and politics were united. A year later, after the World Cup, the opposite was the case. Who can say that the trepidation and fatalism of the 1979 referendum fiasco was a negative consequence not unconnected with these syntheses of sport and politics? After all, the 40 per cent rule was described by its opponents as 'moving the goalposts'.[92] Jacobitism as an ideology was positive and dynamic; negatively, it was a failure. Its attractions and defeats lay close together. For Scott and his followers, the latter were emphasized at the expense of the former. Jacobitism's positive legacy was neglected. Yet it was that positive legacy on which sentimental Jacobitism fed. Unless the Jacobite analysis posed a continuing question about Scotland and its future, there would have been no need to sentimentalize and diminish it. It was patronized because it was still potentially powerful, for political failure had not dimmed the myth of the Stuarts. The victory lay in the defeat: because the Stuarts were not restored, they could the better act as metaphors for the lack of Scottish statehood. But Jacobitism was far from the 'lost cause' of sentiment; it was a political ideology and a messianic myth of enduring force.[93] The Jacobite cause's own icons of struggle, loyalty, Highland patriotism, sacred kingship, art, fertility, and Episcopacy transmuted themselves into various manners of understanding Scotland's continuing problems of identity. The 'lost cause' account, largely engineered by the imperialists of the nineteenth century, views Jacobitism and indeed all Scottish history as an artefact, the subject of intellectual archaeology or commercial profit. But the fact that Scotland's separate history is clearly not over has been one recognized increasingly in this century: and part of the continuing development of Scottish thought and understanding has come from those who are inheritors of the questions posed by the Jacobite analysis.

The positive, transmuting power of Jacobitism can be seen in the antiquarian dimension of the folk revival. Many of the songs sung or written by 'The Corries' in particular over the last twenty years have clearly been aimed at reviving Jacobite metaphors in a modern context. Demand for these songs can be high at their concerts; and as the stage in the evening comes when they are to be performed, enthusiasm and relief can be seen and heard. Songs like 'The Dawning of the Day' and 'Roses o' Prince Charlie' clearly bring Jacobitism into a contemporary context:

> Come now, gather now, here where the flowers grow,
> White is the blossom as the snow on the ben,
> Hear now, freedom's call, we'll make a solemn vow,
> Vow by the roses o' Prince Charlie.

The white rose is here made the symbol, as it was by MacDiarmid, Compton Mackenzie, and Wendy Wood, of Scottish freedom. In the song, it becomes a focal rallying-call, not only for the Highlander as patriot image which dominates the first verse, but also for Scottish exiles abroad, and the workers of Scotland's industrial cities at home. Jacobitism of the left is combined with that of the right:

> Spirits o' the banished, from far and distant lands. . .
> Return now in glory, and on the silver sands
> Fight for the roses o' Prince Charlie . . . .

> Take your strength from the green fields that blanket peat and coal,
> Ships frae the Clyde have a nation in their hold,
> The water o' life some men need to make them bold,
> Black gold and fishes frae the sea, man.

> Come now, gather now . . .

Here all the elements of the Scottish past and present are adduced with the dominant imprecation being to gather under the Jacobite symbol of the white rose in the struggle for Scottish freedom. (In this context, it is interesting to note that 'The Dawning of the Day' was sung on TV the week before the Govan by-election in 1988.[94]) As well as these contemporary Jacobite songs, the Corries sing many more traditional lyrics. 'Welcome, Royal Charlie', which appears on their 1980 album, *Stovies*, seems to be a favourite. But the words of the original eighteenth-century lyric have been altered in order to highlight not the dynastic politics of Jacobitism then, but their message to the future now:

> Charlie's been too long awa',
> The eagle waits for the bugle's ca',
> But the spirit shines aboon us a',
> For the right belongs to Charlie.[95]

The spirit which recognizes that 'the right belongs to Charlie' is the spirit of a Jacobitism which has endured long after the removal of 'Charlie' from the scene, as Bruce Lenman recognizes in his most recent book on the subject, *The Jacobite Cause*, which acknowledges the continuing power of a call for Charlie being a call for justice.[96] The metaphor and symbols endure. The Charles Edward Stuart exhibition at the Royal Scottish Museum in 1986–7 was entitled 'I Am Come Home', stressing the patriotic element in Jacobitism. The idea of the Prince as a deliverer returning from abroad is a potent one, strongly associated as it now is with the theme of exile, so close to the facts of life for many Scots over the last 250 years.[97]

The way in which Jacobite metaphors continue to suffuse the interpretation of other areas of Scottish history is evident from the Corries' most successful song, 'Flower of Scotland', which has become the unofficial national anthem for many in the twenty years since its appearance. The subject of the song is Bannockburn: but its reading of Scottish history is fundamentally Jacobite in kind, with a tone which sounds uneasily the notes of both lament and celebration. The question, 'When will we see your like again?' vaguely echoes the terms of Jacobite laments for Charles though ostensibly it is asked of the Scots Army at Bannockburn, those who fought fought for 'Their wee bit hill and glen': a Highlander as patriot image from the eighteenth century, not a description of the composition of Bruce's army. The land 'that is lost now', where 'autumn leaves lie thick and still', is post-Culloden Scotland, the images of lost fertility echoing the Jacobite analysis. The third stanza, with its positive note that '. . . we can still rise now, /And be the nation again', is a warning against a sentimental reading of the past, and expresses a hope for a positive reading of the past suitable to present circumstances, a theme the Corries often harp on. The Scotland of 'Flower of Scotland' is one of Jacobite images, though Bannockburn is its subject.[98]

The success of this and other manifestations of the Jacobite analysis in various contemporary guises bears witness to the chameleon nature of myth in culture. As times change in their demands, myth changes in its expressions. But the myth survives.

From early times, the Stuart myth claimed to be a pan-Scottish myth, an account of the nature of Scotland's royal and cultural identities. In the seventeenth century, the Covenanters strongly rejected this myth of origin, antiquity, and authority; but as Scotland's religious liberty came to triumph at the expense of her political identity (as it had threatened to do since 1560), the balance swung the other way, and the Stuart myth gained in attractiveness. The Jacobite images of the Highlander as patriot, of history as liberty (a continuing struggle), and of the sacred king and fertile nation, all played a powerful role in maintaining and developing national consciousness. The traditional song itself helped to enable a traditionally Scottish literature to be preserved. The defeat of Culloden in 1746 was gradually to become a metaphor of national loss, a tragic culmination to the struggle for liberty with England. It was not so in fact; but was and is within the parameters of the myth. Like the Clearances, Culloden has developed its own autonomy as a political fairy-tale (not that we should use the term pejoratively). It was ultimately in vain that pro-Union writers attempted to turn Jacobitism, and Scottish history itself, into a sentimental memento: the older myths retaliated in neo-Jacobite nationalism, and subsequently and more potently, in a socialism which had learnt from the Jacobite analysis. At a political level, its inheritors are found on left and right; below a political level, Jacobitism perseveres in the monitory voice of loss, its warnings turned into prophecies in a Scotland still dominated by exile and emigration. At Aberdeen University's Elphinstone Parliament, the Jacobites are equated with the SNP; and although the modern SNP has often failed to take on board the Jacobite analysis, the equation between Jacobitism and nationalism, on a historical level at least, is an easy one to make. That it remains so, and that the iconic status of Charles Edward remains potent after two and a half centuries, is a triumph for the agenda Stuart propaganda set itself in aiding the creation of the Stuart myth.

Predicting the future for this epic story is difficult. The history of Jacobitism, while still a major field of study, may be increasingly outside the direct interests of a younger generation of Scots (although Charles Edward has a book in the Ladybird series to himself: there is not one for all the Scottish kings put together). Yet folk-song, and even pop such as the Proclaimers' 'Letter from America', show the power of the Jacobite experience and the experiences it spawned. Books on more well-worn Jacobite topics continue to sell. The Sunday papers can still refer to Charles as an unsuccessful hero who nearly delivered his country; Jacobite cruises ply Loch Ness, and 'Jacobite clansmen' stage mock battles. On a more commercial note, the shortbread tin and whisky bottle display the major adherents to the Cause in every delicatessen or off-licence.

No one can argue that the Stuart myth is a major issue of our time. But is it a major premise of Scotland's psychological and cultural inheritance? I hope this book has done something to answer that question. Scotland's history, even in the 1970s and 1980s, is full of Derbys which were retreated from:

> Hauf his saul a Scot maun use
> Indulgin' in illusions,
> And hauf in gettin' rid o' them
> And comin' to conclusions
> Wi' the demoralisin' dearth
> O' onything worth while on Earth . . .

The Stuart myth was neither the illusion fostered in the nineteenth century, nor was its conclusion Culloden. It is a question which partakes of both these qualities, and its analysis remains a question, 'What if?' 'Prosperity to Scotland and no Union' was the legend on the swords of the Forty-Five. It did not come true: but the assumptions which lay behind it continued to echo in Scottish culture, trying conclusions down the years with the long adjournment of 1707.[99]

Notes

Introduction

1 T. H. Huxley, quoted in Ronald Holmes, *The Legend of Sawney Bean* (London, 1975), 3; Edwin Muir, *Scott and Scotland* (Edinburgh, 1936), 160; Pierre Joannon, 'The Royal House of Stuart', *Royal Stuart Review* 7(1) (1988), 15–16 (16).

2 Robin Gwyndorf, 'The cauldron of regeneration: continuity and function in the Welsh folk epic tradition', in Bo Alanquist, Seamas O'Cathan, and Padraig O'Healain (eds), *The Heroic Process: Form, Function and Fantasy in Folk Epic* (Dublin, 1987), 413–51 (443–44).

3 The Reverend J. M. Charles-Roux, I. C., 'Charles I: the sovereign saint', *Royalist Focus* 1 (1986), 8, 10, one of the latest examples of the *Eikon Basilike* tradition.

4 The present conflict in eighteenth-century historiography (Clark v. Speck, Dickinson) is ample evidence of this. See W. Speck's *The Butcher* (Oxford, 1981), J. C. Clark's *English Society 1688–1832* (Cambridge, 1985), and *The Clark Newsletter* (Autumn 1989), 6–7.

5 Gwyndorf, op. cit., 437.

6 Elizabeth Jenkins, *The Mystery of King Arthur* (London, 1975), 167; Daniel Szechi, 'The Jacobite theatre of death', in Eveline Cruickshanks and Jeremy Black (eds), *The Jacobite Challenge* (Edinburgh, 1988), 57–73 (69).

7 Jenkins, op. cit., 168–9.

8 Cf. Beverley Taylor and Elisabeth Brewer, *The Return of King Arthur* (Cambridge, 1983), 3, 73, 162; F. Marion McNeill, *The Silver Bough*, 4 vols (Glasgow, 1957), I, 77.

9 Richard Barber, *The Figure of Arthur* (Worcester and London, 1972), 80ff., 108ff., 122.

10 ibid., 109. Cf. John MacInnes, 'Twentieth-century recordings of Scottish Gaelic heroic ballads', *The Heroic Process*, 101–30 (105).

11 Anon., 'Irish Jacobite songs', in *The Royalist* VII: 3 (1896), 41–6 (45).

12 MacInnes, op. cit., 105.

13 Lucy McDiarmid, *Saving Civilization* (Cambridge, 1984), 37.

14 Christopher Harvie, 'Legalism, myth and national identity in Scotland in the imperial epoch', *Cencrastus* 26 (1987), 35–41 (38); cf. also Mary Ellen Brown, 'The study of folk tradition', in *The History of Scottish Literature* ed. Cairns Craig, 4 vols (Aberdeen, 1988), III, 397–409.

15 Magnus Maclean, *The Literature of the Celts* (London, Glasgow, and Dublin, 1902), 196.

NOTES

1 The divided myth and the drift to Union

1 For a discussion of Carew's masque see Earl Miner, *The Cavalier Mode from Jonson to Cotton* (Princeton, 1971), 54ff; Abraham Cowley, *Poems*, ed. A. R. Waller (Cambridge, 1905), 425; Baillie quoted in Audrey Cunningham, *The Loyal Clans* (Cambridge, 1932), 270.

2 David M. Vieth (ed.), *The Complete Poems of John Wilmot, Earl of Rochester* (New Haven and London, 1979), 134.

3 This and other statements of Voltaire's are adduced and discussed in Marquise Campana de Cavelli, *Les Derniers Stuarts à Saint-Germain-en-Laye* (London and Edinburgh, 1871), 6ff.

4 For example: G. M. Trevelyan in *England Under the Stuarts* (London, 1928), who terms the Highlanders 'barbarians'; and Charles Petrie, who went so far the other way as to write *If*, a fantasy of Jacobite victory in 1745. Recent historiographical battles between Clark, Speck, Cruickshanks, Dickinson, etc. confirm how controversial a field Jacobitism remains. Cf. the discussion in J. C. Clark's *Revolution and Rebellion* (Cambridge, 1986), 40, 62–6, 94, 111.

5 Susan Maclean Kybett, *Bonnie Prince Charlie* (London, 1988), is a good example of the potential strength of present-day antipathy to the Stuarts.

6 Cf. Eveline Cruickshanks, *Political Untouchables* (London, 1979); Eveline Cruickshanks and Jeremy Black (eds), *The Jacobite Challenge* (Edinburgh, 1988); Paul Monod, 'For the king to enjoy his own again', unpublished Ph.D. thesis, Yale University, 1985.

7 For a discussion of the Stuart dynasty as Arthur restored, see Elizabeth Jenkins, *The Mystery of King Arthur* (London, 1975). Cf. also Dryden's *King Arthur* (1691), and the other Arthurian plays of the 1690s as political documents. These are discussed in Beverley Taylor and Elisabeth Brewer, *The Return of King Arthur* (Cambridge, 1983).

8 Maryann McGuire, *Milton's Puritan Masque* (Athens, Georgia, 1983), 75.

9 Charles Carlton, *Charles I: The Personal Monarch* (London, 1983), 149–53, 209–11, 347.

10 McGuire, op. cit., 108.

11 ibid., 75.

12 Frank McLynn, *Charles Edward Stuart* (London, 1988), 183.

13 Ian Fletcher, *W. B. Yeats and His Contemporaries* (Brighton, 1987), 107–10.

14 Margaret Barnard Pickel, *Charles I as Patron of Poetry and Drama* (London, 1936), 60.

15 ibid., 1, 94.

16 C. V. Wedgwood, *Poetry and Politics under the Stuarts* (Cambridge, 1960), 34; cf. Douglas Brooks-Davies, *Pope's Dunciad and the Queen of Night* (Manchester, 1985), 17ff.

17 James Turner, *The Politics of Landscape* (Oxford, 1979), 101.

18 Robert Herrick, *The Poetical Works*, ed. L. C. Martin (Oxford, 1956), 211.

19 Turner, op. cit., 1, 5, 91, 95, 97, 185.

20 Sorley MacLean, in Malcolm MacLean and Christopher Carrel (eds), *As an Fhearrann* (London, 1986), 9.

21 Cf. David Norbrook, *Poetry and Politics in the English Renaissance* (London, 1984), 191–2; Brooks-Davies, op. cit., 80; M. G. Walker, 'Andrew Marvell and Thomas, 3rd Lord Fairfax: some aspects of their relationship 1650–53', unpublished D. Phil. thesis (Oxford, 1953), 27.

22 Wedgwood, op. cit., 172.

23 Sir George Mackenzie, *Religio Stoici. Friendly Address to Phanatics* (publisher

not known, no date), 6ff.; Burke, speech of 6 February 1772, cited Cunningham, op. cit., 339.

24 For a discussion of the cultural challenge posed by the 'Covenanting dynamic', see Allan I. MacInnes's essay, 'Scottish Gaeldom 1638–51: the vernacular response to the Covenanting dynamic', in *New Perspectives on the Politics and Culture of Early Modern Scotland*, ed. John Dwyer, Roger Mason, and Alexander Murdoch (Edinburgh, no date), 59–94.

25 The idea of the Community of the Realm of Scotland is identified and explored in Geoffrey Barrow's magnificent *Robert Bruce*, 3rd edn (Edinburgh, 1988).

26 It was the Scots who showed more enthusiasm in the Union discussions of 1603–5. Cf. B. L. Galloway, *The Union of England and Scotland 1603–1608* (Edinburgh, 1986), *passim*.

27 Dugald Stewart, quoted in Frank T. Galter, 'On the literary value of some Scottish Presbyterian writings in the context of the Scottish Enlightenment', in Dietrich Strauss and Horst W. Drescher (eds), *Scottish Language and Literature, Medieval and Renaissance* (Frankfurt, 1986), 175–92 (175).

28 MacInnes, op. cit., 67–70.

29 ibid., 76ff.; cf. A. A. Whyte, 'Scottish Gaelic folksongs 1500–1800', unpublished M. Litt. thesis (Glasgow, 1974), 162ff.

30 Gordon Donaldson, *Scotland James V to James VII* (Edinburgh and London, 1965), 337.

31 Galter, op. cit., 175.

32 Hugh Ouston, 'York in Edinburgh: James VII and the patronage of learning in Scotland, 1679–1688', in Dwyer *et al.*, op. cit., 133–55 (133–9).

33 F. C. Turner, *James II* (London, 1948), 185.

34 ibid., 327; J. R. Jones, *The Revolution of 1688 in England* (London, 1972), 127, 166ff.

35 Raymond Crawfurd, *The King's Evil* (Oxford, 1911), 112.

36 Cf. Turner, op. cit., 333ff., for a discussion of this in the context of the Magdalen College controversy.

37 The Earl of Perth, quoted in Donaldson, op. cit., 382. For a discussion of the composition of James's armed forces, see John Childs, *The Army, James II and the Glorious Revolution* (Manchester, 1980).

38 Andrew Marvell, *The Poems and Letters*, ed. H. M. Margoliouth, 2 vols (Oxford, 1971), I, 92.

39 John Dryden, *The Poems and Fables*, ed. James Kinsley (London, 1962), 328, 356, 430. Cf. Isabel Rivers, *The Poetry of Conservatism* (Cambridge, 1973), 160ff.

40 *The Laws and Acts Made by the First Parliament of Our Most High and Dread Sovereign James VII*, ed. George, Viscount Tarbet, Lord MacLeod, Castlehaven, *et al.* (Edinburgh, 1731), 4.

41 ibid., 3.

42 As can be seen from his actions towards the young James at the time of the Treaty of Ryswick (1697) and thereafter, when there was considerable likelihood that James might after all succeed to his father's crown.

43 Jones, op. cit., 260–1.

44 Turner, op. cit., 422.

45 Clark, op. cit., 3.

46 Donaldson, op. cit., 380.

47 Turner, op. cit., 497.

48 Trevelyan, op. cit., 416.

49 Bruce Lenman, *The Jacobite Cause* (Glasgow, 1986), 7.

50 Cf. Bruce Lenman, 'The Scottish Episcopal clergy and the ideology of Jacobitism', in Eveline Cruickshanks (ed.), *Ideology and Conspiracy: Aspects of Jacobitism 1689–1759* (Edinburgh, 1982), 36–48.

51 Claverhouse, lamenting his lack of support in 1689. Cf. Magnus Linklater and Christian Hesketh, *For King and Conscience* (London, 1989).

52 Anon., 'A letter to a member of The Convention of States in Scotland' (Edinburgh, 1689), 6–7.

53 Linklater and Hesketh, op. cit., 157.

54 Anon., *An Account of the Proceedings of the Meeting of the Estates in Scotland* (London, 1689), 1, 8, 11.

55 Cf. 'A letter to a member of The Convention of States', 6.

56 A. M. Birke, in K. G. Saur, *England und Hanover: England and Hanover*, ed. Adolf M. Birke and Kurt Kluxen, Prince Albert Studies vol. 4 (Munich and London, 1986), 11–13 (11).

57 *An Account of the Present Persecution of the Church in Scotland* (London, 1690), 2; 'A narrative of the late treatment of the Episcopal ministers' (London, 1708), ii, iii, 17. Cf. also John Wilkes, *History of England* (London, 1768), I, 5.

58 Lucy McDiarmid, *Saving Civilization* (Cambridge, 1984), 37.

59 Cf. Murray Pittock, 'Jacobite literature: love, death, violence', in Paul Dukes and John Dunkley (eds), *Culture and Revolution* (London, 1990), 33–45.

60 William Donaldson, *The Jacobite Song* (Aberdeen, 1988), ix.

61 Cf. here John Lorne Campbell, *Highland Songs of the Forty-Five* (Edinburgh, 1933) with Murray Pittock, *New Jacobite Songs of the Forty five* (Oxford, 1989), for a comparison of the similarities of Lowland and Highland viewpoints.

62 Bruce Lenman, *The Jacobite Risings in Britain 1689–1746* (London, 1980), 75.

63 Turner, op. cit., 497.

64 George, Viscount Tarbet, op. cit., 697–725. This volume also includes the text of Acts up to and including Union. For the best discussion of Hamilton's role in events, see John Gibson, *Playing the Scottish Card* (Edinburgh, 1988).

65 Cf. W. R. and V. B. MacLeod (eds), *Anglo-Scottish Tracts 1701–14: A Descriptive Checklist*, University of Kansas libraries series 44 (Morgantown, 1979).

66 Cf. Nicholas Rogers, 'Riot and popular Jacobitism in early Hanoverian England', in Eveline Cruickshanks (ed.), *Ideology and Conspiracy, Aspects of Jacobitism 1689–1759* (Edinburgh, 1982), 70–88. This subject is also extensively discussed in Monod, op. cit.

67 Sir Thomas Craig, *Scotland's Soveraignty Asserted*, ed. George Ridpath (London, 1695), xxii–xxiii, 146, 376–7.

68 James Anderson, *Scotland Independent* (Edinburgh, 1705), 18, 263.

69 Donaldson, op. cit., ix; cf. Cassell's *History of Britain* (London, 1923), and the work of P. Hume Brown, Trevelyan, and others, including J. H. Plumb's discussion of Scotland in *The Growth of Stability* (London, 1967).

70 W. R. and V. B. MacLeod, op. cit.

71 Cf. David Nichol Smith (ed.), *The Oxford Book of Eighteenth Century Verse* (Oxford, 1977), 190.

72 Quoted in Monod, op. cit., 34.

73 Cf. ibid., 81ff.

74 ibid., 83; Murray Pittock, *New Jacobite Songs*, discusses precisely the issues Monod raises here.

75 'Lord Pitsligo's Apologia' [The Memsie Copy], MS 2740/4/18/2, Aberdeen University Library.

76 Cf. Murray Pittock, 'Jacobite songs', in *The Jacobite*, Spring 1990, 2–13. Also Monod, op. cit., 81.
77 Cf. Monod, op. cit., 116ff., 134ff.
78 ibid., 83, 93, 104. Other writers such as Swift, who was by no means clearly Jacobite, tellingly compared the Revolution with the Civil War.
79 John Butt (ed.), *The Poems of Alexander Pope* (London, 1965), 800.
80 Monod, op. cit., 1, 102.
81 Quoted in P. H. Scott, *1707: The Union of Scotland and England* (Edinburgh, 1979), 1.
82 Galter, op. cit., 175–92 (176).
83 *The Smoaking Flax Unquenchable* (1706), 2. Discussed by Galter, op. cit., 181–2.
84 John S. Gibson, *Playing the Scottish Card* (Edinburgh, 1988), 81ff.
85 Anon., *Villpone: Or, Remarks on Some Proceedings in Scotland* (publisher not known, 1707), 16, 22, 28, 29.
86 This facet of Scott's work is clearly seen in the underlying social change which isolates the Jacobite age in *Waverley, The Bride of Lammermoor*, and *Redgauntlet*. In *Scott and Scotland* (1936), Edwin Muir suggests that the last novel is the most profound manifestation of Scott's personal beliefs available.
87 David Daiches, *The Paradox of Scottish Culture* (London, 1964), 13–14.
88 ibid., 27. See Douglas Duncan, *Thomas Ruddiman* (Edinburgh and London, 1965), for a wider discussion of this area.
89 Daiches, op. cit., 95; Donaldson, op. cit., ix.
90 Duncan, op. cit., 18, 70.
91 Cf. Norval Clyne, *The Scottish Jacobites and Their Poetry* (Aberdeen, 1887), 19ff.
92 Duncan, op. cit., 151; Donaldson, op. cit., 9.
93 Duncan, op. cit., 150; cf. Murray Pittock, 'Rights of nature: the ideal images of Jacobite ruralism', in *British Journal of Eighteenth Century Studies* (1990). Note also in this context Monod, op. cit., 118–20, and 'An Epistle from a student at Oxford to the Chevalier' (London, 1717), 3–5.
94 Lenman, *The Jacobite Cause*, 51.
95 Monod, op. cit., 161–70.
96 Cf. Donaldson, op. cit., 5ff.
97 National Library of Scotland, Rosebery Collection, Ry. 111. a.10.f.71 NLS MS 2092.f.38; Donaldson, op. cit., 11ff.
98 Donaldson, op. cit., 9, 12; *A Second Book of Scottish Pasquils* (Edinburgh, 1828), 71.
99 *A Second Book of Scottish Pasquils*, 73, 82, 97.
100 ibid., 25; *A Third Book of Scottish Pasquils* (Edinburgh, 1828), 92.
101 'A recipe from a famous physician how to make a true Scotts Whigg', MS 2222, Aberdeen University Library.
102 MSS 2222 and 2718, Aberdeen University Library, show many examples of this. The trend is discussed in Monod, op. cit., 86ff.
103 NLS MS 488.f.46 and 2960.f.48 show the range and durability of some of these broadsides.
104 James Hogg, *The Jacobite Relics of Scotland*, 2 vols (Edinburgh, 1819–21), I, xi.
105 The need to respond to such portrayals can be seen in the way a greater degree of Scottish national unity in the Middle Ages is argued for in recent books like *The Middle Ages in the Highlands*, ed. Loraine MacLean (Inverness, 1981).
106 Quoted by Galter, op. cit., 188.

107 Clark, op. cit., 66, 94. Cf. also Clark's chapter, 'On moving the middle ground: the significance of Jacobitism in historical studies', in Cruickshanks and Black, op. cit., 177–88. For the reference to 'barbarians', see Trevelyan, op. cit., 455.
108 Gibson, op. cit., 30.

2 Good corn upon the rigs?
The underground world of Jacobite culture in eighteenth-century Scotland

1 G. S. Macquoid (ed.), *Jacobite Songs and Ballads* (London, no date), 153.
2 John Daly (ed.), *Reliques of Irish Jacobite Poetry* (Dublin, 1844), 37n.
3 Cf. Paul Monod, 'For the king to enjoy his own again', unpublished Ph.D. thesis (Yale, 1985), 104ff.; MSS 2222, 2740/4/18/1/16, Aberdeen University Library.
4 Cf. Monod, op. cit., 538.
5 ibid., 118, 135.
6 ibid., 120; James Hogg, *The Jacobite Relics of Scotland*, 2 vols (Edinburgh, 1819–21), I, 55, 100.
7 William Donaldson, *The Jacobite Song* (Aberdeen, 1988), 49ff.
8 Hogg, op. cit., I, 130, 145; 'A Song for Joy of our ancient race of Stewarts', *Four New Songs, and a Prophecy* (no publisher, no date), National Library of Scotland, Rosebery Pamphlets, 1–2–85.
9 Hogg, op. cit., I, 3.
10 'The Battle of *Preston*. To the Tune of *Killiecranky*', National Library of Scotland, MS 488.f.46.
11 William Donaldson, 'The Jacobite song in 18th and early 19th century Scotland', unpublished Ph.D thesis (Aberdeen, 1974), 24, 131.
12 Aberdeen University Library, MS 2222: forthcoming as M. Pittock (ed.), *New Jacobite Songs of the Forty-five* (Oxford, Voltaire Foundation).
13 'The Happy Lady', PRO, SP 35/31/154.
14 Cf. Pat Rogers, '"The Enamelled Ground": the language of heraldry and natural description in *Windsor Forest*', in *Pope: Recent Essays*, ed. Maynard Mack and James Winn (Brighton, 1980), 159–76; Pat Rogers, *An Introduction to Pope* (London, 1975), 25, 46; Isaac Kramnick, *Bolingbroke and His Circle* (Cambridge, Massachusetts, 1968), *passim*.
15 Isabel Rivers, *The Poetry of Conservatism* (Cambridge, 1973), x, 172; Douglas Brooks-Davies, *Pope's Dunciad and the Queen of Night* (Manchester, 1985), 166–7.
16 Alexander Robertson of Struan, *Poems* (Edinburgh, 1749), 241–6, 270, 291, 296.
17 ibid., 89, 114, 117; Rivers, op. cit., 188, 192–3.
18 Cf. Theodore Napier (ed.), *The Fiery Cross* (Edinburgh, 1901–12); and Ian Fletcher, 'The white rose rebudded: neo-Jacobitism in the 1890s', in *W.B. Yeats and His Contemporaries* (Brighton, 1987), 83–123.
19 Hogg, op. cit., I, 91, 119.
20 ibid., I, 57; II, 146.
21 Monod, op. cit., 87, 105–6, 118.
22 ibid., 51, 125–6, 134–5, 170–1. Also Paul Monod, 'The politics of matrimony', in Eveline Cruickshanks and Jeremy Black (eds), *The Jacobite Challenge* (Edinburgh, 1988), 24–41 (34).
23 Cf. Frank McLynn, *Charles Edward Stuart* (London, 1988), 314.
24 Monod, 'For the king', 256, 513.
25 ibid., 662.
26 Hogg, op. cit., I, 14.

27 Burns Martin and John Oliver (eds), *The Works of Allan Ramsay Volume I* [Poems, 1721], Scottish Text Society (New York and London, 1972), 37.

28 David Daiches, *The Paradox of Scottish Culture* (London, 1964), 11–14, 27.

29 ibid., 16; McLynn, op. cit., 47.

30 Daiches, op. cit.; cf. Donaldson, *The Jacobite Song*, 12–14, 24ff.

31 Martin and Oliver, op. cit., xviii, xx; Daiches, op. cit., 28.

32 Daiches, op. cit., 35, 53.

33 Allan H. Maclaine, *Allan Ramsay* (Boston, 1985), ix.

34 Martin and Oliver, op. cit., xviii–xxii.

35 ibid., 28.

36 ibid., 29.

37 Maclaine, op. cit., *passim*.

38 Martin and Oliver, op. cit., 169; Hogg, *The Jacobite Relics of Scotland* (Paisley, 1874), 223–4n.

39 Alexander Kinghorn and Alexander Law (eds), *The Works of Allan Ramsay Volume III (Poems Miscellaneous and Uncollected)* (New York and London, 1972), 81ff., 193, 196; Maclaine, op. cit., 104.

40 David Daiches, *The Scottish Enlightenment* (Edinburgh, 1986), 18, 19.

41 Maclaine, op. cit., 42, 55ff.

42 Cf. 'Mr. Addison turned Tory', By a Gentleman of Oxford (London, 1713); James Anderson Winn, *John Dryden and His World* (New Haven, 1987), 484–5, 488 (see Brooks-Davies, op. cit., 50, 88, for Jacobite readings of Turnus); *Ascanius or the Young Adventurer* (London, 1746); *Ascanio o El Jova Aventurero* (Madrid, no date).

43 Douglas Duncan, *Thomas Ruddiman* (Edinburgh and London, 1965), 11, 18, 21, 70, 150.

44 Geoffrey Barrow, *Robert Bruce*, 3rd edn (Edinburgh, 1988), 88; Cf. Donaldson, *The Jacobite Song*, 72ff., for a view of how this strain influenced Burns.

45 Duncan, op. cit., 11, 18.

46 Daiches, *The Scottish Enlightenment*, 19; Duncan, op. cit., 150.

47 Monod, 'For the king to enjoy his own again', 142; Daiches, *The Scottish Enlightenment*, 85.

48 Monod, 'For the king', 71, 155–70.

49 Donaldson, *The Jacobite Song*, 31, 35.

50 Cf. Daniel Szechi, 'The Jacobite theatre of death', in Cruickshanks and Black, op. cit., 57–73 (69), for an introduction to this argument.

51 The Pitsligo Papers, MSS 2740/4/18/1/16, Aberdeen University Library.

52 *Songs of Scotland. A Selection by John Reid* (no publisher, 1908), 149, 185.

53 Cf. John Lorne Campbell, *Highland Songs of the Forty-Five* (Edinburgh, 1933), 246–7, 287; see George Pratt Insh, *The Scottish Jacobite Movement* (Edinburgh and London, 1952), 174–5, for a suggestion on how Macpherson may have been influenced by this mood.

54 Mary Beacock Fryer, *Allan Maclean: Jacobite General* (Toronto, 1987), 114, 116, 130.

55 James Hogg, *The Jacobite Relics of Scotland*, 2 vols (Edinburgh, 1819–21), I, 194.

56 *Jacobite Songs* (no publisher, no date [contemporary]), 7.

57 Cf. *A Full Collection of All Poems upon Charles, Prince of Wales* (Edinburgh, 1745), 3, 5–6, 22, and *passim*.

58 Charles Petrie, *The Jacobite Movement: The Last Phase* (London, 1950), 95–6.

59 Lorne Campbell, op. cit., 3ff.

60 Figures from *Muster Roll of Prince Charles Edward Stuart's Army*, ed. Alastair

Livingstone of Bachuil, Christian W. H. Aikman, and Betty Stuart Hart (Aberdeen, 1984). For confirmation of the popular version a visit to the National Trust for Scotland video at Culloden is instructive.

61 Monod, 'For the king', 167ff.
62 ibid., 292, 405, 412.
63 Cf. Magnus Maclean, *The Literature of the Highlands*, new edn (Glasgow, 1904), 22.
64 *Scotland's Glory and Her Shame*, By a Well-wisher to The Good Old Cause, 2nd edn (no publisher, 1786), 8, 9, 35.
65 Cf. Barrow, op. cit., *passim*.
66 *Scotland's Glory*, 100.
67 *A Full Collection of All Poems upon Charles, Prince of Wales*, 5, 6, 9, 22.
68 *The Poems of Alexander MacDonald*, ed. Rev. A. MacDonald and Rev. Dr A. MacDonald (Inverness, 1924), 121; Lorne Campbell, op. cit., 169, 175. I quote the relevant translations.
69 Derick S. Thomson, *Introduction to Gaelic Poetry* (London, 1974), 165, 167, 169, 191, 196; Lorne Campbell, op. cit., 108–9, 113, 115, 143, 145.
70 Lorne Campbell, op. cit., 5–7.
71 ibid., 7n.; *The Poems of Alexander MacDonald*, 118–19.
72 *The Poems of Alexander MacDonald*, 69, 97, 125; Lorne Campbell, op. cit., 73.
73 *The Poems of Alexander MacDonald*, 161.
74 ibid., 329; Lorne Campbell, op. cit., 287–90.
75 The Corries, 'Flower of Scotland', in *Live From Scotland Volume* 2 (Glasgow, 1974).
76 *Poems on Several Occasions* (no publisher, 1750), 18, 19, 22.
77 *Songs of Scotland*, 198–201.
78 ibid., 148–50. Cf. The Corries, 'Legends of Scotland' (no publisher, no date), side 1.
79 Cf. Donaldson, *The Jacobite Song*, 88.

3 The invention of Scotland

1 Thomas Crawford, 'Political and protest songs in eighteenth-century Scotland I: Jacobite and anti-Jacobite', *Scottish Studies* 14 (1970), 1–33 (33).
2 *Poems of Ossian*, ed. John MacQueen, 2 vols (Edinburgh, 1971), II, 397.
3 Ruaridh Mor, 'An Bratach Uaine and An feadan Dubh of Clann Mhurich', *The Jacobite*, Summer 1989, 7–9.
4 Cf. Frank McLynn, *Charles Edward Stuart* (London, 1988), 435–7.
5 George Pratt Insh, *The Scottish Jacobite Movement* (Edinburgh and London, 1952), 168, 169, 174.
6 Derick S. Thomson, 'Macpherson's *Ossian*: ballads to epics', in Bo Alanquist, Seamus O'Cathan, and Padraig O'Healain (eds), *The Heroic Process: Form, Function and Fantasy in Folk Epic* (Dublin, 1987), 243–64 (264).
7 Andrew Hook, 'Scotland and romanticism: the international scene', in *The History of Scottish Literature* vol. 2, ed. A. Hook (Aberdeen, 1987), 307–21 (312, 315, 318).
8 ibid.; Pratt Insh, op.cit., 175.
9 Pratt Insh, op.cit., 176–7, 187.
10 John MacInnes, 'Twentieth-century recordings of Scottish Gaelic heroic ballads', in Alanquist *et al.*, op. cit., 101–30 (105).
11 Thomson, op.cit., 243–64 (253); Magnus Maclean, *The Literature of the Celts* (London, Glasgow, and Dublin, 1902), 197, 250.

12 John Simpson, 'The Cause of the '45', in Lesley Scott-Moncreiff (ed.), *The '45: To Gather an Image Whole* (Edinburgh, 1988), 1–13 (12); William Gillies, 'The Prince and the Gaels', same volume, 53–72 (61).
13 Gillies, op.cit., 70.
14 *Poems of Ossian*, I, 81–2, 106–8, 205, 442, 505–6; II, 397, 405–6.
15 ibid., 527ff., 588–9.
16 Thomson, op.cit., 261–2.
17 Bailey Saunders, *The Life and Letters of James Macpherson* (London, 1894), 183, 225, 280; Pratt Insh, op.cit., 177, 183.
18 James Kinsley (ed.), *The Poems and Songs of Robert Burns*, 3 vols (Oxford, 1968), I, 348.
19 Edwin Muir, *Collected Poems* (London, 1960), 98.
20 Cf. Paul Monod, 'For the king to enjoy his own again', unpublished Ph.D. thesis (Yale, 1985), 20, 472, 513, 532. The connections between Jacobitism and freemasonry are instructive in this regard.
21 This phrase originates with the Jacobite historian Frank McLynn, who makes much of the revolutionary status of Charles Edward's army and leadership in his *Charles Edward Stuart* (London, 1988).
22 William Donaldson, *The Jacobite Song* (Aberdeen, 1988), 2, 68.
23 Cf. Eric Richards, *A History of the Highland Clearances*, 2 vols (London, 1985), II, 46; Iain Fraser Grigor, *Mightier than a Lord* (Stornoway, 1979), 20ff.
24 Donaldson, op.cit., 89.
25 Gordon Bryan (ed.), *Scottish Nationalism and Cultural Identity in the Twentieth Century* (Westport, Connecticut, 1984), x.
26 Donaldson, op.cit., 87.
27 Kinsley, op.cit., 1, 637–8. I am indebted to Dr Donaldson for his recognition of the specially ambivalent qualities of this song, first discussed by him in his 1974 Aberdeen Ph.D. thesis.
28 J. De Lancy Ferguson and G. Ross Roy (eds), *The Letters of Robert Burns*, 2 vols (Oxford, 1985), II, 236.
29 It is instructive to compare Barbour's 'Fredome' with Burns's 'Liberty' as nationalist concepts. The continuing argument over Burns's politics shows how difficult he is to pin down over deliberately anachronistic uses of contemporary concepts.
30 Douglas Duncan, *Thomas Ruddiman* (Edinburgh and London, 1965), 41ff., 70, 170; David Daiches, *The Scottish Enlightenment* (Edinburgh, 1986), 18–19.
31 This is from one set of 'Welcome, Royal Charlie' (James Hogg, *The Jacobite Relics of Scotland*, 2 vols (Edinburgh, 1819–21), II, 144).
32 Cf. H. J. Hanham, *Scottish Nationalism* (London, 1969), 69.
33 This version of the song is discussed by Crawford, op.cit., 13.
34 Walter Scott, *Redgauntlet*, Waverley Novels XVIII (London, 1901), 505. Cf. the MS in the National Library of Scotland.
35 William Sharp, 'Walter Scott's land', *Harper's Monthly Magazine*, vol. 105 (June 1902), 3–12 (7).
36 A combination of credulity and quick temper is found in all these figures: cf. *The Bride of Lammermoor* (London, 1988 (1906)), 33ff.
37 Cf. E. P. Thompson, *Whigs and Hunters* (Harmondsworth, 1985), for a discussion of repressive legislation in the 1720s and its connection to perceived Jacobitism. The issue is also discussed in Monod, op.cit., 413–24, and by Eveline Cruickshanks and Howard Erskine-Hill in 'The Waltham Black Act and Jacobitism', *Journal of British Studies*, 24 (1984), 358–65.
38 That Scott knew of the true fate of his model for Bradwardine can be seen from his foreword to Alexander Lord Pitsligo, *Thoughts concerning Man's*

Condition and Duties in This Life ed. Lord Medwyn, 4th edn (Edinburgh and London, 1854).

39 Cf. John Prebble, *The King's Jaunt* (London, 1988), 365.

40 Cf. ibid., 103.

41 Cf. Derrick McClure, *Why Scots Matters* (Edinburgh, 1988), 7–13.

42 William Blake, *The Complete Poems*, ed. Alicia Ostriker (Harmondsworth, 1979), 182.

43 William Donaldson, 'The Jacobite song in eighteenth and early nineteenth-century Scotland', unpublished Ph.D. thesis (Aberdeen, 1974), 434.

44 Christopher Harvie, in Alan Bold (ed.), *Sir Walter Scott* (London and New Jersey, 1983), 17–42 (31).

45 Wendy Wood papers, ACC 7980/2, National Library of Scotland.

46 Prebble, op.cit., 18, 123, 211, 269.

47 ibid., 19, 97, 100.

48 ibid., opening chapters for a discussion of this question.

49 ibid., 9, 170.

50 ibid., 251. Cf. the later activities of James Grant (Hanham, op.cit., 76ff.), the antiquarian aspects of whose nationalism were closely linked to Jacobitism.

51 Andrew D. Hook, 'Scotland and America revisited', in *Scotland, Europe and the American Revolution*, ed. Owen Dudley Edwards and George Shepperson (Edinburgh, 1976), 83–8 (88).

52 Hogg, op. cit., 101.

53 Thomas Crawford, 'James Hogg: the play of region and nation', in Douglas Gifford (ed.), *The History of Scottish Literature*, vol. 3, 4 vols (Aberdeen, 1988), 89–103 (103).

54 James Hogg, *The Three Perils of Woman*, 3 vols (London, 1823), III, 123, 275–6, 324–7, 343.

55 ibid., 325, 327, 335, 339, 371; James Hogg, *The Private Memoirs and Confessions of a Justified Sinner*, with an introduction by André Gide (London, 1947), 12.

56 Hogg, *Confessions*, 19–20, 26, 47.

57 Donaldson, *The Jacobite Song*, 105; James Hogg, *The Works of the Ettrick Shepherd: Poems and Ballads* (London, no date), 415; a version of 'The Highlander's Farewell' which appears in Hogg, *Relics*, I, 186.

58 Francis Jeffrey, writing in *The Edinburgh Review* (August 1820), 154–7.

59 Hogg, *Relics*, I, 194.

60 This is clear from the relationship Hogg draws between Jacobitism and the Clearances identified and discussed by Donaldson, *The Jacobite Song*, 105ff.

61 Hogg, *Poems and Ballads*, 380; James Hogg, *Selected Poems*, ed. Douglas S. Mack (Oxford, 1970), 142.

62 Hogg, *Poems and Ballads*, 280, 283, 410, 413, 417, 423; *Relics*, I, 156.

63 Muir, op. cit., 98; Hogg, *Relics*, II, 427.

64 Donaldson, *The Jacobite Song*, 103; *Relics*, II, 90–2.

65 Hogg, *Poems and Ballads*, 415.

4 Reality and romance

1 Hugh MacDiarmid and Lewis Grassic Gibbon, *Scottish Scene* (London, 1934), i; *The Greig-Duncan Folk Song Collection Volume 3*, ed. Patrick Shuldham-Shaw, Emily B. Lyle, and Peter A. Hall (Aberdeen, 1983), 323; John Mercer, *Scotland: The Devolution of Power* (London, 1978), 137.

2 Cf. Keith Webb, *The Growth of Nationalism in Scotland* (Glasgow, 1977), 35, for a discussion of nationalist aspects of the Disruption.

3 Mercer, op. cit., 62.

4 Cf. Paul Monod, 'For the king to enjoy his own again', unpublished Ph.D. thesis (Yale, 1985); Mercer, op. cit., 135.
5 Cf. *Legitimist Kalendar 1895*, ed. Marquis de Ruvigny et Raineval (London, 1895), 1.
6 Andrew Noble, 'Highland history and narrative form in Scott and Stevenson', in A. Noble (ed.), *Robert Louis Stevenson* (London and New Jersey, 1983), 134–87 (152).
7 Ian A. Olson, 'Gavin Greig's lecture to the Scottish National Song Society, November 1909. A failure of nerve?', *Northern Scotland* 7(2), 1987, 151–8 (156).
8 Webb, op. cit., 34ff.
9 Anon., 'Irish Jacobite songs', in *The Royalist* VII: 3 (1896), 41–6 (43); Margaret Steele, review of *Highland Songs of the Forty-Five*, ed. John Lorne Campbell, *Scottish Historical Review* 65 (1), 1986, 90–1 (91).
10 Cf. in this context Yeats's view as discussed in Lucy McDiarmid, *Saving Civilization* (Cambridge, 1984), 37. Cf. also Howard Erskine-Hill, 'Literature and the Jacobite cause', in *Ideology and Conspiracy*, ed. Eveline Cruickshanks (Edinburgh, 1982), 49–69.
11 Sydney and Olive Checkland, *Industry and Ethos in Scotland 1832–1914* (London, 1984), 3, 7, 166.
12 Michael Fry, *Patronage and Principle* (Aberdeen, 1987), 3–4.
13 Magnus Maclean, *The Literature of the Highlands*, new edn (Glasgow, no date), 22.
14 Delia Miller, *Queen Victoria's Life in the Scottish Highlands Depicted by her Watercolour Artists* (London, 1985), 8.
15 Beverley Taylor and Elisabeth Brewer, *The Return of King Arthur* (Cambridge, 1983), 3, 15, 16, 21.
16 Miller, op. cit., 15, 25–6, 88.
17 ibid., 19, 134; Tom Nairn, *The Enchanted Glass* (London, 1988), 68.
18 Miller, op.cit., 69–70. Cf. Malcolm MacLean and Christopher Carrell, *As an Fhearann* (Glasgow, 1986), 39.
19 William Donaldson, *The Jacobite Song* (Aberdeen, 1988), 110, 113.
20 George Skene, 'The heirs of the Stuarts', *Quarterly Review* (June 1847), 57–85 (85).
21 John Sobieski and Charles Edward Stuart, *Lays of the Deer Forest*, 2 vols (Edinburgh and London, 1848), I, 269, 361–2, 367.
22 ibid., 368.
23 G. Ross Roy, 'Jacobite literature of the eighteenth century', *Scotia* I (1977), 42–55 (53); MacDonald (tr. Blackie), quoted in J. G. Mackay, 'After Culloden', *The Celtic Magazine* 20 (1912), 144–6, 171–3, 182–4, 202–3 (183); Andrew Dewar Gibb, *Scotland Resurgent* (Stirling, 1950), 170.
24 Cf. Neil Gunn, *Butcher's Broom* (London, 1977 (1934)).
25 David Stewart of Garth, *Sketches of the Character, Manners, and Present State of the Highlanders of Scotland* (Edinburgh, 1822; 2nd edn 1825). The latter edition was critical of the landlords.
26 Garth, quoted in Eric Richards, *A History of the Highland Clearances*, 2 vols (London, 1985), II, 46.
27 Richards, op. cit., II, 231, 239; MacLean and Carrell, op. cit., 5.
28 Neil Gunn, quoted in MacLean and Carrell, op. cit., 10; Iain Fraser Grigor, *Mightier than a Lord* (Stornoway, 1979), 14; Tony Dickson (ed.), *Scottish Capitalism* (London, 1980), 91.
29 Grigor, op. cit., 20.
30 MacLean and Carrell, op. cit., 21; Dewar Gibb, op. cit., 170.

31 MacLean and Carrell, op. cit., 39.
32 ibid., 41; Grigor, op. cit., 20–1.
33 Derek Cooper, *Hebridean Connection*, quoted in Richards, op. cit., II, 177.
34 Cf. *Ris A' Bhruthaich: Somhairle MacGill-eain*, ed. William Gillies (Stornoway, 1985), 64–5.
35 Cf. Richards, op. cit., II, 239; Grigor, op. cit., 33–5.
36 Audrey Cunningham, *The Loyal Clans* (Cambridge, 1932), 352ff.
37 Margaret Steele, op. cit.
38 W. R. Lawson (1884), quoted in Richards, op. cit., II, 83; Sorley Maclean in Maclean and Carrell, op. cit., 9.
39 Richards, op. cit., II, 68; MacLean and Carrell, op. cit., 6; Fry, op. cit., 105ff.
40 MacDiarmid and Grassic Gibbon, op. cit., 242; cf. *Selected Essays of Hugh MacDiarmid*, ed. Duncan Glen (London, 1969), 230.
41 Cf. H. J. Hanham, *Scottish Nationalism* (London, 1969), 79; Fry, op. cit., 4.
42 Fry, op. cit.; cf. Mercer, op. cit., 135–7.
43 Cf. Webb, op. cit., 33–5.
44 ibid., 34; Mercer, op. cit., 137.
45 Webb, op. cit., 35; Hanham, op. cit., 76.
46 Hanham, op. cit., 73, 77; Fry, op. cit., 206.
47 Webb, op. cit., 37; cf. Donaldson, op. cit., 86–7.
48 Isobel Murray, 'James Grant's *The Romance of War* and the "military novel"', *Northern Scotland* 6 (1985), 183–92 (188, 191).
49 Briefly discussed in William Donaldson, 'The Jacobite song in 18th and early 19th century Scotland', unpublished Ph.D. thesis (Aberdeen, 1974), 45, where George Lockhart is cited; and by John Gibson in *Playing the Scottish Card* (Edinburgh, 1988).
50 James Hogg, *The Jacobite Relics of Scotland*, 2 vols (Edinburgh, 1819–21), II, 431.
51 Cf. Frank McLynn, *The Jacobites* (London, 1985), for this reading of the Earl Marischal.
52 William Edmondstoune Aytoun, *Lays of the Scottish Cavaliers* (Edinburgh and London, 1870), 89–92.
53 Hanham, op. cit., 78; Checkland, op. cit., 166.
54 Hanham, op. cit., 78–9.
55 ibid., 79–80; *The Times*, 4 December 1856.
56 William Ferguson, *Scotland 1689 to the Present* (Edinburgh, 1968), 335–6.
57 Christopher Harvie, *Scotland and Nationalism* (London, 1977), 33; Ferguson, op. cit., 322, 378.
58 Harvie, op. cit., 40.
59 ibid., 39; Hanham, op. cit., 81.
60 Harvie, op. cit., 24, and Hanham, op. cit., 69, discuss Burns's codification of this approach, as I myself have done above (see chapter 3 pp. 82–4).
61 R. L. Stevenson, *The Young Chevalier: A Fragment* (no publisher, no date).
62 Anon., *The Fiery Cross* 43: 3 (1912), 8.
63 Hanham, op. cit., 88–9.
64 ibid., 86–8. The work of Theodore Napier and Ruaraidh Erskine was later to bear this out.
65 Checkland, op. cit., 166.
66 Cf. Grigor, op. cit., 33–5; Richards, op. cit., II, 83, 91, 98.
67 Cf. Murray Pittock, 'Decadence and the English tradition', unpublished D.Phil. thesis (Oxford, 1986), 156.
68 Cf. Robert Peters, 'Swinburne: a personal essay and a polemic', in Richard A.

Levine (ed.), *The Victorian Experience: The Poets* (Athens, Ohio, 1982); cf. Pittock, op. cit., 104–5.

69 Cf. Gordon Bryan (ed.), *Scottish Nationalism and Cultural Identity in the Twentieth Century* (Westport, Connecticut, 1984), 22; cf. *Fiery Cross* (April 1905), 3.

70 Fry, op. cit., 105.

71 Stevenson, op. cit.; Theodore Napier, *The Fiery Cross* 3 (1901), 5.

72 J. G. Nelson, *The Early Nineties: A View from the Bodley Head* (Cambridge, Massachusetts, 1971), 178.

73 *Catalogue of the Exhibition of the Royal House of Stuart* (London, [1888]), 118ff.; Anon., 'The Royal House of Stuart', *All the Year Round* (February 1889), 133–6; Ian Fletcher, *The Collected Poems of Lionel Johnson* (New York and London, 1982), xli.

74 Herbert Horne, editorial, *The Century Guild Hobby Horse* (4: 1889), 1–8 (1, 3).

75 Unsigned review of Reginald Palgrave's *Oliver Cromwell*, *The Royalist*, 10 (16 January 1891), 149, 152 (149).

76 *Ris A' Bhruthaich: Somhairle MacGill-eain*, 20.

77 Philip O'Leary, '"What stalked through the post office?": Pearse's Cu Chulain', in John T. Koch and Jean Ritmueller (eds), *Proceedings of the Harvard Celtic Colloquium*, III (Cambridge, Massachusetts, 1983), 21–38 (23, 31).

78 Neo-Jacobite papers of Ian Fletcher, Reading University Library; Fletcher, op. cit., 32.

79 Neo-Jacobite papers of Ian Fletcher.

80 *Legitimist Kalendar 1895*, 60. The poem was Lionel Johnson's 'By the statue of King Charles at Charing Cross' (Fletcher, op. cit., 11–12).

81 Ian Fletcher, 'The white rose rebudded: neo-Jacobitism in the 1890s', in *W. B. Yeats and his Contemporaries* (Brighton, 1987), 83–123 (118).

82 Cf. *The Royalist*, III(4) (30 July 1892), 49–50.

83 *The Legitimist Kalendar for 1898*, ed. Marquis de Ruvigny et Raineval and Cranston Metcalfe (London, 1898), 63; *The Legitimist Kalendar for 1899*, ed. Marquis de Ruvigny et Raineval (London, 1899), 67; Alastair Stuart, 'The White Cockade', *Munsey's Magazine* (June 1902), 421–6 (426).

84 Ian Fletcher, 'The white rose rebudded: neo-Jacobitism in the 1890s', in *Journal of the Francis Thompson Society*, 4/5 (1974), 17–52 (28–30).

85 Andrew Lang, 'The Tenth of June 1715', *Everybody's Magazine*, June 1901.

86 Bernard Kelly, *The Conqueror of Culloden* (London, 1903), 75.

87 Fletcher, *W.B. Yeats and His Contemporaries*, 102, 103, 107; cf. Colonel S. Dewe White, 'Revival of Jacobitism', *The Westminster Review*, 146:4 (1896), 417–26 (417); W.G. Blaikie Murdoch, *The Renaissance of the Nineties* (London, 1911), 3.

88 Frederic Harrison, *Memories and Thoughts* (London, 1906), 68, 82.

89 *The Legitimist Ensign* 3 (1901), xii; *The Jacobite* IV(5) (1903), 33; IV(7), 52; *The Legitimist Kalendar for 1899*, 67; C. S. Millard, letter of 31 October 1905, Legitimist Jacobite League Miscellaneous Papers, Bodleian Library 2776c2.

90 Allen Upward, *Treason*, 3rd edn (London, 1904), title-page, 39; Allen Upward, *The Fourth Conquest of England* (London, 1905), 44, 52.

91 Unsigned review of Allen Upward, *High Treason*, in *The Jacobite*, IV, 11, 12 (1903), 76; W. G. Blaikie Murdoch, *The Royal Stuarts in their Connection with Art and Letters* (Edinburgh, 1908), 19.

92 Theodore Napier, *The Royal House of Stuart: A Plea for its Restoration. An Appeal to Loyal Scotsmen*, Legitimist Jacobite League Publications no. 17 (Edinburgh and London, 1898), 17, 31.

NOTES

93 G. W. T. Omond, *The Early History of the Scottish Union Question* (Edinburgh and London, 1897); James Mackinnon, *The Union of Scotland and England* (London, 1896), 501–24 (523).
94 Wilmott Dixon, *The Jacobite Episode in Scottish History and its Relative Literature* (Edinburgh, Glasgow, and London, 1874), 2.
95 Andrew Dewar Gibb, *Scotland Resurgent* (Stirling, 1950), 243–6.
96 Dixon, op. cit., 143.
97 Pittendrigh Macgillivray, *Memories of the '45* (Edinburgh, 1911), 3, 4, 9.
98 Theodore Napier, *The Fiery Cross* 1 (Edinburgh, 1901), 2, 6.
99 Anon., 'Distinguished Jacobite's gift', in *The Jacobite*, I(5) (1920), 18.
100 Keith Webb, *The Growth of Nationalism in Scotland* (Glasgow, 1977), 39–40; Fry, op. cit., 102–5ff.
101 Hanham, op. cit., 93.
102 ibid., 121.
103 ibid., 95; Alex Laidlaw, 'The Young Scots Society and Scottish Home Rule' in *The Fiery Cross* 11 (1903), 6.
104 *The Fiery Cross* 1 (1901), 2.
105 ibid., 3ff., and *passim*.
106 ibid., 3, 6.
107 *The Fiery Cross* 3 (1901), 3–4; Hanham, op. cit., 126, 133; W. B. Yeats, *Collected Poems* (London, 1950), 85.
108 *The Fiery Cross* 2 (1901), 8; 3 (1901), 5; 4 (1901), 4–5; 5 (1902), 3; 6 (1902), 8.
109 ibid., 7 (1902), 2, 6.
110 'Strathgarry', editorial, 'A Scottish National Party', *The Fiery Cross* 11 (1903), 2; 12 (1903), 2.
111 ibid., 7 (1902), 2; 10 (1903), 5, 8; 17 (1905), 8.
112 'Jacobus', 'Did King Henry relinquish his claim to the British throne?' *The Fiery Cross*, 13 (1904), 4; Theodore Napier, 'The anniversary of the Battle of Culloden', 15 (1904), 4–5.
113 *The Fiery Cross* 20 (1906), 3–8; 7 (1902), 5; Hanham, op. cit., 121.
114 Fry, op. cit., 128; Webb, op. cit., 39.
115 Hanham, op. cit., 123; Harvie, op. cit., 43, 45.
116 Hanham, op. cit., 123, 125.
117 ibid., 135, 142.

5 A nation once again?
Scotland since 1918

1 Duncan Glen, *Hugh MacDiarmid and the Scottish Renaissance* (Edinburgh and London, 1964), 4; Sydney Goodsir Smith, *Collected Poems* (London, 1975), 47; Hugh MacDiarmid, 'A Scots Communist looks at Bonny Prince Charlie', *Scots Independent* (August 1945), 1; F. W. Robertson, 'Re-appraising the Forty-Five', *Scots Independent* (April 1944), 4.
2 Cf. Duncan Glen (ed.), *Selected Essays of Hugh MacDiarmid* (London, 1969).
3 Glen, *Hugh MacDiarmid and the Scottish Renaissance*, 4–5.
4 Cf. Alan Bold, *Hugh MacDiarmid* (London, 1988), 318–19; Nan Milton (ed.), *John Maclean: In the Rapids of Revolution* (London, 1978), 218.
5 Cf. Hugh MacDiarmid in Alan Bold (ed.), *The Thistle Rises* (London, 1984), 233–43 (242).
6 MacDiarmid, 'A Scots Communist', 1.
7 Bold, *Hugh MacDiarmid*, 124, 228.
8 Hugh MacDiarmid, *Complete Poems 1920–1976*, ed. Michael Grieve and W. R.

179

Aitken, 2 vols (London, 1978), I, 157; G. Gregory Smith, *Scottish Literature: Character and Influence* (London, 1919).
9 Cf. MacDiarmid's 1968 speech at a 1320 Club symposium in Bold (ed.), *The Thistle Rises*, 233–43.
10 MacDiarmid, *Complete Poems*, I, 213, 273.
11 Mary Helen Thuente, *W. B. Yeats and Irish Folklore* (New Jersey, 1980), 198ff.
12 Lucy McDiarmid, *Saving Civilization* (Cambridge, 1984), 37.
13 MacDiarmid, *Complete Poems*, I, 469ff.
14 ibid., 228, 274.
15 ibid., 476; Bold, *The Thistle Rises*, 60.
16 Hugh MacDiarmid and Lewis Grassic Gibbon, *Scottish Scene* (London, 1934), 139–40.
17 Cf. G. M. Trevelyan, *England Under the Stuarts* (London, 1982), and P. Hume Brown's *History of Scotland*, attacked both by Fionn MacColla and John Lorne Campbell, in *Highland Songs of the Forty-Five* (Edinburgh, 1933), xviii–xx.
18 Cf. Margaret Barnard Pickel, *Charles I as Patron of Poetry and Drama* (London, 1936).
19 Cf. Edwin Muir, *Scott and Scotland* (Edinburgh, 1936), 150, 153, 159; Murray Pittock, 'Edwin Muir and Scottish nationalism', in *Edwin Muir: Centenary Assessments*, ed. D. S. Robb and C. J. Maclachlan (Aberdeen, 1990), 38–46.
20 Muir, op. cit., 150, 153.
21 Edwin Muir, *Collected Poems* (London, 1960), 97, 228–9; Murray Pittock, 'This is the place: Edwin Muir and Scotland', *Scottish Literary Journal* 14:1 (1987), 53–73.
22 David Morrison (ed.), *Essays on Fionn MacColla* (Thurso, no date), 5, 20.
23 ibid., 14.
24 Lorne Campbell, op. cit., xix–xx.
25 Alan Bold, 'And the Cock Crew', in Morrison, op. cit., 38–45 (41).
26 Andrew Dewar Gibb, *Scotland Resurgent* (Stirling, 1950), 178.
27 Cf. Norman Allan, *Scotland: The Broken Image* (Ottawa, 1982), 17ff.; *Scots Independent*, 1927–8, *passim*.
28 John Rafferty, quoted in Morrison, op. cit., 35 (Fionn MacColla: 'Mein Bumpf').
29 C. M. Grieve (Hugh MacDiarmid), 'Wider aspects of Scottish nationalism', *Scots Independent* II(1) (1927), 3–4; L. M. G., 'The "Elusive Gael" – and the Highland delusion', *Scots Independent* II(6), (1928), 94–5.
30 *Scots Independent* II(8) (1928), 125–6; III(2) (1929), 143; IV(7) (1930), 85.
31 Compton Mackenzie, *Prince Charlie* (Edinburgh, 1932), 75, 155, 197.
32 H. J. Hanham, *Scottish Nationalism* (London, 1969), 147.
33 William Power, 'The next step in world politics: a United States of Europe', *Scottish Opinion* 2 (1947), 11.
34 F. W. Robertson, writing in *Scots Independent* (April 1944), 4. Cf. also F. W. Robertson's *The Scottish Way 1746–1946* (publisher not known, 1946).
35 Robertson, *The Scottish Way 1746–1946*, 1; Buchan, quoted by Christopher Harvie, writing in *Cencrastus* 26 (1987), 35–41 (40); Malcolm Chapman, *The Gaelic Vision in Scottish Culture* (London, 1978), 23.
36 Francis Russell Hart and J. B. Pick, *Neil M. Gunn: A Highland Life* (London, 1981), 108.
37 ibid., 95.
38 Cf. Tom Scott, writing in *Agenda* (double issue: 'Hugh MacDiarmid and Scottish poetry') (1968), 20; Ruaraidh Erskine, *Changing Scotland* (Montrose, 1931).
39 Michael Parnell, *Eric Linklater* (London, 1984), 123.

NOTES

40 Hanham, op. cit., 180; Joy Hendry, *The Way Forward* (Edinburgh, 1980), 15.
41 Cf. John Mercer, *Scotland: The Devolution of Power* (London, 1978), 150ff.
42 Hanham, op. cit., 154; *Scots Independent* III (1928–9), 59.
43 Anon., 'Soirée of the White Cockade-Edinburgh. 16th June 1979', in *Beauceant* 3(2) (1979), 5.
44 Hanham, op. cit., 145, 150, 155, 157.
45 ibid., 142–4; *Scots Independent* VII (1933), 150.
46 *Scots Independent* VII (1933), 124–5, 156, 172; VIII (1933), 12.
47 J. M. MacCormick, 'A new National Covenant', *Scots Independent* IV(8) (1930), 100; Neil MacCormick, 'Constitutionalism and constitutions', in *What Scotland Wants: Ten Years On*, Unit for the study of government in Scotland at Edinburgh University (Edinburgh, 1989), 3–11 (3).
48 *Scots Independent* (1936), nos 2 (2), 3; 2 (4), 1; William L. Miller, *The End of British Politics?* (Oxford, 1981), 57.
49 Hanham, op. cit., 157; *Scots Independent* VII (1933), 68; VIII (1933), 25; (1935) nos 1 (4), 1.
50 Christopher Harvie, *Scotland and Nationalism* (London, 1977), 51, 122; Neil Gunn, letter of 3 April 1933 to T. H. Gibson, quoted in Hart and Pick, op. cit., 114; ibid., 110; cf. William Ferguson, *Scotland 1689 to the Present* (Edinburgh, 1968), 378.
51 H. C. MacNeacail, 'William Wallace: hero, patriot, statesman, martyr', *Scots Independent* VI (1932), 151–8 (151); Glen, *Selected Essays of Hugh MacDiarmid*, 228.
52 Hanham, op. cit., 175, 179.
53 Compton Mackenzie in *The Royal Stuart Calendar 1931*, ed. David Ross Fotheringham, 3.
54 *Scots Independent* (October 1947), 1; Iain Crichton Smith, *The Exiles* (Manchester and Dublin, 1984), 26.
55 Cf. William L. Miller, *The End of British Politics?* (Oxford, 1981).
56 Cf. the discussion of Hume Brown and Trevelyan's work above. A modern manifestation of the fierce partisanship still surrounding the period can be found in the opening pages of J. C. Clark's *Revolution and Rebellion* (Cambridge, 1986).
57 MacDiarmid (C. M. Grieve), 'A Scots Communist looks at Bonny Prince Charlie', 1.
58 I am thinking here in particular of the work of Paul Monod and Frank McLynn (*Charles Edward Stuart* (London, 1988)).
59 Cf. Mick Hume and Derek Owen, *Is There A Scottish Solution?* (London, 1988), 87 and *passim*.
60 Cf. Frank McLynn, profile in *Times Higher Education Supplement*, 23 September 1988, 18; Ian B. Cowan, 'The inevitability of Union – a historical fallacy?', *Scotia* V (1981), 1–8.
61 The phrase is Philip Larkin's, from his 1982 interview in *The Observer*.
62 Cf. Clark, op. cit., 45ff., 66; J. H. Plumb, *The Growth of Political Stability in England 1675–1725*, (London, 1967), 18.
63 Paul Monod, 'For the king to enjoy his own again', unpublished Ph.D. thesis (Yale, 1985), 662ff.
64 Tom Nairn, *The Enchanted Glass* (London, 1988), 219.
65 Donald Smith, 'You may well ask: nine decades of Mitchison', *Cencrastus* 13 (1983), 14–17 (17).
66 ibid.
67 George MacBeth, *My Scotland: Fragments of a State of Mind* (London and Basingstoke, 1973), 17, 33; *Agenda* double issue: 'Hugh MacDiarmid and Scottish poetry' (1968), 93.

68 Ailie Munro, *The Folk Music Revival in Scotland* (London, 1984), 47.

69 ibid., 50, 80, 153, 155.

70 Cf. Wendy Wood papers, National Library of Scotland ACC 7980/1/15.

71 Hugh MacDiarmid, in Bold, *The Thistle Rises*, 233–43 (242); also Duncan Glen (ed.), *Selected Essays of Hugh MacDiarmid* (London, 1969), 171–6; J. M. Reid, *Scotland's Progress* (London, 1971), 150.

72 Sydney Goodsir Smith, *Collected Poems* (London, 1975), 199.

73 Tom Crawford, review of Ailie Munro's *The Folk Music Revival in Scotland*, *Scottish Literary Journal* Supplement 25 (1986), 27–32 (29).

74 G. W. R. Grant, 'The '45: a disastrous mistake', in Lesley Scott-Moncreiff (ed.), *The '45: To Gather an Image Whole* (Edinburgh, 1988), 23–34 (25).

75 John McGrath, *The Cheviot, the Stag and the Black, Black Oil* (London, 1981), xxvi, xxvii.

76 ibid., 42, 54–5.

77 ibid., 48.

78 Malcolm Chapman, *The Gaelic Vision in Scottish Culture* (London, 1978), 21.

79 Neal Ascherson, 'Devolution diary', in *Cencrastus* 22 (1986), 3–14 (11); Wendy Wood papers, National Library of Scotland, ACC 7980/2; The Corries, *Live from Scotland Volume* 1 (Pan-Audio, 1974).

80 Miller, op. cit., 25.

81 Wendy Wood papers, National Library of Scotland, ACC 7980, Box 26.

82 Miller, op. cit., 33; *Scots Independent*, 13 November 1965, 1; editorial, *Scots Independent*, 18 November 1967, 1; *Scots Independent*, 9 March 1968, 8.

83 *Scots Independent*, 27 January 1968, 1; 2 March 1968, 8; 18 May 1968, 6; 1 June 1968, 4; 22 June 1968, 5; 20 July 1968; 17 May 1969, 5; 9 May 1970.

84 Cf. Hanham, op. cit., 162ff.

85 Wendy Wood, 'Yours sincerely for Scotland' (MS), Wendy Wood papers, National Library of Scotland, ACC 8197/2.

86 Wendy Wood papers, National Library of Scotland, ACC 7980/2.

87 Cf. Gordon Bryan (ed.), *Scottish Nationalism and Cultural Identity in the Twentieth Century* (Westport, Connecticut, 1984), x; Hugh MacDiarmid, 'The upsurge of Scottish nationalism', in Glen, *Selected Essays of Hugh MacDiarmid*, 228–32 (228–9).

88 Cairns Craig, 'Visitors from the stars: Scottish film culture', *Cencrastus* 11 (1983), 6–11 (8–9); Hume and Owen, op. cit., 87; The Corries, 'The Dawning of the Day' (Pan-Audio, 1982).

89 This is true even of good recent work like Peter Womack's *Improvement and Romance* (Basingstoke, 1989).

90 Cf. McLynn, *Charles Edward Stuart*, 181, and *passim*.

91 Cf. Petrie's *If* and my own review of Kybett's book in *British Journal of Eighteenth Century Studies* 13: 1 (1990), 107.

92 This particular metaphor surely reaches its ultimate expression in the last part of John McGrath's *Border Warfare*, which represents the development of modern Scottish politics as a football match.

93 Scott-Moncrieff, op. cit., dustjacket, xi.

94 The Corries, *Live From Scotland Volume* 1 (Pan-Audio, 1974).

95 The Corries, *Stovies* (1980).

96 Bruce Lenman, *The Jacobite Cause* (Glasgow, 1986), conclusion.

97 Cf. Norman Murray, *The Celtic Tragedy* (Montreal, 1919–21); Donald Macaulay (ed.), *Modern Scottish Gaelic Poems* (Edinburgh, 1976), 186.

98 The Corries, *Live From Scotland Volume* 1 (Pan-Audio, 1974).

99 MacDiarmid, *Complete Poems 1920–1976*, I, 157.

Select bibliography

Anon., *An Account of the Proceedings of the Meeting of the Estates in Scotland*, London, 1689.

——, 'Irish Jacobite songs', *The Royalist* VII: 3, 1896.

——, 'A letter to a member of The Convention of States in Scotland', Edinburgh, 1689.

——, 'The Royal House of Stuart', *All the Year Round*, February 1889.

——, 'Soirée of the White Cockade-Edinburgh. 16th June 1979', *Beauceant* 3(2), 1979.

——, *Villpone: Or, Remarks on Some Proceedings in Scotland*, publisher not known, 1707.

Aberdeen University Library, MSS 2222, 2718.

An Account of the Present Persecution of the Church in Scotland, London, 1690.

Agenda, 1968.

Alanquist, Bo, O'Cathan, Seamas, and O'Healain, Padraig (eds), *The Heroic Process: Form, Function and Fantasy in Folk Epic*, Dublin, 1987.

Allan, Norman, *Scotland: The Broken Image*, Ottawa, 1982.

Allardyce, Colonel James (ed.), *Historical Papers Relating to the Jacobite Period 1699–1750*, 2 vols, Spalding Club, Aberdeen, 1895.

Anderson, James, *Scotland Independent*, Edinburgh, 1705.

The Appeal of the Episcopal Clergy in Scotland to the Lords in Parliament, publisher not known, 1718.

Ascanio o El Jova Aventurero, Madrid, no date.

Ascanius or the Young Adventurer, London, 1746.

Ascherson, Neal, 'Devolution diary', *Cencrastus* 22, 1986.

Aytoun, William Edmondstoune, *Lays of the Scottish Cavaliers*, Edinburgh and London, 1870.

Barber, Richard, *The Figure of Arthur*, Worcester and London, 1972.

Barrow, Geoffrey, *Robert Bruce*, 3rd edn, Edinburgh, 1988.

Beauceant, 1979.

Blackie, J. S., *The Language and Literature of the Scottish Highlands*, Edinburgh, 1876.

Blaikie Murdoch, W. G., *The Spirit of Jacobite Loyalty*, Edinburgh, 1907.

——, *The Royal Stuarts in their Connection with Art and Letters*, Edinburgh, 1908.

——, *The Renaissance of the Nineties*, London, 1911.

Blake, William, *The Complete Poems*, ed. Alicia Ostriker, Harmondsworth, 1979.

Bold, Alan (ed.), *Sir Walter Scott*, London and New Jersey, 1983.

—— (ed.), *The Thistle Rises*, London, 1984.

——, *Hugh MacDiarmid*, London, 1988.

Bolingbroke, Viscount, *Letters on the Spirit of Patriotism*, London, 1749.

The Book of the Lamentations of Charles the Son of James, Edinburgh, 1746.

Boulton, Harold, *Prince Charlie in Song*, London and Edinburgh, 1934.

Brooks-Davies, Douglas, *Pope's Dunciad and the Queen of Night*, Manchester, 1985.

Brown, Gordon, *Maxton*, Edinburgh, 1986.

Brown, Mary Ellen, 'The study of folk tradition' in *The History of Scottish Literature*, general ed. Cairns Craig, 4 vols (vol. III), Aberdeen, 1988.

Bryan, Gordon (ed.), *Scottish Nationalism and Cultural Identity in the Twentieth Century*, Westport, Connecticut, 1984.

Butt, John (ed.), *The Poems of Alexander Pope*, London, 1965.

Campana de Cavelli, Marquise, *Les Derniers Stuarts à Saint-Germain-en-Laye*, London and Edinburgh, 1871.

Carlton, Charles, *Charles I: The Personal Monarch*, London, 1983.

Carruthers, R., *The Highland Note-Book*, Edinburgh, 1843.

Catalogue of the Exhibition of the Royal House of Stuart, London, no date [1888].

A Cat May Look upon a King, Amsterdam, 1714.

Cencrastus, vol. 11, 1983; 13, 1983; 22, 1986; 26, 1987.

The Century Guild Hobby Horse, 4, 1889.

Chapman, Malcolm, *The Gaelic Vision in Scottish Culture*, London, 1978.

Charles-Roux, J. M., 'Charles I: the sovereign saint', *Royalist Focus* 1, 1986.

Checkland, Sydney, and Checkland, Olive, *Industry and Ethos in Scotland 1832-1914*, London, 1984.

Childs, John, *The Army, James II and the Glorious Revolution*, Manchester, 1980.

Clark, J. C., *English Society 1688–1832*, Cambridge, 1985.

——, *Revolution and Rebellion*, Cambridge, 1986.

——, 'On moving the middle ground: the significance of Jacobitism in historical studies', in Eveline Cruickshanks and Jeremy Black (eds), *The Jacobite Challenge*, Edinburgh, 1988.

Clyne, Norval, *The Scottish Jacobites and Their Poetry*, Aberdeen, 1887.

Cowan, Ian B., 'The inevitability of Union – a historical fallacy?', *Scotia* V, 1981.

Cowley, Abraham, *Poems*, ed. A. R. Waller, Cambridge, 1905.

Craig, Cairns, 'Visitors from the stars: Scottish film culture', *Cencrastus* 11, 1983.

—— (ed.), *The History of Scottish Literature*, 4 vols, Aberdeen, 1987–8.

Craig, Sir Thomas, *Scotland's Soveraignty Asserted*, ed. George Ridpath, London, 1695.

Crawford, Thomas, 'Political and protest songs in eighteenth-century Scotland I: Jacobite and anti-Jacobite', *Scottish Studies* 14, 1970.

—— (ed.), *Love, Labour and Liberty: The Eighteenth Century Scottish Lyric*, Cheadle Hulme, 1976.

——, review of Ailie Munro's *The Folk Music Revival* in *Scottish Literary Journal*, Supplement 25, 1986.

——, 'James Hogg: the play of region and nation', in *The History of Scottish Literature*, vol. 3, ed. Douglas Gifford, Aberdeen, 1988.

Crawfurd, Raymond, *The King's Evil*, Oxford, 1911.

Crichton Smith, Iain, *The Exiles*, Manchester and Dublin, 1984.

Croker, T. Crofton, *The Historical Songs of Ireland*, London, 1841.

Cruickshanks, Eveline, *Political Untouchables*, London, 1979.

—— (ed.), *Ideology and Conspiracy: Aspects of Jacobitism 1689–1759*, Edinburgh, 1982.

Cruickshanks, Eveline, and Black, Jeremy (eds), *The Jacobite Challenge*, Edinburgh, 1988.

Cruickshanks, Eveline, and Erskine-Hill, Howard, 'The Waltham Black Act and Jacobitism', *Journal of British Studies*, 24, 1984.

Cunningham, Audrey, *The Loyal Clans*, Cambridge, 1932.

Curtis, Tony, *Wales: The Imagined Nation*, Bridgend, 1986.

Daiches, David, *The Paradox of Scottish Culture*, London, 1964.

——, *The Scottish Enlightenment*, Edinburgh, 1986.

Daly, John (ed.), *Reliques of Irish Jacobite Poetry*, Dublin, 1844.

De Lancy Ferguson, J., and Ross Roy, G.(eds), *The Letters of Robert Burns*, 2 vols, Oxford, 1985.

Dewar Gibb, Andrew, *Scotland Resurgent*, Stirling, 1950.

Diamond Cut Diamond: The Lamentations of the Nonjuring Clergy, &c, 2nd edn, London, 1724.

Dickinson, H. T., *Liberty and Property*, London, 1977.

Dickson, Tony (ed.), *Scottish Capitalism*, London, 1980.

Dixon, Wilmott, *The Jacobite Episode in Scottish History and its Relative Literature*, Edinburgh, Glasgow, and London, 1874.

Donaldson, Gordon, *Scotland James V to James VII*, Edinburgh and London, 1965.

Donaldson, William, 'The Jacobite song in 18th and early 19th century Scotland', unpublished Ph.D. thesis, Aberdeen, 1974.

——, *The Jacobite Song*, Aberdeen, 1988.

Dryden, John, *The Poems and Fables*, ed. James Kinsley, London, 1962.

Duncan, Douglas, *Thomas Ruddiman*, Edinburgh and London, 1965.

The Edinburgh Review, August 1820.

'An epistle from a student at Oxford to the Chevalier', London, 1717.

Erskine, Ruaraidh, *Changing Scotland*, Montrose, 1931.

Erskine-Hill, Howard, 'Literature and the Jacobite cause', in Eveline Cruickshanks (ed.), *Ideology and Conspiracy*, Edinburgh, 1982.

Ferguson, William, *Scotland 1689 to the Present*, Edinburgh, 1968.

Fergusson, Robert, *Works*, Edinburgh, 1805.

Fieldhouse, H. N., 'Bolingbroke's share in the Jacobite intrigue of 1710–14', *English Historical Review*, 1937.

The Fiery Cross, ed. Theodore Napier, Edinburgh, 1901–12.

Fletcher, Ian, 'The white rose rebudded: neo-Jacobitism in the 1890s', *Journal of the Francis Thompson Society* 4/5, 1974.

——, *The Collected Poems of Lionel Johnson*, New York and London, 1982.

——, *W. B. Yeats and His Contemporaries*, Brighton, 1987.

Fotheringham, David Ross (ed.), *The Royal Stuart Calendar 1931*, publisher not known, no date.

Four new songs, and a Prophecy, National Library Scotland, Rosebery Pamphlets, 1–2–85, publisher not known, no date.

Fry, Michael, *Patronage and Principle*, Aberdeen, 1987.

Fryer, Mary Beacock, *Allan Maclean: Jacobite General*, Toronto, 1987.

A Full Collection of All Poems upon Charles, Princes of Wales, Edinburgh, 1745.

Fulton, Robin (ed.), *A Garioch Miscellany*, Loanhead, 1986.

Galloway, B. L., *The Union of England and Scotland 1603–1608*, Edinburgh, 1986.

Galter, Frank T., 'On the literary value of some Scottish Presbyterian writings in the context of the Scottish Enlightenment', in Dietrich Strauss and Horst W. Drescher (eds), *Scottish Language and Literature, Medieval and Renaissance*, Frankfurt, 1986.

Garioch, Robert, *Complete Poetical Works*, ed. Robin Fulton, Edinburgh, 1983.

Gibson, John, *Playing the Scottish Card*, Edinburgh, 1988.

Gillies, William (ed.), *Ris A' Bhruthaich: Somhairle MacGill-eain*, Stornoway, 1985.

Glen, Duncan, *Hugh MacDiarmid and the Scottish Renaissance*, Edinburgh and London, 1964.
——(ed.), *Selected Essays of Hugh MacDiarmid*, London, 1969.
Goodsir Smith, Sydney, *Collected Poems*, London, 1975.
Grigor, Iain Fraser, *Mightier than a Lord*, Stornoway, 1979.
Gunn, Neil, *Butcher's Broom*, London, 1977 (1934).
Hanham, H. J., *Scottish Nationalism*, London, 1969.
'The happy lady', PRO, SP 35/31/154.
Harrison, Frederic, *Memories and Thoughts*, London, 1906.
Hart, Francis Russell, and Pick, J. B., *Neil M. Gunn: A Highland Life*, London, 1981.
Harvie, Christopher, *Scotland and Nationalism*, London, 1977.
Hendry, Joy, *The Way Forward*, Edinburgh, 1980.
Herrick, Robert, *The Poetical Works*, ed. L. C. Martin, Oxford, 1956.
Hogg, James, *The Jacobite Relics of Scotland*, 2 vols, Edinburgh, 1819–21.
——, *The Jacobite Relics of Scotland*, Paisley, 1874.
——, *The Three Perils of Woman*, 3 vols, London, 1823.
——, *The Private Memoirs and Confessions of a Justified Sinner*, with an introduction by André Gide, London, 1947.
——, *Selected Poems*, ed. Douglas S. Mack, Oxford, 1970.
——, *The Works of the Ettrick Shepherd: Poems and Ballads*, London, no date.
Holmes, Ronald, *The Legend of Sawney Bean*, London, 1975.
Hook, Andrew, 'Scotland and America revisited', in Owen Dudley Edwards and George Shepperson (eds), *Scotland, Europe and the American Revolution*, Edinburgh, 1976.
——, 'Scotland and romanticism: the international scene', in *The History of Scottish Literature*, vol. 2, ed. Andrew Hook, Aberdeen, 1987.
Houston, R. A., and Whyte, I. D. (eds), *Scottish Society 1500–1800*, Cambridge, 1989.
Hume, Mick, and Owen, Derek, *Is There A Scottish Solution?*, London, 1988.
The Jacobite, 1902– .
The Jacobite (New Zealand), 1919– .
Jacobite Minstrelsy, Glasgow, 1829.
Jenkins, Elizabeth, *The Mystery of King Arthur*, London, 1975.
Jones, J. R., *The Revolution of 1688 in England*, London, 1972.
Kelly, Bernard, *The Conqueror of Culloden*, London, 1903.
Kenyon, J. P., *Revolution Principles: The Politics of Party 1689–1720*, Cambridge, 1977.
Kinsley, James (ed.), *The Poems and Songs of Robert Burns*, 3 vols, Oxford, 1968.
Kramnick, Isaac, *Bolingbroke and His Circle*, Cambridge, Massachusetts, 1968.
Kybett, Susan Maclean, *Bonnie Prince Charlie*, London, 1988.
Lang, Andrew, 'The tenth of June 1715', *Everybody's Magazine*, June 1901.
——, *Prince Charles Edward Stuart: The Young Chevalier*, London, New York, and Bombay, 1903.
The Legitimist Ensign 1900– .
Legitimist Kalendar 1895, ed. Marquis de Ruvigny et Raineval, London, 1895.
The Legitimist Kalendar for 1898, ed. Marquis de Ruvigny et Raineval and Cranston Metcalfe, London, 1898.
The Legitimist Kalendar for 1899, ed. Marquis de Ruvigny et Raineval, London, 1899.
Lenman, Bruce, *The Jacobite Risings in Britain 1689–1746*, London, 1980.
——, 'The Scottish Episcopal clergy and the ideology of Jacobitism', in Eveline Cruickshanks (ed.), *Ideology and Conspiracy*, Edinburgh, 1982.

——, *The Jacobite Cause*, Glasgow, 1986.

Leruez, Jacques, *L'Ecosse une nation sans état*, Lille, no date.

Levine, Richard A. (ed.), *The Victorian Experience: The Poets*, Athens, Ohio, 1982.

Linklater, Eric, *The Prince in the Heather*, London, 1965.

Linklater, Magnus, and Hesketh, Christian, *For King and Conscience*, London, 1989.

Livingstone, Alastair, Aikman, Christian W. H., and Hart, Betty Stuart (eds), *Muster Roll of Prince Charles Edward Stuart's Army*, Aberdeen, 1984.

Lock, F. P., *Swift's Tory Politics*, London, 1983.

Lorne Campbell, John, *Highland Songs of the Forty-Five*, Edinburgh, 1933.

Macaulay, Donald (ed.), *Modern Scottish Gaelic Poems*, Edinburgh, 1976.

MacBeth, George, *My Scotland: Fragments of a State of Mind*, London and Basingstoke, 1973.

McClure, Derrick, *Why Scots Matters*, Edinburgh, 1988.

MacCormick, Neil, 'Constitutionalism and constitutions', in *What Scotland Wants: Ten Years On*, Unit for the study of government in Scotland, Edinburgh, 1989.

MacDiarmid, Hugh, 'A Scots Communist looks at Bonny Prince Charlie', *Scots Independent*, August 1945.

——, *Complete Poems 1920–1976*, ed. Michael Grieve and W. R. Aitken, 2 vols, London, 1978.

MacDiarmid, Hugh, and Grassic Gibbon, Lewis, *Scottish Scene*, London, 1934.

McDiarmid, Lucy, *Saving Civilization*, Cambridge, 1984.

MacDonald, Alexander, *The Poems*, ed. Rev. A. MacDonald and Rev. Dr A. MacDonald, Inverness, 1924.

MacEwen, Sir Alexander Malcolm, *The Thistle and the Rose*, Edinburgh, 1932.

Macgillivray, Pittendrigh, *Memories of the '45*, Edinburgh, 1911.

McGrath, John, *The Cheviot, the Stag and the Black, Black Oil*, London, 1981.

McGuire, Maryann, *Milton's Puritan Masque*, Athens, Georgia, 1983.

MacInnes, Allan I., 'Scottish Gaeldom 1638–51: the vernacular response to the Covenanting dynamic', in John Dwyer, Roger Mason, and Alexander Murdoch (eds), *New Perspectives on the Politics and Culture of Early Modern Scotland*, Edinburgh, no date.

Mackay, J. G., 'After Culloden', *The Celtic Monthly* 20, 1912.

Mackenzie, Compton, *Prince Charlie*, Edinburgh, 1932.

Mackenzie, Sir George, *Religio Stoici. Friendly Address to Phanatics*, no publisher, no date.

MacKillop, James, *Fionn MacCumhaill: Celtic Myth in English Literature*, Syracuse, NY, 1986.

Mackinnon, James, *The Union of Scotland and England*, London, 1896.

Maclaine, Allan H., *Allan Ramsay*, Boston, 1985.

Maclean, Magnus, *The Literature of the Celts*, London, Glasgow, and Dublin, 1902.

——, *The Literature of the Highlands*, new edn, Glasgow, 1904.

MacLean, Malcolm, and Carrell, Christopher, *As an Fhearann*, London, 1986.

MacLeod, W. R., and MacLeod, V. B., *Anglo-Scottish Tracts 1701–1714: A Descriptive Checklist*, University of Kansas libraries series no. 44, Morgantown, 1979.

McLynn, Frank, *The Jacobites*, London, 1985.

——, *Charles Edward Stuart*, London, 1988.

——, 'Profile', in *Times Higher Education Supplement*, 23 September 1988.

McNeill, F. Marion, *The Silver Bough*, 4 vols, Glasgow, 1957.

Macquoid, G. S. (ed.), *Jacobite Songs and Ballads*, London, no date.

Maitland, F. W., *The Constitutional History of England*, Cambridge, 1911.

Marvell, Andrew, *The Poems and Letters*, ed. H. M. Margoliouth, 2 vols, Oxford, 1971.

Mercer, John, *Scotland: The Devolution of Power*, London, 1978.

The Middle Ages in the Highlands, ed. Loraine MacLean of Dochgarroch, Inverness, 1981.

Miller, Delia, *Queen Victoria's Life in the Scottish Highlands Depicted by her Watercolour Artists*, London, 1985.

Miller, William L., *The End of British Politics?*, Oxford, 1981.

Milton, Nan (ed.), *John Maclean: In the Rapids of Revolution*, London, 1978.

Miner, Earl, *The Cavalier Mode from Jonson to Cotton*, Princeton, 1971.

Monod, Paul, 'For the king to enjoy his own again', unpublished Ph.D. thesis, Yale, 1985.

——, 'The politics of matrimony', in Eveline Cruickshanks and Jeremy Black (eds), *The Jacobite Challenge*, Edinburgh, 1988.

Mor, Ruaridh, 'An Bratach Uaine and An Feadan Dubh of Clann Mhurich', *The Jacobite*, summer 1989.

The Morning Star. A Poem, London, 1746.

Morrison, David (ed.), *Essays on Fionn MacColla*, Thurso, no date.

'Mr. Addison turned Tory', By a Gentleman of Oxford, London, 1713.

Muir, Edwin, *Scott and Scotland*, Edinburgh, 1936.

——, *Collected Poems*, London, 1960.

Munro, Ailie, *The Folk Music Revival in Scotland*, London, 1984.

Murray, Isobel, 'James Grant's *The Romance of War* and the "military novel"', *Northern Scotland* 6, 1985.

Murray, Norman, *The Celtic Tragedy*, Montreal, 1919–21.

Nairn, Tom, *The Enchanted Glass*, London, 1988.

Napier, Theodore, *The Royal House of Stuart: A Plea for its Restoration. An Appeal to Loyal Scotsmen*, Legitimist Jacobite League Publications no. 17, Edinburgh and London, 1898.

——(ed.), *The Fiery Cross*, Edinburgh, 1901–12.

'A narrative of the late treatment of the Episcopal ministers', London, 1708. National Library of Scotland, Rosebery Collection Ry. 111; MS 2092; MS 488.f.46; MS 2960.f.48.

Nelson, J. G., *The Early Nineties: A View from the Bodley Head*, Cambridge, Massachusetts, 1971.

Neo-Jacobite papers of Ian Fletcher, Reading University Library.

Noble, Andrew (ed.), *Robert Louis Stevenson*, London and New Jersey, 1983.

Norbrook, David, *Poetry and Politics in the English Renaissance*, London, 1984.

O'Leary, Philip, '"What stalked through the post office?"': Pearse's Cu Chulain', in John T. Koch and Jean Ritmueller (eds), *Proceedings of the Harvard Celtic Colloquium*, III, Cambridge, Massachusetts, 1983.

Ollard, Richard, *The Image of the King*, London, 1979.

Olson, Ian, 'Gavin Greig's lecture to the Scottish National Song Society, November 1909. A failure of nerve?', in *Northern Scotland* 7(2), 1987.

Omond, G. W. T., *The Early History of the Scottish Union Question*, Edinburgh and London, 1897.

O'Tuama, Sean (ed.), *The Gaelic League Idea*, Cork and Dublin, 1972.

Ouston, Hugh, 'York in Edinburgh: James VII and the patronage of learning in Scotland 1679–1688', in John Dwyer, Roger Mason, and Alexander Murdoch (eds), *New Perspectives on the Politics and Culture of Early Modern Scotland*, Edinburgh, no date.

Parnell, Michael, *Eric Linklater*, London, 1984.

Petrie, Charles, *The Jacobite Movement: The Last Phase*, London, 1950.

Pickel, Margaret Barnard, *Charles I as Patron of Poetry and Drama*, London, 1936.

The Pious Life and Sufferings of the Reverend Dr. Henry Sacheverell, publisher not known, 1710.

Pitcairn, Archibald, *Good News From Scotland*, publisher not known, 1712.

Pitsligo, Lord Alexander, *Thoughts concerning Man's Condition and Duties in This Life*, ed. Lord Medwyn, with a foreword by Walter Scott, 4th edn, Edinburgh and London, 1854.

Pitsligo, Papers, Aberdeen University Library MSS 2740/4/18/1–2.

Pittock, Murray, 'Decadence and the English tradition', unpublished D.Phil. thesis, Oxford, 1986.

——, 'This is the place: Edwin Muir and Scotland', *Scottish Literary Journal* 14: 1, 1987.

——, *New Jacobite Songs of the Forty-five*, Oxford, 1989.

——, 'Edwin Muir and Scottish nationalism', in *Edwin Muir: Centenary Assessments*, ed. D. S. Robb and C. J. Maclachlan, Aberdeen, 1990.

——, 'Jacobite literature: love, death, violence', in Paul Dukes and John Dunkley (eds), *Culture and Revolution*, London, 1990.

——, 'Jacobite Songs', *The Jacobite*, Spring 1990, 2–13.

——, 'Rights of nature: the ideal images of Jacobite ruralism', *British Journal of Eighteenth Century Studies* 13:2, 1990.

Plumb, J. H., *The Growth of Political Stability in England 1675–1725*, London, 1967.

Poems of Ossian, ed. John MacQueen, 2 vols, Edinburgh, 1971.

Poems on Several Occasions, publisher not known, 1750.

Popery and Slavery, Edinburgh and London, 1714.

Power, William, 'The next step in world politics: a United States of Europe', *Scottish Opinion* 2, 1947.

Pratt Insh, George, *The Scottish Jacobite Movement*, Edinburgh and London, 1952.

Prebble, John, *The King's Jaunt*, London, 1988.

Presbyterian Persecution Examined, Edinburgh, 1707.

Ramsay, Allan, *Works*, 3 vols, New York and London, 1972.

Reid, J. M., *Scotland's Progress*, London, 1971.

Reliques of Irish Jacobite Poetry, tr. Edward Walsh, 2nd edn, Dublin, 1866.

Richards, Eric, *A History of the Highland Clearances*, 2 vols, London, 1985.

Rivers, Isabel, *The Poetry of Conservatism*, Cambridge, 1973.

Robertson, of Struan, Alexander, *Poems*, Edinburgh, 1749.

Robertson, F. W., *The Scottish Way 1746–1946*, publisher not known, 1946.

Rogers, Nicholas, 'Riot and popular Jacobitism in early Hanoverian England', in Eveline Cruickshanks (ed.), *Ideology and Conspiracy*, Edinburgh, 1982.

Rogers, Pat, *An Introduction to Pope*, London, 1975.

——, '"The Enamelled Ground"': the language of heraldry and natural description in *Windsor Forest*', in *Pope: Recent Essays*, ed. Maynard Mack and James Winn, Brighton, 1980.

Ross, Anne, *The Folklore of the Scottish Highlands*, London, 1976.

Ross Roy, G., 'Jacobite literature of the eighteenth century', *Scotia* I, 1977.

The Royalist, 1891–.

Royal Stuart Review, 1986; 7(1), 1988.

Sanford Terry, Charles, *The Jacobites and the Union*, Cambridge, 1922.

Saunders, Bailey, *The Life and Letters of James Macpherson*, London, 1894.

Saur, K. G., *England und Hanover: England and Hanover*, ed. Adolf M.Birke and Kurt Kluxen, Prince Albert Studies vol. 4, Munich and London, 1986.

Scotland's Glory and Her Shame, By a Well-wisher to The Good Old Cause, 2nd edn, publisher not known, 1786.

Scotland's Grievance, Edinburgh, 1746.

Scots Independent, 1927–.
Scott, P. H., *1707: The Union of Scotland and England*, Edinburgh, 1979.
Scott, Walter, *Redgauntlet*, London, 1901.
——, *The Bride of Lammermoor*, London, 1988 (1906).
Scottish nationalism (papers of Archie Lamont), National Library of Scotland ACC 9290.
Scott-Moncreiff, Lesley (ed.), *The '45: To Gather an Image Whole*, Edinburgh, 1988.
Scottish Pasquils, A Second Book of, Edinburgh, 1828.
Scottish Pasquils, A Third Book of, Edinburgh, 1828.
The Secret History of the Calves-Head Club, 7th edn, London, 1709.
Sedgwick, Romney, *The History of Parliament: The House of Commons 1715–1754*, London, 1970.
Sharp, William, 'Walter Scott's land', in *Harper's Monthly Magazine*, vol. 105, June 1902.
Sherburn, George, *Roehenstart*, Edinburgh and London, 1960.
Shuldham-Shaw, Patrick, Lyle, Emily B., and Hall, Peter A., *The Greig-Duncan Folk Song Collection Volume 3*, Aberdeen, 1983.
Skene, George, 'The heirs of the Stuarts', *Quarterly Review*, June 1847.
Smith, David Nichol (ed.), *The Oxford Book of Eighteenth Century Verse*, Oxford, 1977.
Smith, Donald, 'You may well ask: nine decades of Mitchison', *Cencrastus* 13, 1983.
Smith, G. Gregory, *Scottish Literature: Character and Influence*, London, 1919.
Snyder, Edward D., *The Celtic Revival in English Literature 1760–1800*, Cambridge, Massachusetts, 1983.
Sobieski, John, and Stuart, Charles Edward, *Lays of the Deer Forest*, 2 vols, Edinburgh and London, 1848.
Songs of Scotland. A Selection by John Reid, publisher not known, 1908.
Speck, W. A., *Society and Literature in England 1700–60*, Dublin, 1983.
Starr, Nathan Comfort, *King Arthur Today*, Gainesville, Florida, 1954.
Steele, Margaret, review of John Lorne Campbell (ed.), *Highland Songs of the Forty-Five*, in *Scottish Historical Review* 65 (1), 1986.
Stevenson, R. L. *The Young Chevalier: A Fragment*, publisher not known, no date.
Stuart, Alastair, 'The White Cockade', *Munsey's Magazine*, June 1902.
Swire, Otta F., *The Highlands and their Legends*, Edinburgh and London, 1963.
Szechi, Daniel, 'The Jacobite theatre of death', in Eveline Cruickshanks and Jeremy Black (eds), *The Jacobite Challenge*, Edinburgh, 1988.
Tarbet, Viscount George, *et al.*, *The Laws and Acts made by the First Parliament of Our Most High and Dread Sovereign James VII*, Edinburgh, 1731.
Taylor, Beverley, and Brewer, Elisabeth, *The Return of King Arthur*, Cambridge, 1983.
Thompson, E. P., *Whigs and Hunters*, Harmondsworth, 1985.
Thomson, Derick S., *The Gaelic Sources of Macpherson's 'Ossian'*, Aberdeen University Studies no. 130, Edinburgh, 1951.
——, *Introduction to Gaelic Poetry*, London, 1974.
Thuente, Mary Helen, *W. B. Yeats and Irish Folklore*, New Jersey, 1980.
'To His Royal Highness, CHARLES, Prince of Wales, &c. A Poem', publisher not known, 1745.
Trevelyan, G. M., *England Under the Stuarts*, 14th edn, London, 1928.
Turner, F. C., *James II*, London, 1948.
Turner, James, *The Politics of Landscape*, Oxford, 1979.

Upward, Allen, *Treason*, 3rd edn, London, 1904.

——, *The Fourth Conquest of England*, London, 1905.

Vieth, David M. (ed.), *The Complete Poems of John Wilmot, Earl of Rochester*, New Haven and London, 1979.

Walker, M. G., 'Andrew Marvell and Thomas, 3rd Lord Fairfax: some aspects of their relationship 1650–53', unpublished D.Phil. thesis, Oxford, 1953.

Webb, Keith, *The Growth of Nationalism in Scotland*, Glasgow, 1977.

Wedgwood, C. V., *Poetry and Politics under the Stuarts*, Cambridge, 1960.

The Weesils. A Satyrical Fable, London, 1691.

Weinbrot, Howard D., *Augustus Caesar in 'Augustan' England*, Princeton, 1978.

Wendy Wood Papers, National Library of Scotland ACC 7980/2.

——, 'Yours sincerely for Scotland' (MS), ACC 8197/2.

The Westminster Review, 1896.

Whyte, A. A., 'Scottish Gaelic folksongs 1500–1800', unpublished M.Litt. thesis, Glasgow, 1974.

Wilkes, John, *History of England*, London, 1768.

Winn, James Anderson, *John Dryden and His World*, New Haven, 1987.

Womack, Peter, *Improvement and Romance*, Basingstoke, 1989.

INDEX

A Drunk Man Looks at the Thistle
  (MacDiarmid) 136
'A Marching Song' 57
Act anent Peace and War 25, 32
Act of Security 25, 26, 32
Act of Settlement 25
Act of Union 149;
  and the Disruption 112
Addison, Joseph 58
'Advice to a Painter' 49
Aeneas and His Two Sons 58
Aeneid 58
Alasdair, Alasdair MacMhaighstir
  [Alexander MacDonald] 66–7, 69, 76,
  105, 136
Albert, Prince 103, 108
*All Hail, the Scottish Worker's
  Republic!* (Maclean) 135
'An Suithneas ban' (Ross) 70
Anglicanism 9–14;
  and Nonjurors 29;
  Oxford Movement and Episcopal
  Church 116
anti-imperialism, and nationalism
  129–31
antiquarianism: and nationalism 34–5,
  54, 73, 116;
  and nostalgia 102
Appeal to Loyal Scotsmen (Napier) 126
Arnold, Matthew 121
Arthur, King 1–4;
  and Henry VII 3;
  James I and Britain 3;
  compared with Stuarts 97;
  and Victorian mediaevalism 103
Ascanius, or the Young Adventurer 58
Ascherson, Neal 156
Aughrim, battle 24
Auld Alliance 146
'Auld Lang Syne' 71;

a Jacobite song 83
Auldearn, battle 45
'Away with Prince Hannover' 48
Aytoun, W.E. 115, 128, 149

Badenoch 73
Balmerino, Lord 60
Balmoral 104
Bannockburn Rally, institution 130
Beattie, James 66
Begg, James 113
Belhaven, Lord 35–6
Black Act 53
'Blackbird, The' 47, 102
Blackie, John Stuart 111
Blaikie Murdoch, W. 124, 126, 147
Boer War, links with nationalism 130
'Bonnets o' Blue, The' 99–100
'Bonny Dundee' (McGrath) 155
'Bony Scot, The' 57
Border Warfare (McGrath) 155, 161
Boswell, James, and Jacobite images 64
Boulton, Harold 141
Bradwardine, Baron 58
'Braes o' Killiecrankie, The' 46
British Army 62–3, 71;
  in Clearances 108;
  and Jacobite song 99–100
British state, and its foundation-myths
  39;
  use of Jacobite images for own
    purposes 72, 99–101
Britishness of Scotland 150
'Broom of Cowden Knowes, The' 47
Bruce, Robert 27, 36, 40, 43, 63, 65, 66;
  like Charles Edward 118;
  complement of Wallace 59, 118;
  in 'Scots Wha Hae' 82–3
Bruce, The (Barbour) 82
Buchan, John 145

'Burial March of Dundee' (Aytoun) 115
Burns, Robert 79ff., 101, 134–5
Burns, William 117
Byron, Lord, and Jacobites as freedom-
fighters 64

Calvinism 34;
impact on Scottish history 140
Cameronians 24
'Canadian Boat Song, The' 105–6
'Carle, Now the King's Come' 89
Catholicism 18–20;
and anti-Jacobite feeling 125;
and historical nationalism 65
Cavalier/Puritan dichotomy 121
Celtic communism 111, 149, 153, 161;
and MacDiarmid 134
Celtic Magazine, The 119
Celtic nationalism 133
Celtic Twilight 102;
positive effects 121–2
Celticism, vision of Scotland
99ff., 106–8
Charles I 2;
and Anglican Church 9–14, 29;
and fertility symbolism 11–12;
and Horatian Ode 57;
iconography 52;
opposition to Presbyterianism 140
Charles II 8;
and Covenanters 16–17;
and oak-tree images 42, 52;
opposition to Presbyterianism 140;
and Royal Touch 17
Charles Edward Stuart 8, 62, 134–5,
138–9, 150ff.;
and fertility imagery 44, 50,
52–3, 68–9;
opposition to Presbyterianism 140;
and Roman Republicanism 36,
52–3, 58–9
'Charlie is my Darling' 44
Chartism 112
Cheviot, the Stag and the Black, Black
Oil, The (McGrath) 141, 155–6
Church of Scotland and the Clearances
113
Churchill, Winston, and Home Rule
132, 157
Civil War 11–12, 47
clans: Hogg's attitude 96–8;
opposition to Covenanters 14–15;
patriot image 43;

sexual prowess 44ff.;
support for Dundee 24
Clan Scotland 147
Clark, Angus 136
Claverhouse (Viscount Dundee) 24,
35, 58, 88
Clearances 49, 80, 90, 105ff;
Hogg's attitude 80, 92ff;
Scott's attitude 86
Community of the Realm of Scotland
14, 82
Confessions of a Justified Sinner
(Hogg) 92
Constitutional Convention 159
Constructive Recusancy Act 53
Cope, General Sir John 74
Cornish Parliament 151
Corries, The 156, 160, 162ff.
Covenanters 7, 22–3;
and Cromwell 15–16;
and Highlands 16;
Hogg's sympathy 51
and National Covenant 13ff.;
and Scottish liberty 39
Cowley, Abraham 10, 12
Crawford, Tom 73, 154
Crofting Act 111
Crofting Commission, and the Jacobite
analysis 119–20
Cromdale, battle 24, 45
Cromwell, nineteenth-century interest
121
Cuchulainn 1, 148
Culloden 61ff., 75;
and nationalist consciousness 119
'Culloden Day' 67
cultural nationalism 146, 149
Cunninghame Graeme 111
Cycle Club, the 53, 122

Darien scheme 22, 27;
and Jacobite ideology 62
Declaration of Arbroath 82
Declarations of Indulgence 18
deer hunting, and Clearances 106–8
Denham, John 12
Dewar Gibb, Andrew 106, 148
Disclothing Act 119
Disruption 112–13
Divine Right of Kings 21
'Donald Macgillavry' (Hogg) 91, 97
Donn, Rob 67
Douglas (Home) 74

Dryden, John 20, 35;
and Jacobitism 49
Duffus, Lord 47
Dundee, Viscount 24, 35, 58, 88
Dunkeld 24

Easy Club 55
Edict of Toleration 53
Edinburgh, and James II 17;
and George IV's visit 88–90
Edward VII, and Jacobite opposition
125, 129–30
Egypt, like England 67
England: claims of sovereignty 26–7;
conflation with Britain 39;
and pressure for Union 24–5;
rejection of conflation 117, 128
Enlightenment 73
Episcopal Church in Scotland 14,
16, 142;
custodian of Scottish tradition 55;
disestablished 22;
and nationalism 38;
opposition to Union 23–31
patriotic nature 142;
Queen Victoria's attitude 103;
reconciliation with Anglicanism 116;
sacred Jacobite lyric 47–50;
and social elite 18–19;
support for Jacobitism 22ff., 47;
surviving Jacobite sentiments
151, 162
Erastianism, and Scottish kirk 14ff.,
22–23, 30;
and Union 59
erotic Jacobite song 46
exile 105ff.
Eucharist, and Jacobite imagery 70

famine in Scotland 41
Fergusson, Robert 61, 79
Fiery Cross, The (Napier) 127–8, 130–1
Fingal 75, 78
Fionn MacCumhail 1, 4–6, 45;
once and future king 141;
Prince Albert 103;
Scottish Arthur 154;
Scottish legends 75;
as symbolic exile 110;
and Victorian huntsman 108
fin de siècle and Jacobitism 124
Fletcher of Saltoun 32;

and the federalist position 126
'Flower of Scotland' (The Corries)
163–4
Folk Music Revival in Scotland, The
(Munro) 153
Frazer, J.G. 5
Free Church of Scotland 112–14
Freemasons 52
French Revolution 79, 113;
avoidance 143
Froude, J.A. 39

Gaeltacht 16, 87;
Jacobite poetry 62, 64ff.;
poetry 109;
population loss 107, 109
Garscadden, by-election 158
'General Cope's defeat at Gladsmuire'
48
'Geordie Whelps' Testament' 51
George IV, and visit to Edinburgh
88–90, 114
George V, opinions about Jacobitism 63
Gibbon, Lewis Grassic 112;
and Jacobitism 139–40
Gillies, William 136
Glencoe 37
Glyndwr, Owain 1–2
Govan, by-election (1988) 163
Grant, James 128;
and Royal Arms controversy 113–15
'Great James, come kiss me now' 44
Gunn, Neil 145, 148
Guth na Bliadhna 132, 145

Halkerton Muir 66
'Hame, Hame, Hame' 71
Hamilton, by-election 157
Hamilton, Duke of 26
Hanoverian State 82
Haughs of Cromdale, The' 45
Hay, George Campbell 145
Henry VII 3
Henry VIII 13
Herrick, Robert 11
'Hey Johnnie Cope!' 90
High Church 52, 116
Highland Songs of the Forty-Five
(Campbell) 141
'Highland Laddie, The' 44ff., 57
Highlander as patriot 55, 62–3
'Highlander, The' 78

'Highlander's Farewell, The' (Hogg)
47, 94, 106
Highlands 66ff.
historical revisionism 9, 28, 39, 47
Hogg, James 51, 91ff.;
  attitude to Clearances 80, 92ff.
Home Rule All Round 111, 126
Horatius 58
Huxley, T.H. 1

'I Will Go' 71, 155
Independent Labour Party 135
Insurrection of 1820 90, 113, 154
Israel, like Scotland 60, 67
'Is Scotland to get Home Rule?'
  (Waddie) 118

Jacobite, The 127
Jacobite claimants, recent 123, 146, 160
Jacobite culture, growth 38, 41ff.
Jacobite ideology, sacred character
  30–3, 70;
  and Clearances 110–11;
  dual vision 152ff.;
  and fertility imagery 41–3, 66–9;
  importance of martyrdom 60;
  and Macpherson 74–5;
  and modern nationalism 122–3,
    136–8, 142, 151–3, 156, 160ff.;
  and Republicanism 116–17;
  and Roman Republicanism 35–7;
  and song-culture 44ff., 79;
  survival 114ff.
  survival into nineteenth century
    100–1ff.
Jacobite Relics 51, 94–5
Jacobite song, aggressive 46
Jacobitism 9, 13, 41, 49;
  and Episcopal ideology 22, 47;
  nineteenth-century 99ff.;
  nostalgia and sentimentality 70–2;
  and opposition to Union 23ff.;
  and Queen Victoria 103;
  Scott's writing 84ff.;
  surviving today 150ff.
'Jacobitism of the Left' 79, 135,
  153, 161
James VI and I 3
James VII and II 8;
  and Catholicism 18–20
  and Church of England 18–20;
  in Edinburgh 17–18;
  frees Quakers 18;

opposition to Presbyterianism 140;
  as symbolic exile 110;
  and Toleration 19, 53
James VIII ['the Old Pretender'] 25, 30,
  38–9, 70, 82;
  gentle character 69;
  Presbyterian support for 32;
  propaganda 52, 59
'Jamie Come Home' 47
'Jessie's Dream' 71
Jonson, Ben 11

Killiecrankie 24, 148
King, Dr William 59
king over the water 1
king's two bodies 30–1
Ku Klux Klan 112
Kulturstaat 72

Labour Party, and Home Rule 128,
  135, 145
Lang, Andrew, and neo-Jacobitism 123
Laud, William, Archbishop of
  Canterbury 9, 16;
  and 'beauty of holiness' 10–11
Lays of the Deer Forest (Sobieski
  Stuarts) 104
Lays of the Scottish Cavaliers (Aytoun)
  115
Legitimist Jacobite League, the
  122–3, 127
Liberal Party 145
Linklater, Eric 145, 146, 148
'Loch Lomond' 47
'Lochaber No More' 57
Lockhart of Carnwath, George 58, 132
Lord of Misrule 51
Louis XIV 19
Louis XVI 100
Lovat, Lord (Simon Fraser) 39
Lowlands 66–7
Loyal Songs 64

MacBeth, George 152
MacColla, Fionn 141
MacCormick, John and 1950 Covenant
  147–8, 157
MacDiarmid, Hugh (Christopher
  Grieve) 134ff., 142–3, 145–6,
  150, 162;
  and cultural nationalism 149, 153
MacDonald Douglas, Ronald 153
Macgillavray, Pittendrigh 127

McGrath, Tom 141ff., 155
Mackenzie, Lady Compton 146
Mackenzie, Sir Compton 139, 149, 162;
  elected Lord Rector, Glasgow
    University 143;
  and Jacobitism 143
Mackenzie, Sir George, Lord Advocate
  13, 17;
  support for the Stuarts 58
MacLachlainn, Iain 68
MacLaren, Duncan 113, 117
MacLean, Colonel Allan 62
Maclean, John 135, 149
'Maclean's Welcome, The' (Hogg) 97
MacNeill, D.H. 143
Macpherson, James 72, 73ff.;
  reputation 119
Mary, Queen of Scots 7
Mist's Journal 52
Mitchison, Naomi 145, 152
Montrose, James Graeme, Marquess of
  15, 45, 88;
  claimed as nationalist 143
'Moorhen, The' 47
Motherwell by-election 1945 148, 156
Muir, Edwin 1, 79, 140–1, 145,
  148, 154

'Na Casagan Dubha' (Rob Donn) 67
Nairn, Tom 152
Napier Commission 111
Napier, Theodor 120, 122, 126, 127ff.,
  135, 141, 142–4, 145, 146, 149
Naseby, battle 119
National Association for the
  Vindication of Scottish Rights 112–13,
  117, 144
National Party of Scotland 145–6, 148
National Trust for Scotland 148
nationalism, Irish 1, 145–6;
  and Scottish nationalism
    nineteenth-century 117;
    twentieth-century 148
nationalism, Scottish, and Jacobite
  cause 24–5, 27, 33–5, 38–9, 43;
  revival of 112–13, 114ff.;
  Scott's conflation with Jacobitism 85
nationalism, Welsh 1, 148
neo-Jacobitism 120ff., 135, 144, 146
Neoplatonism 9
noble savage 43
Nonjurors 29, 53;
  last surviving 100

'Oh! Why I left my Hame' 61
'On the Death of Marshal Keith' 78
'Oran Mu Bhliadhna Thearlaich' 69
Order of the Thistle 17
Order of the White Rose 122;
  programme 123
Ossian 4, 43, 63, 73ff.
Oxford Movement 116, 120

Pan-Celtic Congress 130
Paoli, Pasquale 64
Pearse, Patrick 1, 134;
  and Celtic Twilight 122;
  and Neil Gunn 145
Peerage Bill 53
Pitcairne, Archibald 35, 58
Pitsligo, Lord (Alexander Forbes) 30;
  in Scott's work 85;
  and Stuart myth 61
Pope, Alexander 31, 51, 67, 107;
  and Jacobitism 49
popular culture 38, 41ff.
Power, William 143–4
Presbyterianism 14, 19, 27;
  compromise with Union 59;
  and Disruption 112–13;
  hostile feeling 38;
  and nationalist feeling 65;
  negative impact on Scotland 140;
  pro-Jacobite 32;
  propaganda 55;
  Queen Victoria's attitude 103–4;
  and Union 29–31
Proclaimers, The 165
propaganda, pro- and anti-Union
  24ff., 32–4

Radcliffe Library 59
Ramsay, Allan 35–6, 51, 54ff.
referendum of 1979 154;
  and World Cup 162
Registration Act 53
Reichstaat 72
Republicanism, and Jacobitism
  114–15
Revolution of 1688 2, 8–9, 47, 53, 121;
  constitutional effects 25–7;
  definition 21;
  and myth of British state 151ff.
Riot Act 53
Rising of 1708 26
Rising of 1715 43, 47, 58, 149
Rising of 1745 149

Robertson of Struan, Major General
   Alexander 49ff.
Robertson, F.W. 134, 143–4
Romanticism, and Jacobitism 79–80
romanticization of Scotland 106–9
'Roses o' Prince Charlie' (The
   Corries) 162
Ross, William 70
Royal Arms controversy 114
Royal Oak 4, 42
Royal Stuart Society 123
Royalist, The 120ff.
Ruaridh Erskine of Mar 126–7, 132,
   135–6, 144, 147, 159
Ruddiman, Thomas 35–6;
   Keeper of Advocates Library 59;
   and patriotic publishing 58–9
   prints Ramsay's work 55
Ruskin, John and neo-Jacobitism 120

sacred Jacobite song 46ff., 70
Saltire Society 148
Scaevola 58
'Scotland First' (MacDonald) 153
Scotland's Glory and Her Shame 65
Scotland's Sovereignty Asserted (Sir
   Thomas Craig) 27
Scoto-Latinists 34–6, 54, 57, 59, 74
Scots Independent 142, 147–8, 150
Scots language 55, 66
'Scots Wha Hae' 82
Scott, Tom 152
Scott, Sir Walter 31, 34, 54, 84ff.;
   and Highland cult 143;
   and MacDiarmid 136
Scotticisms (Beattie) 66
Scottish Estates 20, 21, 24–5;
   abolition of 151;
   and the propaganda war 28, 32–3
Scottish Home Rule Association 111,
   128, 144, 149
Scottish identity 1;
   claims of English supremacy 26–8;
   and Covenant 15;
   divided character, eighteenth century
      and today 54;
   and eighteenth-century
      antiquarianism 34–5
   and ethnic conflict 86–7;
   and Jacobitism 151;
   romanticized 99–104, 106–9;
   Scott's analysis 84ff.;
   subsumed into British state 72

Scottish Legitimists 153
Scottish National League 130, 136, 147
Scottish National Party 135, 138,
   144, 145ff.;
   establishment suggested 128–9, 131;
   future 156ff.;
   and Jacobitism 147–8
Scottish Nationalist, The 132
Scottish Nationalist Movement 145
Scottish Office, move to Edinburgh 148
Scottish Party 146
Scottish Patriot, The 132
Scottish Patriotic Association 130–1
Scottish Patriots 153, 160
Scottish renaissance 134ff., 146, 154
Scottish Review 145
Scottish Rite 53
Scottish Secretaryship, restoration
   117, 128
Scottish song-culture 36–8, 41ff.
Scottish Wars of Independence, The
   (William Burns) 117
Septennial Act 53
Sherriffmuir, battle 148
Siol Nan Gaidheal 146
Smith, Gregory and Caledonian
   Antisyzygy 136
Smith, Iain Crichton 150, 152
Smith, Sydney Goodsir 134, 145, 154
Smuggling Act 53
Sobieski Stuarts 104–5
Society of King Charles the Martyr 124
Solemn League and Covenant, the 16
songs 41ff.
Soutar, William 141
'Sow's Tail to Geordie, The' 51
Spence, Lewis 145–6
Stevenson, Robert Louis 118, 120
Stewart, Colonel John Roy 64, 136;
   poetry 66–7
Stewart of Garth 107
Stone of Scone, removal 157
'Struan's Farewell to the Hermitage' 49
Stuart, Charles Edward *see* Charles
   Edward Stuart
Stuart Exhibition of 1889 121
Stuart myth 1;
   and curse of Covenanters 91;
   and dynasty 7–9;
   endurance 150ff.;
   and fertility symbolism 4–6, 41–3;
   nature symbolism under Charles I
      11–12;

and popular song 35–7, 41ff.;
   and Union 30–3
'Stuarts of Appin, The' (Hogg) 94
Sutherland Clearances 107, 111
Swift, Jonathan 49, 67, 107
Swinburne, Algernon Charles 120

'Tartan Curtain' 82
Tea-Table Miscellany, The 57
Temora 75, 78
Templars 53
'Tenth of June 1715, The' (Lang) 123
Three Perils of Woman, The (Hogg) 91
Toleration Act 53
1320 Club 146, 153, 157
topographical poem 11–12
Tories 30
Touching for the King's Evil 17, 19, 41
Townley, Colonel Francis 60
Towton, battle 119

Union: Belhaven's speech 35–6;
   creeping legitimation 58–60;
   and Disruption 112–13;
   effect on Scottish culture 41ff.;
   historiographical bias 39;
   opposition to 30–3;
   pressure for 26;
   Scott's attitude 84–5
Union of England and Scotland
   (Mackinnon) 126
Unionism 22, 34–5;
   and political necessity 24ff.
United Scotsmen 112

Victoria, Queen 99;
   and Balmoral 102–4;
   and Jacobitism 103
Villpone and the Union argument 32–4
Virgil 58
'Vision, The' 57
Voltaire and the Stuarts 8

Wallace, Sir William 27, 36, 40,
   134, 148;
   aligned with Charles Edward
      Stuart 161;
   Celtic nationalist 96;
   eighteenth-century symbol 58–9, 71;
   English reaction 116;
   and myth of Bruce 140;
   nineteenth-century icon 102, 112,
      116, 118
Wallace, The (Blind Harry) 82
Wallace Monument 116
Wars of Independence 57, 81;
   likened to Stuart cause 118
'Welcome, Royal Charlie' 163
Welsh Youth Movement 147
'What's A' The Steer, Kimmer?' 61
Whigs 21, 38, 47;
   and commercialism and tyranny
      49–50, 67;
   use of Republican images 58
'White Cockade, The' (Ross) 70
White Rose 146
'Whurry Whigs awa' man' 66
'Will Ye No Come Back Again?' 47
William of Orange 21–3, 41;
   offer to restore James VIII 25;
   propaganda against 31, 37
'Windsor Forest' 51
Wood, Wendy 127, 134, 135, 139,
   146, 147, 153, 159, 162
Worcester, battle 63

'Ye gods who Justice Love' 57
'Ye Jacobites by name' 81
Yeats, W.B. 5, 24;
   and MacDiarmid 138;
   and Macpherson 74;
   and Scottish renaissance 145
Young Ireland, and Scottish nationalism
   116
Young Scots Society 128